Digital Strategies in a Global Market

Natalia Konina
Editor

Digital Strategies in a Global Market

Navigating the Fourth Industrial Revolution

palgrave
macmillan

Editor
Natalia Konina
Moscow State Institute of International Relations (MGIMO University)
Moscow, Russia

ISBN 978-3-030-58266-1 ISBN 978-3-030-58267-8 (eBook)
https://doi.org/10.1007/978-3-030-58267-8

This Palgrave Macmillan imprint is published by the registered company Springer Nature Switzerland AG
The registered company address is: Gewerbestrasse 11, 6330 Cham, Switzerland

Preface

This book is inspired by ideas of Klaus Schwab about the Fourth Industrial evolution and represents an academic attempt to evaluate its impact on business strategy, marketing, management, sustainability innovation, and various kinds of activities of international companies. The depth and dynamism of changes in the global economy and business in direction to singularity have considerably increased during the pandemic of COVID-19. This book written by a big group of Russian and international researchers from different Universities and research centers represent the views and ideas of how in a changing global digital environment international firms seek to adopt to the challenges and opportunities posed by a rapidly transforming digital world. Through the lens of macro and microanalysis this book provides European and Russian case studies connected with management and business transformation in digital market as well digital aspects of oil and gas, retail, hotel, FMCG and agri-business.

Moscow, Russia Natalia Konina

Acknowledgments

Moscow State Institute of International Relations (MGIMO University), Moscow, Russia.

The authors are grateful to REGION Group (Moscow, Russia) for financial support in the implementation of research projects.

Contents

Notes on Contributors

Ekaterina Bostoganashvili is Assistant Professor at the Department of Management, Marketing and Foreign Economic Activities, MGIMO University. She is the author of several academic papers on management, marketing and digital economy. Her major research interest lies in the areas of economic activities, digitalization, international e-commerce and e-business.

Olga Butorina is Corresponding Member of the Russian Academy of Sciences, Deputy Director for Research at the Institute of Europe, Russian Academy of Sciences, Moscow. She received her Ph.D. from MGIMO-University in Moscow in 1987 and was a fellow at the Institute of Europe in 1989–2003. Research interests include European integration, Euro and the European Monetary Union. Professor Butorina has founded the Department of European Integration in MGIMO-University and served as Chair from 2003 through 2012. She has advised the Federal Assembly, State Duma, Russian Ministry of Foreign Affairs and the Bank of Russia. Her many contributions to the literature include "European Integration" (textbook, ed.), "International Currencies: The Integration and Competition", "An Economic History of the Euro", chapters and articles in professional journals.

Anna Churakova is Master of Science in Luxury Management and Marketing at Emlyon Business School (France), and postgraduate student at the Department of Management, Marketing and Foreign Economic

Activities, MGIMO-University. Her research interests focus on the global hotel industry, marketing of Russian and international hospitality companies, particularly of luxury hotel brands, digital marketing, and empirical marketing.

Anastasia Erokhina is Master in International Management, Institute of Business Studies, the Russian Presidential Academy of National Economy and Public Administration, and Master in Management, NEOMA Business School Programme Grande Ecole. Her research interests focus on modern management practices and trends and also include management control and finance related aspects of management.

Alexander Gaponenko is Professor at the Institute of Business Studies (RANEPA). He holds a Doctorate degree from RANEPA. He is also Academic Director of DBA Programme. His academic expertise includes theoretical aspects of management. He has published many books and articles on those issues. He has more than 20 years of experience in research and lecturing on strategic and knowledge management. His research interests also include management by values issues.

Oleg Gavryushin is Rector of the Institute of International Trade and Law, post-graduate student of the Department of Foreign Trade Transactions Technology, Russian Foreign Trade Academy, has publications on the development of international e-commerce, its supranational regulation, the involvement of large financial groups and retailers in e-commerce in Russia, and the development of Russian export models through e-commerce.

Since 2003—founder and head (up to the present time) of the non-profit educational high school—the Institute of International Trade and Law. His current professional and research interests include international and cross-border e-commerce.

Valentina Gerasimenko is Doctor Habilitatus, Professor, Head of Marketing Department, Director of the Research center for market analysis and pricing and Head of M.B.A. programs at the Faculty of Economics of Lomonosov Moscow State University. She teaches courses on Marketing and Pricing policy, has professional activity in the field of digital market transformation, consumer behavior models, new marketing and branding technologies. She has published many books and articles on those issues and also supervises Master's and Ph.D. theses.

Marina Gregorić, Ph.D. is Associate professor at University North, Koprivnica, Croatia. The courses she teaches are Selective forms of Tourism, Marketing strategies, Corporate communications, and Human resource management. She was Foreign Associate, former Dean and Vice dean at European Business School in Zagreb. She was an international visiting lecturer at the Plekhanov Russian University of Economics in Moscow; Faculty of Tourism, hospitality, and sport. She was external associate at Polytechnic of Međimurje in Čakovec, Croatia; Management of Tourism and sports. Previously, she was a module coordinator at Stenden University in Doha, Qatar; Faculties of Hospitality, Tourism and International Business Management. She has published over 70 scientific and professional papers. She is a member of the editorial board of international scientific journals. She is Senior Manager in domestic and international markets, with 25 years of experience in business (financial and commercial sectors). She is a member of the expert panel in initial accreditation and re-accreditation of study programs with Croatian Agency for Science and Higher Education.

Sergey Gutnik is Doctor in Physics and Mathematics, Associate Professor at the Department of Mathematics, Econometrics and Information Technologies, MGIMO-University, where he teaches courses in Informatics, Mathematical and Computer Simulations in Digital Economy. He is the author of more than 50 scientific publications and 5 textbooks. His main research interests include symbolic-numeric methods for differential and polynomial equations, computer algebra and machine learning methods for simulation and modeling. He has more than 30 years of experience in computer science and banking information technology.

Alina Ignatieva is Professor of the Department of Management at MGIMO-University, Candidate of Economic Sciences, and Honorary Worker of Higher Professional Education of the Russian Federation. During 35 years the author has published more than 100 scientific papers on the problems of modern management, in particular, on the problems of improving the management mechanism in socio-economic systems. The author's sphere of scientific interests is related to the research and design of strategic management systems of modern organizations and the development of organizational and administrative management models.

Peter Khaiter is an Associate Professor in the School of Information Technology at York University, Toronto, Canada. He received his B.Sc.

and M.Sc. degrees in Economic Cybernetics, M.Sc. degree in Environmental Studies and Ph.D. degree in Mathematical Modeling/Information Technology. His main research areas include sustainable development, environmental informatics and economics, mathematical and simulation modeling, quantitative methods for sustainability appraisal, ecosystem services, dynamics and stability, systems of environmental monitoring, and applications of Artificial Intelligence and optimization methods. He is an author and editor of numerous publications on these issues, including a recent book *Sustainability Perspectives: Science, Policy and Practice*, Springer Verlag (2020).

Natalia Konina is Doctor in Economics, Professor and since 2016—Head of Department of Management, Marketing and Foreign Economic Activities at Moscow State Institute of International Relations (MGIMO University). She received her Ph.D. from MGIMO-University in Moscow in 1991 and further continued her scientific research with Doctoral Thesis in 2009. With more than 30 years of experience in researching and business consulting, specializing in different aspects of international management, geoeconomics, competition and competitiveness, and transnational corporations. Her current research interests are focused on the dynamics of business environment in digital era, globalization and digitalization, modern strategies of big multinational corporations, global value chains, digital transformation of companies, and evolution of management in post-industrial society. Her many contributions to the literature include "Management: Theory, Practice and International Aspect" (textbook, ed.), "Management of International Firms: How to Win in Competition", "Competitiveness of the Firms in the Global World", chapters and articles in professional journals. A Vice-Head of joint Dissertation Council MGIMO University—RUDN University, Moscow.

Julia Kovalchuk is Dr.Sc. (Econ), Chief Researcher of Asset Management Department at Moscow State Institute of International Relations (MGIMO University) and Professor of the Department of Energy Service and Energy Saving Management at Moscow Aviation Institute (National Research University). Choosing strategic aspects of industrial development as a scientific priority, she has long specialized in industrial modernization, including reindustrialization. She has accumulated a wealth of experience in strategic research of the high-tech industry, including competition and cooperation factors. Her current research interests include digital transformation of companies and value creation in the digital arena.

Elena Nozdrenko is Head of the Department of Advertising and Social and Cultural Activities of the Siberian Federal University. He has a Ph.D. (theory and history of culture), Associate Professor. She has 20 years of research and teaching experience in advertising, public relations, imageology, and self-management. She is the author of many publications on communication technologies, marketing, social and cultural management, etc.

Raisa Nozdreva is Honored Scientist of Russian Federation, Doctor in Economics, Professor of the Department of Management, Marketing and Foreign Economic Activities, MGIMO-University. A well-known Russian researcher with more than 45 years of publishing activity, she is the author of more than 180 publications in Russian and foreign publishing houses in marketing theory, international marketing, general management, crisis management. Her research interests extend also to Japan (economy, foreign trade, and planning system) as well as different aspects of Marketing. She is an expert of United Nations in the field of public administration, a member of Japan Marketing Association and Japan Strategic Management Association and also a member of editorial board of journal Marketing in Russia and Overseas.

Vladimir Osipov is Doctor in Economics, Professor of Asset Management Department at MGIMO- University (Russia) and also Visiting Professor of School of Economics and Management at Beijing Jiaotong University (China). He is the Member of American Law and Economics Association, Editorial Boards Member of several scientific Journals. He has published over 160 articles in professional journals and sixteen books as author, co-author, editor, and co-editor. His primary research expertise embraces institutional policy and public administration. He is Vice-Head of Dissertation Council of Lomonosov Moscow State University.

Maria Pokrovskaya is postgraduate student at Institute of Business Studies, the Russian Presidential Academy of National Economy and Public Administration. She is Lecturer at College of Economic International Relations. Her research interest lies in the area of management by values.

Elena Ponomareva is Ph.D. in Economics, Associate Professor in MGIMO-University at School of Management, Marketing and Foreign Economic Affairs. She started her academic and scientific career in 1998 in MGIMO in the field of marketing. She is the author of the textbook "Brand-management" (2006, 2018) as well as articles and scientific reports on Branding, Advertising and Strategic Communications. She started her practical experience in 1998 in Ford Motor Company as Marketing Assistant, then she had more than 10 year experience in the position of Commercial Director and Head of Interactive Services Department in the media-holding Red Square LLC. She has a special reward—a letter of honor, signed by the Russian President V. Putin.

Nikolay Revenko is Ph.D. in politics, former carrier diplomat, Minister Extraordinary and Plenipotentiary. Now he is Lead Research Fellow at the Institute for Research of International Economic Relations of the Financial University. His research interests include digital economy, economic cooperation within international organizations and associations, the European Union, migration policy, export controls. He is author of numerous articles, co-author and editor of several monographs.

Lilia Revenko is Doctor in Economics, Professor at the Department of International Economic Relations and Foreign Economic Affairs of MGIMO University. She teaches courses on economic environment, global commodity markets and prices, government-business cooperation in export regulation, global markets for agricultural products. She also is moderator of business role-playing games on determining the price of a foreign trade contract and decision-making in foreign economic activity. Her research interests include current trends in the development of global commodity markets, global food market, food security, sustainable development, export controls. She is author and editor of numerous monographs and articles.

Ante Rončević, Ph.D. is Associate professor at University North, Koprivnica, Croatia. The author was born in Jasenice, Croatia, in 1964 and Lives in Zagreb. B.A., M.Sc. and Ph.D. in Economics levels were achieved at the Graduate School of Economics and Business, additional pedagogy & psychology education gained at the Faculty of Philosophy, University of Zagreb. The author also completed post-graduate Economic Advisor studies at Joint Vienna Institute and took part in many scientific and professional international conferences. The author has published more than seventy scientific and/or professional papers. Before becoming a professor at University North, work experience gained at various manufacturing and service companies as well as government financial and non-financial institutions. The author works as a visiting professor at several universities in Croatia and is a Winner of "Mijo Mirković" Award for scientific contribution.

Yuri Savinov is Professor at the Department of International Trade Transaction Technology, Russian Foreign Trade Academy. His research interests extend to a wide range of problems: international trade in high-tech goods, the development of Russian exports of these goods, the impact of international industrial cooperation on the expansion of exports for certain goods, the effectiveness of foreign trade transactions, use of digital technologies in foreign trade, state support for exports and a number of other areas. His current research interests include foreign trade in finished goods and raw materials, international e-commerce, commercial document flow in e-business, and outsourcing in international trade.

Anastasia Sheveleva is Doctor in Economics, Associate Professor, Professor at the management, marketing and foreign economic activities department, Deputy Dean of the Faculty of International Business and Business Administration at Moscow State Institute of International Relations (MGIMO-University). She has 20 years of experience in research and lecturing on Management of the oil and gas companies, Economics of the companies of the fuel and energy complex and a whole range of other disciplines. She is the author of more than 120 publications related to management and economic issues. Her current research interests include the ways to improve the efficiency of companies, primarily in the oil and gas complex.

Tatiana Skryl is Associate Professor at the Department of Economic Theory, Plekhanov Russian University of Economics, Moscow, Russia. She holds her Ph.D. in Economic theory. Her current professional and research interests include regional development, industry policy, public administration, and Russia's post-crisis development. She is currently a member of the Dissertation Council (industry and economic safety specialization).

Dmitry Stapran is Doctor in Economics, Director of Strategy & Operations, consultancy practice at PwC Russia. For over 5 years Dmitry has been focused on research of sourcing strategies, boundaries of the firm and sources of competitive advantage of companies in different industries. He gained insights for his research from the 5 years of consulting experience, 11 years of operational practice in leading Russian energy companies as well as from knowledge gained at various institutions: Dmitry is the alumnus of Harvard business school, IMD business school and Kingston business school and a visiting professor in leading Russian universities, has legal degree and Ph.D. in Historical Sciences.

Igor Stepnov is Dr.Sc. (Econ), Head of Asset Management Department at Moscow State Institute of International Relations (MGIMO University) and Professor of the Corporate finance and Corporate Governance at Financial University under the Government of the Russian Federation. With more than 30 years of experience in researching the dynamics of production and economic systems and businesses consulting to innovative development, he formed the theory of organizational platform of interaction, which includes an original model of strategic development of companies. His current research interests are focused on the dynamics of digital ecosystems and their elements, such as pricing and profit control in business models, investment attractiveness of digital business and digital asset management, digital business models design.

George Stonehouse is a well-known researcher in the field of management, strategies and change management and multinational business, Professor, Ph.D., Director, Consultant, Author and Developer, Professor Emeritus International Strategic Management. During the13 years he acted as a Dean of Edinburgh Napier University Business School. providing Academic and Research Leadership in the Business Schools, led major research projects in International Education, Primary Healthcare, Organizational Learning, SME Strategy, Strategy in the Airline Industry, and International Business and Culture. His main research areas include Strategic Management, Leadership, International Business, Culture, Change Management, Creativity, Strategic Knowledge Management, Management Education, Research Methods and Methodology, Digitalization and Multinational Corporations. He is an author and editor of numerous publications on these issues, including books *Global and Transnational Business- Strategy and Management*, with Dr. J. Hamill, D. Campbell and Dr. A. Purdie, John Wiley Publishing, *Business Strategy: An*

Introduction, with D.Campbell and W. Houston, Butterworth - Heinemann, *Strategic Management for Travel and Tourism*, with N. Evans and D. Campbell, Butterworth—Heinemann.

Evgeniya Taranovskaya is Associate Professor at the Department of Finance, Monetary and Credit Relations, Russian Foreign Trade Academy. She worked as Dean of Professional Refresher Department, Professor in Accounting in Moscow High School of International Business, Chief-Accountant in JSC Promstroytema, General Director of RAM-Engineering. Her scientific interests include the issues of export financing and its state support, the development of the international investment process, the terms of payment in foreign trade contracts, and international trade and economic activities.

Pavel Trifonov is Associate Professor at Financial University under the Government of the Russian Federation, Faculty the Higher School of Management. He is also a leading researcher for Institute of industrial policy and institutional development at Financial University under the Government of the Russian Federation, Academic Director for the Masters' Programme on Operation Management. He has more than 15 years of experience in research and lecturing on operation management, industrial development, e-commerce and global value chains. He has worked as a consultant for in the largest Russian companies in the automotive and electrical engineering sector.

Sergey Tyaglov is Doctor in Economics, Professor at the Department of Economics of the Region, Industries and Enterprises Faculty of Economics and Finance at Rostov State University of Economics. He is also Honorary Worker of Higher Education of the Russian Federation, member of the Expert Advisory Council under the Chairman of the Chamber of Control and Accounts of the Rostov Region, expert of the Russian Science Foundation on regional and sectoral economics, author of over 200 scientific papers on regional and sectoral economics, environmental economics, modeling of social and economic and ecological-economic development, published in publications indexed in international and domestic databases.

Irina Vladimirova is Doctor in Economics, Professor of the Department of Management, Faculty of Economics Peoples' Friendship University of Russia (RUDN University). She is also Head of the master's program “International Management”, Deputy Head of the Anglo-Russian program, Institute of World Economy and Business RUDN University. Her current professional and research interests include management, international management, and international business. She has published many books and articles in national and international journals on those issues.

Alexander Yukhno is Lecturer at the Scientific-educational center of MPA programs, Institute of Public Administration and Civil Service of the Russian Presidential Academy of National Economy and Public Administration. He is also the Deputy Head of the Public Council under the Federal Agency for State Property Management of the Russian Federation. He holds a Ph.D. in Law from MGIMO-University. His primary research expertise embraces corporate governance, digital economy, information and communication technologies, international law and finance.

List of Figures

List of Tables

CHAPTER 1

Introduction: At the Dawn of the Fourth Industrial Revolution—Problems and Prospects

Natalia Konina

The Fourth Industrial Revolution has led society into the era of technological singularity, characterized by the changing role of machines and technologies in various aspects of life, which requires rethinking all approaches to management and marketing.

The modern world has a multi-structural character. Along with and in parallel with the realities of the Third Industrial Revolution (computerization and automation), the Fourth Industrial Revolution has been gaining momentum since the end of the twentieth century. The authors of this book consider the industrial revolution as an abrupt step, which suddenly increased the complexity of the technological structures associated with several technical, technological, social, institutional, and other developments, caused by radical changes in the productive forces due to innovations.

N. Konina (✉)
Moscow State Institute of International Relations (MGIMO University),
Moscow, Russia

N. Konina (ed.), *Digital Strategies in a Global Market*,
https://doi.org/10.1007/978-3-030-58267-8_1

The merging of cyber-physical technologies within the Fourth Industrial Revolution is characterized by the speed, scale, and systemic nature of socio-economic consequences. The most important technologies already being implemented in the Fourth Industrial Revolution include the Internet of Things (IoT); artificial intelligence; sensors, collecting and evaluating Big Data in real-time; Big Data and analytics; robots with greater autonomy and flexibility; autonomous vehicles; 3D printing; virtual and augmented reality; cloud computing; online platforms; software as a service; quantum computers; smart materials; blockchain; and a number of other technologies. The Fourth Industrial Revolution is changing the economic landscape and boundaries of industries and transforming the traditional business environment, creating new markets while destroying existing businesses; these developments make it possible to understand how companies create value, manage changes, and lay the basic principles for creating and implementing strategies. Fundamentally, this era is changing traditional approaches to fundamental issues—how to reach customers, how to compete and guarantee growth and sales (Baldwin 2016).

It should be noted that the speed of technological changes and innovations has been increasing significantly since 2015. The development of new technologies of the Fourth Industrial Revolution is now becoming exponential, which has an increasingly diverse and complex effect on reducing transaction costs, production processes, and creating and transforming materials and goods (Deloitte 2015).

Some new technologies will significantly improve transport logistics, as well as coordination between exporters and importers, which will increase trade in goods, services, and digital data (Lopez Gonzalez and Ferencz 2018). According to studies, cross-border B2C e-commerce—but for the coronavirus infection pandemic—could grow to about $1 trillion by 2020. Logistics technology continues to improve significantly. The Internet of Things (IoT) allows delivery services to become more efficient by tracking packages in real-time, while AI autonomously directs vehicles taking traffic into account. Automatic processing of documents significantly speeds up customs processing; for example, at ports, autonomous vehicles can unload, store, and reload containers faster and with fewer errors. Amazon warehouses around the world use about 100 thousand robots, whose productivity is about 4–5 times higher than that of humans, although the skills of the existing robots are still too limited to make warehouses fully automated. Blockchain delivery solutions can reduce transit time and speed up payments. New logistics technologies can reduce delivery and customs clearance times by 16–28%.

Innovative technologies of the next technological mode are increasingly used by TNCs with global value chains around the world, in particular, the German Trumpf (producing laser equipment), the German Siemens (the Internet of Things and medical engineering), the Swiss ABB and the American Amazon (creating robots), the British Rolls-Royce and the American General Electric (creating jet engines), and the American Tesla and the German Daimler, BMW, Volkswagen (dealing with electric vehicles).

An example of implementing the principles of the Fourth Industrial Revolution in practice is Siemens, the largest German TNC (Konina 2018). Siemens sees digitalization as a comprehensive task to increase efficiency: across the entire conglomerate, all internal processes are transferred to digital platforms; digital tools, systems, programmes are introduced; and end-to-end digital value-added chains are built. Siemens makes extensive use of digital twin technology, which means digital twins can be created before physical prototypes; this reduces the time it takes for the product to enter the market, and can significantly improve product quality, while reducing the cost of making efforts to eliminate errors and deviations before the product leaves the production site. As a leader in the Internet of Things (IoT), Siemens is widely developing open innovation through an internal venture capital fund system, and is using partnerships with Alibaba Cloud (a subsidiary of a Chinese digital conglomerate) to promote MindSphere, a digital platform for the Internet of Things.

The transition to the emerging new industrial production system is mainly being influenced by digital technologies. The increasing affordability and reduced prices of ICT products, their wide horizontal distribution, and the internalized interaction of several digital approaches is leading to the emergence of new technologies and ways to use them. The Fourth Industrial Revolution opens doors for business models that take advantage of mass customization, where each product is created as a unique single product (McKinsey 2019).

The integration of digital technologies and other new developments is creating profound changes in almost all industries, creating threats for existing companies and forcing them to modernize business models. Breakthrough technologies and digital innovations stimulate consumer income and demand, and reduce costs, creating areas for inventing new values based on open innovation. Digital globalization and Industry 4.0

key technologies—such as new mobility, artificial intelligence, AR/VR, 3D, cloud computing, business analytics, and social networks—are transforming the global market; they provide great opportunities yet at the same time create serious challenges and unexpected market risks. Many companies from developed countries have faced competition from aggressive high-tech firms from developing countries. The modern economy is characterized by a combination of competition and cooperation, rapid change of priorities, open innovation and the use of cluster opportunities, and the transition to a network-based decentralized management model based on trust and cooperation. The challenges and opportunities in manufacturing, procurement, sales, marketing, and logistics are associated with new ways of creating value.

Digitalization of the economy (*digitalization*)—the widespread use of ICT, digital platforms, and other digital technologies, alongside their integration into the business processes of companies in a growing number of sectors—is making economic systems more complicated; they are transformed into dynamic network systems both at the micro and macro levels. Digitalization has provoked the active use of new information tools, such as cloud computing or Big Data analytics, which are already contributing significantly to GDP (OECD 2017).

The use of data has also transformed manufacturing, fostering a new production revolution (OECD 2016). The widespread use of information has already changed the entire production system. Cross-border data exchange in 2014 was 45 times greater than in 2005, which means a contribution of approximately $2.8 trillion per year to global economic activity, or 3.5% of global GDP (OECD 2017). Moreover, according to the 2014–2022 forecast, the cross-border data exchange may grow another 9 times.

Platform business has become the new ecosystem of the global digital economy. Online platforms are actively developing and capturing an increasing share of promising markets, which affects the markets, consumers, the company's competitive position, the technologies used in production, and marketing. In 2017, the total value of platform-based US companies with a market capitalization of more than $100 million exceeded an estimated $7 trillion, which is 67% more than in 2015 (UNCTAD 2019).

Some global digital platforms have gained very strong market positions in particular segments. For example, about a 90% share of search engines belongs to Google, which is part of the digital conglomerate Alphabet.

Facebook accounts for 66% of the global social media market, making its platform the most popular social network in more than 90% of countries. In China, the WeChat communication network (owned by Tencent) has more than a billion active users, and its payment system, along with Alipay (owned by Alibaba), covers almost the entire Chinese mobile payments market. At the same time, Alibaba accounts for an estimated 60% of the Chinese e-commerce market (UNCTAD 2019).

The digital revolution is having a profound impact on the structure, dynamics, and direction of the global market's evolution. More and more, society is dealing with a single global market for the vast majority of goods and services, rather than with a combination of national economies, or with markets limited by regional economic groupings. Nonetheless, the global market is increasingly acquiring a different dimension, as digital streams are becoming increasingly important. Over the past two decades, the global export of ICT services, now made possible using digital technology, has increased much faster than the entire export of services in general, which indicates the growing digitalization of the global economy. In 2018, the volume of exports of services provided using digital technologies reached $2.9 trillion accounting for 50% of global service exports (UNCTAD 2019).

The digital realities of the Fourth Industrial Revolution contribute to how companies are evolving from hierarchical to network structures. Many industries have faced competition from companies that have implemented breakthrough technologies, including those working in the digital sphere (*digital disruption*) (Skog and Wimelius 2018). Breakthrough innovations completely change the way an industry or market operates, and the state of competition offers customers a network effect or lower cost or other economic benefits, including a unique consumer experience (Christensen et al. 2018). The strongest digital disruptors—like Amazon, Google, Uber, and others—employ combinatorial disruption, creating different values which are mutually reinforcing such as cost value, experience, and platform values (Stonehouse and Konina 2020). The Fourth Industrial Revolution requires companies to become more flexible, approaching a new form of network organizational structure: an edge-based organization. Under this organizational structure, executives and their teams are empowered at the edge of the company, with the freedom to undertake the fast moves necessary for customer satisfaction and new value creation. These edge-based companies are characterized by an innovative organizational culture, cooperative spirit, widely distribute decision-making, and quick reactions to evolving realities in the market (Leodolter 2017).

Among the best examples of building new business opportunities, based on new technologies as the primary revenue driver and facilitator of new business models, are social networks and location awareness. Social media now has a very big impact on business, totally changing approaches to advertising, building brand awareness, and customer loyalty (Appel et al. 2020). According to 2019 social media statistics, there are now 3.2 billion users around the globe, or about 42% of the total population at present. Facebook now has over 650 million users, with 68% of adults based in the US reportedly having a Facebook account. Active social media users increase with every passing generation: 48.2% Baby Boomers, 77.5% Generation X, and 90.4% Millennials have social media accounts. Twitter's volume of visitors is rising at over 80% a year. Social media has a very big impact on business: 73% of online marketers agree that their efforts in implementing a social media marketing strategy for their business have been effective.

According to the authors of this book, the literature on international business has paid little attention to how international companies have implemented digital strategies in the framework of the Fourth Industrial Revolution; the factors and dynamic processes of digital strategy elaboration have been under-represented in such writings. Naturally, international operations impose their complexities on management in the New Digital Era, which can be characterized through additional moderating, intervening, or competitive and strategic factors, with a profound influence on performance abroad. In this book, we want to address the impact of new digital technologies on strategies of international companies, and how these companies will be managed in the future.

Therefore, this volume's overall aim is to shed fresh light on a range of concepts, influential factors, and strategic decisions facing international firms in the situation of the Fourth Industrial Revolution, examining them in their own respective environmental, institutional, and operating conditions and contexts, following some theoretical developments in each of the two parts of the volume.

The broad objective of this volume is to examine a young, but rapidly evolving, field of scholarly inquiry: the impacts of the changing environment of the Fourth Industrial Revolution internally, with a specific focus on a list of selected issues in the digital strategy, management and marketing domain. For all the reasons above, we chose to focus this volume on the fundamental topic of how new emerging technologies influence international firms; their business strategies, elaboration thereof, its implementation, and their intersection and combination with different aspects of economic development at both a macro and a micro level.

This book this volume aim to study not only issues arising but their potential impacts; Part I will look at digital issues concerning firms, institutions, and policymakers from macro or subject lenses, whilst the impact of technologies of the Fourth Industrial Revolution on firms from industry or sector or country viewpoints will be the focus of Part II.

At the beginning of this volume nine-part study of contributions revisit, from a theoretical and/or empirical standpoint, the main theories in the field. These take into consideration macro aspects connected with the Fourth Industrial Revolution, as well as crucial digital technology implementation, ranging from the new concept of marketing in the digital era and institutional aspects of digital transformation to the concrete tools of machine learning and the digital transformation of corporate governance.

Following this introduction, after a review of the institutional framework of digital strategy and digital marketing operations, the discussion turns to the issues in business environments connected with European digital policy and global value chains . This discussion further expands the examination of such subjects as sourcing, networking, advance management, and concrete digital tools connected with data mining and machine learning in digital marketing. A combination of these subjects helps to focus impact strategies, which guides a firm's adaptation of its digital strategy, and paves the path for the firm's overall inclusion in the practicalities of transforming post-industrial economy.

Further Chapters of the volume focus on the specific organizational forms and actions, behaviours and orientations thereof that influence the performance of firms or industries in international markets; these articles are dedicated to several empirical studies on the most pressing contemporary issues in the area of digital strategies implementation in the real activities of companies from different industries on different markets.

Against this backdrop, the volume explores the theoretical and empirical challenges related to concepts of the post-industrial society: digitalization, firm management, organization, marketing, business models, networking, and operations in global markets. The contributors try to reflect upon pressing issues in the field of international business, and question how current management methods and existing business models can be adapted to fit the challenges of ongoing digital transformation.

The authors investigate the business trends most likely to impact the operations of firms in the field of modern marketing, as well as the management of such firms of different sectors; the authors try to identify proper suitable managerial solutions for the challenges and opportunities created by the turbulent and fast-evolving environment of the Fourth Industrial Revolution. A secondary focus is on the methodological challenges for this research field, such as the difficulties in selecting proper goals and performance indicators, and measuring them consistently. Thirdly, the authors want to share their views and research approaches with the wide English-speaking international auditorium.

The contributions cover the most important domains connected with the firm, industry, and country levels for Digital Strategy elaboration, and their further execution in the turbulent global market. The goal of the authors is to gather fresh theoretical analyses and empirical studies, based on the combined research of technological, social, and economic trends, in the pages of a unitary volume, to serve scholars in the field, policymakers, and the public.

Following the introduction, Chapter 2 by Valentina Gerasimenko, is entitled "Digital Marketing Strategy: New Performance and Risks". The author interviewed top managers of different companies operating in Russian markets about digital marketing strategies, tools for implementation, and emerging risks of being resistant to change.

Chapter 3 by Olga Butorina focuses on the external influence of the EU's digital policy through economic lenses. Analysis of the most important political materials of 2015–2020 showed that if the EU's digital policy was initially aimed at overcoming internal barriers, today it is aimed at creating a favourable global digital environment, facilitating the efforts of the EU to become the global regulator.

The following four chapters have a rather specific focus, each narrowing the discussion down to specific institutional macroeconomic issues of digital strategies at the dawn of the Fourth Industrial Revolution.

The author of Chapter 4, Vladimir Osipov, contributes to the discussion of different approaches to the embeddedness of the Fourth Industrial Revolution in national economics and on the global market, which he argues consists of two main paradigms of institutional policy. The author concludes that Natural States pursue a top-down policy to embed institutions of the Fourth Industrial Revolution, but Open Access Order goes radically the other way, implementing a "down-top" path. The digitalization of national economy occurs according to the chosen institutional policy.

The authors of Chapter 5, "Genesis of Network Management Forms During the Fourth Industry Revolution", Tatiana Skryl and Marina Gregorić explore the theoretical and empirical challenges around the concept of network effects on product team operations, in the cluster and the nature of networking among companies in the Fourth Industrial Revolution.

On the topic of a strategic approach, the co-authors of Chapter 6, Alina Ignatieva and Pavel Trifonov, take a look at perspectives on value chains, including the features and possibilities of Russia's involvement in the global value chains in the era of the Fourth Industrial Revolution.

Dmitry Stapran and Igor Stepnov are the authors of Chapter 7, "Sourcing and Digital Strategy Performance of Big Companies in Key Global Markets". This chapter contributes to the discussion of the fundamental concept of sourcing by Russian firms during four different periods in the digital era, based on transaction costs, competitive advantage, trust, and institutional voids.

The author of Chapter 8 "Technologies of the Fourth Industrial Revolution as a Driver of Advancing in Digital Operations Management" Julia Kovalchuk investigates the trends most likely to impact the opportunities and prospects for the development of operational management in the context of the economy's digital transformation.

On the topic of how boards of directors are evolving their activities in digital times, Alexander Yukhno take a look at the different perspectives on the increasing role digital characteristics play in firm's business strategy in Chapter 9 "The Fourth Industrial Revolution and the New Paradigm of Corporate Governance". The author concludes that digital strategy and digital tools significantly expand management capabilities, and the role of the board of directors as a strategic management and oversight body will continue to increase.

Chapter 10 "Application of Data Mining and Machine Learning Methods to Enhance the Effectiveness of Digital Marketing Strategies" written by Sergey Gutnik is devoted to the ways in which data mining and machine learning methods enhance the effectiveness of digital marketing strategies. The author focuses on machine learning algorithms (regression, classification, clustering, decision trees, neural networks) and particularities of their implementation, as well as on the benefits of machine learning in marketing strategies.

In their entirety, these chapters give answers to—as well as ask additional questions about—the aspects of business environments influencing the elaboration and implementation of digital strategies in the global economy. Furthermore, these chapters provide a framework for the further discussion of the impact of digital technology on the activities of modern companies. The chapters have a focus on industry or national specificity. The range of companies and industries under consideration is wide—from digital conglomerates and the digital transformation of oil and gas company management, to the digital characteristics of Western companies' marketing strategies in the Chinese cosmetics market, as well as the impact of digital technologies on value management in Russian companies.

Chapter 11, entitled "The Evolution of Conglomerates in Digital Era: Strategies and Performance", is co-authored by Natalia Konina, Irina Vladimirova and George H. Stonehouse. This chapter offers a comprehensive review of the characteristics of the activities and strategies of digital conglomerates. The authors prove that conglomerates, as a form of integrated business organization in global markets, have not exhausted themselves, but the current stage of the digital revolution has created the prerequisites for the transformation of digital leaders into global digital conglomerates, which, using the network nature of operations and platform features, have managed to increase the efficiency of their operations.

Chapter 12, entitled "Digital Transformation Strategies of Global Oil and Gas Companies: Preparing for the Fourth Industrial Revolution", written by Anastasia Sheveleva, Peter Khaiter, and Sergey Tyaglov, turns to the implementation of digital tools in the management of the biggest oil companies. This chapter discusses the impact of digitalization on the planning, organization, coordination, management, and control processes in oil and gas companies—their main functions of management—as well as identifying the benefits of the use of digital technology in management activities. The research proves that digitalization, despite the debatable nature of the problem, as a whole has a positive impact on the management of oil and gas companies, increasing its effectiveness.

Chapter 13 in the volume, co-authored by Yuriy Savinov, Evgeniya Taranovskaya and Oleg Gavryushin, focuses on the development of e-commerce as a new form of internalizing company activities, facilitating the minimization of expenses for advertising and marketing connected with market entry. The authors note that despite the domination of the most used method of calculating the Return on Investment (ROI), other methods should be applied: in particular, those based on accounting.

Chapter 14, co-authored by Lilia Revenko and Nikolay Revenko, concentrates on the effect of digital platforms on new strategies in the agribusiness sector. The authors suggest that the adaptive process to the platform-based economy depends on several aspects: geographical location and profile, organizational structure, the propensity for innovation, the market environment, and government regulation factors. The article draws attention to the ambiguous influence digital platforms have on articultural business; for example, high-technology companies' improvement in performance is accompanied by the digital divide.

The author of the next Chapter 15 "Retail Business Models in the Era of the Fourth Industrial Revolution" Ekaterina Bostoganashvili identifies both the challenges and the opportunities for the evolution of international big retail firms in these turbulent times.

The next Chapter 16, written by Raisa Nozdreva and Anna Churakova, reviews the practical use of modern digital tools by hospitality companies, and concludes that they are the most important vehicles for the implementation of their empirical marketing strategies. The chapter describes the results of a system analysis of using digital tools by hotel chains, identifies the key digital channels being used to interact with the consumer, and determines the extent of integration among the various channels, as well as the possibility of creating an integrated cross-channel infrastructure.

The authors of Chapter 17 Elena Ponomareva and Elena Nozdrenko focus on the digital transformation of Western companies' marketing strategies in the Chinese cosmetic market. Cosmetic goods marketing is aimed at the millennial generation, which is the predominant target audience, and this marketing requires digitalization in the tools and methods of its communication and distribution. The chapter notes that digital strategies in the cosmetic market in China are a key driver of marketing, as they allow flexibility in responding to ongoing changes and market needs.

Chapter 18 "Management by Values in Digital Transformation Strategies of Russian Companies and the Fourth Industrial Revolution", co-authored by Alexander Gaponenko, Anastasia Erokhina, and Maria

Pokrovskaya, is dedicated to an empirical study of the impact of management by values on the digital business transformation processes of Russian companies.

Chapter 19, Conclusion.

References

Appel, G., Grewal, L., Hadi, R., & Stephen, A. T. (2020). The Future of Social Media in Marketing. *Journal of the Academy of Marketing Science, 48*, 79–95.

Baldwin, R. (2016). *The Great Convergence: Information Technology and the New Globalization*. Cambridge: The Belknap Press of Harvard University Press.

Christensen, C. M., McDonald, R., Altman, E. J., & Palmer E. (2018). Disruptive Innovation: An Intellectual History and Directions for Future Research. *Journal of Management Studies, 55*(7), 1043–1078.

Deloitte. (2015). *Industry 4.0: Challenges and Solutions for the Digital Transformation and Use of Exponential Technologies*. Zurich: Deloitte.

Konina, N. (2018). Evolution of the Largest Multinational German Companies. *Sovremennaya Evropa, 2*(81), p. 49-59

Leodolter, W. (2017). *Digital Transformation Shaping the Subconscious Minds of Organizations: Innovative Organizations and Hybrid Intelligences*. Cham: Springer.

Lopez Gonzalez, J., & Ferencz, J. (2018). *Digital Trade and Market Openness* (OECD Trade Policy Tapers, No. 217). Paris: OECD Publishing. https://doi.org/10.1787/1bd89c9a-en.

McKinsey Global Institute. (2019). *Globalization in Transition: The Future of Trade and Value Chains* (Report). Available at: https://www.mckinsey.com/featured-insights/innovation-and-growth/globalization-in-transition-the-future-of-trade-and-value-chains.

OECD. (2016). *An OECD Horizon Scan of Megatrends and Technology Trends in the Context of Future Research Policy*. Copenhagen: DASTI.

OECD. (2017). *The Next Production Revolution: Implications for Governments and Business*. Paris: OECD Publishing.

Skog, D. A., & Wimelius, H. (2018). Digital Disruption. *Business & Information Systems Engineering, 60*, 431–437.

Stonehouse, G. H., & Konina, N. Y. (2020). *Management Challenges in the Age of Digital Disruption*. Conference Paper. Conference: Proceedings of the 1st International Conference on Emerging Trends and Challenges in the Management Theory and Practice (ETCMTP 2019). https://doi.org/10.2991/aebmr.k.200201.001.

UNCTAD. (2019). *Digital Economy Report 2019*. New York: United Nations Publication.

CHAPTER 2

Digital Strategy Implementation in Marketing: New Performance and Risks

Valentina Gerasimenko

Introduction

Digital technologies are becoming an integral element of contemporary life, as this sphere is expanding very quickly. Global digital growth shows a million new people around the world coming online every day. 45% of the world's population are now social media users: a whopping 3.5 billion people (Global Digital Report 2019). According to Mediascope, in 2019 the Runet audience reached 93 million people, growing over the past three years by 7%. According to data for 2018–2019, 76% of the Russian population aged 12 and over used the internet at least once a month (Mediascope News 2019).

More and more potential consumers spend a long time on social media and use mobile applications, possibly even integrating them into their work and household tasks; consumer behavior and consumer choice models are changing dramatically.

The growth of the scale and forms of digital communications is inevitably followed by the development of electronic markets and digital

V. Gerasimenko (✉)
Lomonosov Moscow State University, Moscow, Russia

N. Konina (ed.), *Digital Strategies in a Global Market*,
https://doi.org/10.1007/978-3-030-58267-8_2

management strategies, based on the use of technologies for collecting big data and automating their processing. Russia is, in terms of volumes and growth rates of the e-commerce market, one of the ten leading companies in the world. According to Yandex.Market, in 2019 trade turnover exceeded a trillion per year (Sahno 2019). This, in turn, creates the conditions for the emergence of new business models and management tools, primarily in the field of market interactions and marketing.

Marketing is also becoming very dynamic as markets become digitalized. Modern companies are facing global environmental changes, the most serious of which include technological and competitive changes that require quick adaptation to the emergence of virtual tools and new IT solutions. Therefore, new methods of strategic competitive analysis on the internet are emerging (Gerasimenko and Golovanova 2018). Employees '39; competencies are changing: businesses need internet analytics, software specialists, digital logistics, and digital marketing strategies.

There is also growing scientific interest in the socio-economic consequences of using digital technologies in management. As a rule, the main aspect affecting this issue is the threat of reduced employment due to the digitalization of management and the replacement of human labor with machine labor (World Economic Forum 2016). Foreign studies predict that in the next 15–20 years, about 30–40% of jobs in advanced economies are likely to be cut (Valenduc and Vendramin 2016). It is assumed that there is a causal relationship between technological innovations (such as machine learning and robotics), and productivity growth. Productivity increases not only due to new technologies, but also due to organizational and labor changes that may be instigated by their application (Freddi 2017).

As for company management, digitalization is becoming a condition of competitiveness, especially for high-tech companies. Using digital strategies, the company detects market trends, creates new consumer values, reduces marketing costs, and finds insights for promotion in the digital environment (Gerasimenko 2019). Digital transformation simultaneously affects several areas in the organization, and there are many stakeholders involved in determining the transformation strategy: for example, marketing, IT, product development, strategic management, or HR. All these groups need to develop an understanding of the digital transformation priorities. Research results (Berghaus and Back 2016) have shown that most companies are already using digital technologies in management. However, creating a personalized customer experience based on big data analysis or process automation shows lower results.

According to research by Russian experts (Smirnov 2019), the main factors pushing businesses to start digital transformation are changed customer preferences (55%), prospects for developing in new markets (53%), and increased competitive pressure (49%). Most companies need to win new market shares, increase revenue, reduce costs, rebuild, diversify their businesses, build up from competitors, and sometimes change completely (Gorlin 2019).

According to Russian surveys, more than 80% of companies consider digital transformation critical (Koptelov 2016). However, the desire to transform often is not based upon real understanding, and this is one of the main reasons for failure in digital marketing. Transformation without reference to the real needs, tasks, and problems of the business is a utopian idea. At best, the company has a vision of the business model and processes, and their way of thinking remain unchanged; in this case, the implementation tools become more complex and more expensive. According to expert estimates, the employees of many companies are not sufficiently prepared for digital transformation (Dudareva 2018). Sometimes, top management starts implementing changes, middle management does not support them, and employees do not understand what is happening at all.

Companies implementing digital technologies face similar problems in different countries. This was shown, in particular, by a recently published study by the New York Times. "The biggest barrier to getting technology rolled out is the organizational resistance to adoption," said Eric Brignolfsson, the head of the Digital Economy Initiative, Massachusetts Institute of Technology, "so companies need a strategy not only for how to get it to work, but also how to get the work force behind it getting rolled out" (Condliffe 2019). Digitalization of markets requires companies to initiate the changing of their business models and creating new competencies for employees (Gerasimenko and Molchanova 2017).

Therefore, researchers should pay special attention to the current trends of digitalization in management and marketing, as well as to problems such as resistance to change and challenges for management. These issues require special research and analysis.

Methodology

In order to understand which areas of digital marketing and management strategies are being implemented in Russian companies and what competencies are under development by Russian managers, the author conducted 2 surveys of managers in 2019 and in 2020.

The methodology of the research is an electronic anonymous survey. The target group and the survey participants are top managers, and managers of large and medium-sized businesses. The survey was conducted among graduates of MBA programs of the faculty of Economics of Moscow State University, a homogeneous group of people representing the target audience of the survey. 132 people took part in the survey 2019, including 44% of top managers and 56% of heads of divisions and departments. About half of them represented various companies registered in Moscow and Saint Petersburg (both Russian and foreign), while the rest were companies represented in the regions of Russia, as well as several of our graduates from neighboring countries of Kazakhstan and Azerbaijan (about 10%). The second study, conducted in July 2020, aimed to examine the impact of restrictions related to the COVID-19 pandemic in April–July 2020 on the use of digital technologies in management and marketing. The same target group was used, and the same research methodology and questionnaire were applied. A total of 131 people from the same group of respondents took part in the 2020 survey.

The homogeneity of the target audience ensured that the study was representative, as did the fact that graduates of MSU (the country's top university) MBA programs are advanced managers with modern competencies and knowledge of strategic management and marketing. We set the purpose of the surveys to find out how these top Russian managers evaluate the content, current value, and implementation of digital strategies and tools in management and marketing, and how they assess relevant competencies and risks in this area and what changes have been observed under the influence of the challenges caused by the COVID pandemic.

Results

Through the study in 2019, it was possible to understand how top managers and company leaders evaluate their implementation of digital strategies in company management. We wanted to evaluate the understanding of market digitalization and the use of digital technologies and strategies in different companies. Therefore, the question was the following: "If you imagine an organization in your market that makes the most of the current opportunities of digital technologies in the development and implementation of market strategies, how would you assess the situation in your company?" It should be noted that only 8% consider the situation excellent, while 39% call it good. More than half of respondents (53%) rated the actual use of digital strategies in their companies as merely satisfactory (31%) or even unsatisfactory (23%). According to the survey, digital tools and strategies have been used most successfully over the past three years in the areas of working with clients through a corporate website (27%), managing customer relationships through CRM systems (21%), Or actively developing technologies for working in social networks (17%). At the same time, other areas—including such important areas as logistics management—are still poorly covered by digital technologies.

In companies where digital strategies have been introduced into management and marketing, the majority of respondents believe that the effect meets expectations (58%) or even exceeds expectations (10%); for this large number the effect is evaluated very positively.

This makes us think about the pace and contradictions of digitalization in companies. If managers evaluate such efficiency so highly, a logical question arises: why is the transition to digital management strategies so slow, according to the same top managers and business leaders? What is holding back this process: the lack of technology, or the employees themselves? Why are there still obstacles? In our survey we tried to get answers from managers to these complex questions.

It should be noted that the range of digital strategic management tools available today in management and marketing is widely esteemed by business representatives. These are, first of all, big data and business analytics, the use of social networks in marketing, mobile technologies in marketing, multi-channel marketing, and trading technologies. Cloud technologies and interactive interfaces are being introduced. Digital tools—artificial intelligence and machine learning, virtual and augmented reality technologies—are beginning to be actively used in market strategies.

The second study, conducted in July 2020, showed how quickly the situation changes in a crisis. The urgent need arose to manage the work of companies remotely, ensuring all departments, as well as contacts with customers and partners, worked at a distance. This dramatically accelerated the introduction of remote technologies in management and marketing, including the transition to online communications, using modern software products such as Zoom, Microsoft Teams, Google Meet, and other resources. The answer to the question on how managers assessed the range of digital tools available in marketing today looked different now, compared to the estimates in 2019 (see Table 2.1).

In other words, the set of digital management tools available and already being introduced to marketers is quite wide; dealing with these technologies, however, or marketers' willingness to use them, proves less successful. This implies the need to analyze the causes for this, and search for ways to overcome these obstacles to management digitalization. As our survey showed, many managers tend to think that management digitalization is slow because of the lack of awareness. Thus, according to respondents' estimates, only 14% of managers have the necessary information to implement digital methods in the company's marketing strategy. The rest reported a lack of information (79%), while many of them noted the prioritization of other business development strategies (34%). At the same time, when it came specifically to their company, the importance of digital management technologies were assessed much more cautiously. Accordingly, only 16% of respondents indicated that digitalization of management and marketing allows them to become market leaders today, and only 13% believe that these technologies allow them to open a fundamentally new line of business.

An interesting transformation has occurred in 2020 in assessing the effectiveness of digital technologies in the management and marketing of a company. If, previously, managers were quite cautious, now top

Table 2.1 Manager assessment of the range of digital tools available in marketing today

Question: "Which digital technologies have an impact on management and marketing today?"	*2019 (%)*	*2020 (%)*
Big data and analytics	20	57
Social media marketing	17	45
Mobile marketing	15	63
Omnichannel marketing	13	34
Cloud technologies	11	36
Interactive interfaces	9	41
Artificial intelligence, machine learning	7	38
Elements of virtual and augmented reality	2	20
Other	7	16

Source Created by the author

Table 2.2 Evaluating the effectiveness of digital strategies in your company

Question: "Evaluate the effectiveness of digital technologies in your company's marketing"	*2019 (%)*	*2020 (%)*
They allow you to achieve some competitive advantage	42	54
The company cannot survive without them	19	40
They make you market leaders	16	34
They allow you to start a fundamentally new line of business	13	22
Difficult to answer	10	8

Source Created by the author

managers were more confident in assessing the effect of their application in all possible directions (see Table 2.2)

The above estimates of effectiveness seem rather cautious. Therefore, it was interesting to find out their causes, analyzing how the survey participants evaluated the problems that managers face when implementing digital strategies. As for the main difficulties in implementing digital strategies, 20% mentioned the lack of qualified managers and marketers; another 19% noted a lack of experience in implementing digital strategies in practice; 18% indicated the poor interaction between the company's divisions; 17% believe that the lack of involvement and employee interest in digitalization is a hindrance; 14% mentioned technological incompetence; and finally, 12% indicated the poorly timed provision of software resources for using big data and other digital technologies in marketing.

It is important to note that today, as the crisis unfurls, managers are seeing the effects of digitalization not only in maintaining competitive advantages (54%) and surviving in a crisis (40%), but in other areas too. The share of managers who are convinced that the active use of modern digital technologies in management and marketing will allow them to become market leaders has grown significantly (34%), and the share of those who believe that digital technologies will help to open a completely new promising business direction has grown (22%).

In general, the managers' view of the problem now seems more optimistic. This confirms the idea that an economic crisis always opens a window for new opportunities and innovative technologies. The dynamics of the described changes in the estimates of available digital management tools are shown in Fig. 2.1.

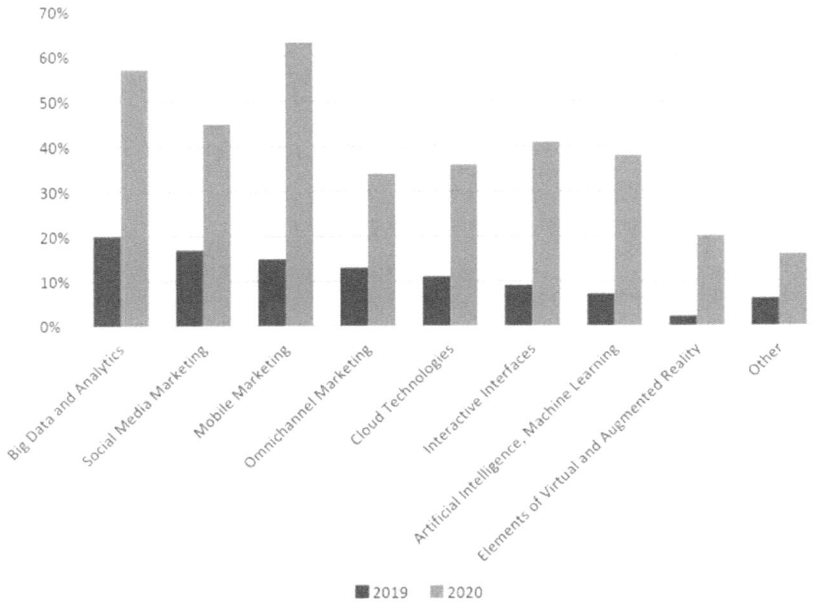

Fig. 2.1 Dynamic of manager assessment of available digital tools 2019/2020 (*Source* Created by the author)

Conclusions/Recommendations

Our study confirms that digitalization is developing rapidly, but unevenly. Managers' assessment of the range of digital tools currently available in management and marketing shows broad prospects for the development of digital strategies.

The estimates in this study show that the effectiveness of digital strategies is not always high, there are currently problems with the implementation of digital strategies, and the main risks in management digitalization lie mainly on the side of management competencies.

Scientific research in this area should bear in mind that new digital strategies emerging in global markets shift the focus of marketing from promoting a product to acquiring and retaining a target consumer through a personalized internet communications system. In this area, we can identify several new areas that will need to be explored soon:

- blurring the line between offline and online trade, developing omnichannel marketing strategies;
- developing cross-border online trading strategies, globalizing markets;
- developing strategies based on the use of Big Data technology and machine learning;
- including mobile technologies in marketing, using social networks for communicating with consumers on mobile devices;
- developing personalization strategies for marketing and sales based on innovative digital solutions and artificial intelligence.

Digitalization of marketing is an irreversible process; it is caused by revolutionary technological changes. The costs of using marketing analytic technologies in the US and UK companies exceed their advertising budgets. For example, Gartner's annual study "CMO Spend Survey for 2018-2019" indicates that the largest share of marketing budgets (29%) was spent on marketing and analytical services in 2018; compared to 2017, the share of investment in technology increased by 7%, while the expenses on paid promotion decreased from 25% in 2017 to 23% in 2018 (Pemberton 2019).

The rapid development of market analytics internet tools based on Big Data processing offers up wide opportunities for their use in developing marketing strategies. Furthermore, practice shows that using analytical internet services entails a reduction in research costs and better reasoning behind managerial decision-making (Gerasimenko 2019; Omiyale 2016). Modern market analytics involve using those information systems that transform raw data into meaningful information, thus helping to reduce uncertainty in decision-making (Torres et al. 2018).

It is important to emphasize that the risk of lacking managerial competency, noted in our study, is global. According to surveys by Hays (a major British recruitment agency), only 18% of marketing leaders rate their digital skills as very good. When it comes to the technical skills that are most lacking, 46% of marketers say they need digital project management skills to successfully automate processes, 57% point to strategic marketing skills, and 70% to data analytics (The Hays 2019).

The difficulties of this process are not yet sufficiently understood. COVID-19 is catalyzing big changes; the shock caused by communication restrictions during this pandemic in 2020 has served as a strong catalyst for the digitalization process in management. "This crisis is bringing to the surface all kinds of innovative ways to use technology and other means to serve customers. In many cases, new solutions and products might have already been in your pipeline or on your mind, but current needs are giving you reason to accelerate development and launch" (Adams and Hart 2020).

The crisis of 2020 has shown that digital technologies in management are a valuable resource for overcoming existing problems and starting future development. Large reserves for cost savings are provided by the transition to cloud infrastructure in company management. In the coming years, more and more organizations will use the services of cloud providers and create cloud services that are necessary for remote work and training. We can expect that companies working in various fields—in particular, in the financial sector, medicine, healthcare, and retail—will gradually come to the "cloud only" model; in other words, using cloud infrastructure will be their only option.

Many companies will invest in machine learning and artificial intelligence. While artificial intelligence is most often used to automate customer service and sales, or to search for and prevent threats, machine learning helps to extract useful information from any data, which means that management decisions can be made based on Analytics, not on intuition.

Significant investments in the development of artificial intelligence systems can be expected in the retail and banking industries. Retailers are investing in customer service automation. The banking industry will invest in developing automated credit scoring systems and preventing threats.

Businesses will make greater use of data from IoT devices to search for hypotheses and forecasts. For example, retailers can use sensors to monitor inventory, saving on staff. Smart shelves have already appeared—they monitor the number of products and give a signal if the products are out of stock or placed incorrectly. With the development of IoT, the amount of data received from smart devices increases, and their processing moves to the cloud. It is important to note that IoT platforms will deliver reliable big data for machine learning.

By processing this data, companies will be able to develop business hypotheses. For example, they may be able to find solutions to attract new customers or increase profits. In this regard, businesses will be interested in cloud IoT services. These will help companies save resources for developing special platforms, quickly implementing Industrial Internet of Things systems without significant costs.

All these trends reflect the current stage of business digitalization across the world and in Russia. In the near future, all new routine operations in infrastructure can be performed through providers of infrastructure and platform cloud services.

Most modern IT systems include high-tech services. This can be a consultation on the architecture of a future product, a service for implementing an Analytics system, renting cloud databases, or outsourcing the company's services management (managed services). In a crisis, new challenges appear for the company's marketers. Digital technologies help to overcome them.

Managers were able to understand, during the crisis of 2020, that the features of anti-crisis team management are a very large number of external changes, whose speed is too high, which forced a switch to short-time management during the crisis using online technologies in management and marketing. These technologies compensate for the almost complete absence of offline communication.

The search for a work-life balance became, perhaps, a great difficulty after switching to remote operation during the crisis. The volume of work in the digital environment has increased many times, with the standard working day having become up to 12 hours. If in the short term this could be attributed to positive changes that contributed to rapid management decision-making, then after a few months fatigue will most likely accumulate and management efficiency will accordingly decrease.

During the period when offline activities were restricted, all companies switched their interaction with clients to a digital channel. Now, the volume of information-emails, ads, and invitations to various online events increases many times. Therefore, the role of information analysis and forms of digital communication with customers to maintain loyalty is increasing.

Social networks have now become one of the main channels for managing brand reputation, which means increasing the role of digital technologies, such as content analysis, in the study of consumer behavior, as well as the development of advertising on social networks.

It is necessary to constantly analyze the activities of competitors on the internet. It is important to use digital methods for competitive analyses of sites, platforms, and price parsing based on Big Data.

For marketing, it is important to analyze what has changed in working with content. In times of crises, non-standard approaches to providing content are in high demand. If a company cannot navigate the new environment and continues to post simple advertising texts describing its products on the internet, it may lose customers.

If a company starts using videos with messages of support from employees—recording videos with product presentations with an emphasis on specific benefits for consumers in the current environment—it has a greater chance not only to survive, but also to acquire new customers and increase the level of loyalty of all its customers. This is why it is important to accompany the company's online events not only with presentations and detailed announcements, but also with video messages, in order to minimize the distance between speakers and listeners. A strategy for conducting online events with a focus on customer needs would be correct in a crisis.

A business that quickly adapts to online management technologies is more likely to survive in the new reality. Many business and everyday tasks require personal contact, even with the help of a webcam. For the management of many companies, virtualization and "zooming" (a term that arose in management due to the name of the Zoom program) have become the new norm of everyday work.

There is no choice: managers and marketers have to continue working even in difficult conditions and adapt to virtualization. The coronavirus has caused a seismic shift in industry around the world, so companies need to look wider and find new opportunities to stay connected, work productively, and restore business.

Online technologies for customer relations help to preserve such industries as fitness, restaurant business, event industry, education, and retail in the conditions of a crisis. Digital technologies help support companies in manufacturing and construction today. Although these industries have been hit hard, they can use remote work opportunities for group discussions and develop ideas to improve productivity. They can study online reviews of 3D materials, product samples, and supplier quotes.

Everyone will have to learn to live in a new way—from small businesses to large industries. Remote work, conferencing, and digital and media tools are skills that need to be mastered in order to get good results. These skills will be useful for a long time, even after this crisis has passed. These skills will open a new era of effective workplace management practices in the future. Virtual connections will become the lifeblood of companies.

The business that understands this more quickly and adapts to it will have a better chance to stay ahead of the changes and survive in the new reality.

New research is needed in this area. To overcome these risks, researchers should monitor and evaluate new technological changes, give as much information as possible and as early as possible in how markets and companies are transforming, and pinpoint who will be affected by the changes and what economic entities will get from them.

Another important area of research is to identify and show how to eliminate behavioral barriers that emerge to technological change. The difference in employee's motivation can also be a barrier to mastering effective technologies: different people want to achieve different indicators, and in digital transformation, new indicators will appear. Such inconsistencies can greatly impede the adoption of digital technology in management. The most urgent tasks for developing modern companies include: forming digital competencies in marketing, coordinating digital interaction between different levels of management, and motivating managers. These areas should be the subject of further economic research.

References

Adams, T., & Hart, R. (2020, June 4). *Redefining B2B Experience: COVID-19 Catalyzes Big Changes*. Consumer & Retail. https://www.strategy-business.com/blog/Redefining-B2B-experience-COVID-19-catalyzes-big-changes?gko=f1e0e&utm_source=itw&utm_medium=itw20200461l&utm_campaign=resp.

Berghaus, S., & Back, A. (2016). Stages in Digital Business Transformation: Results of an Empirical Maturity Study. MCIS 2016 Proceedings. 22. Available at: http://aisel.aisnet.org/mcis2016/22.

Condliffe, J. (2019). Some Workers Hate Robots. Retraining May Change That. *The New York Times*. Available at: https://www.nytimes.com/2019/07/19/technology/amazon-automation-labor.html.

Dudareva, D. (2018). Vnedrenie innovacij v ofise: kak preodolet "soprotivlenie sotrudnikov". *E-xecutive.ru*. Available at: https://www.e-xecutive.ru/management/practices/1989419-vnedrenie-innovatsii-v-ofise-kak-preodolet-soprotivlenie-sotrudnikov.

Freddi, D. (2017). Digitalization and Employment in Manufacturing. Pace of the Digitalisation Process and Impact on Employment in Advanced Italian Manufacturing Companies. *AI & Soc, 33*(1), 393–403.

Gerasimenko, V. (2019). *Value Creation Through Digital Technologies in Product Development on Russian Telecommunications Markets*. Innovation Management, Entrepreneurship and Sustainability, Proceedings of the 7th International Conference in Prague (pp. 220–228).

Gerasimenko, V., & Golovanova, E. V. (2018). Cifrovye instrumenty konkurentnogo analiza: kak izmerit "znanie i interes k brendu v Seti. *Marketing v Rossii i za rubezhom, 4*, 77–100.

Gerasimenko, V., & Molchanova, O. (2017). Global Pressure or National Identity: Strategic Challenges for Russian Business Schools. *Serbian Journal of Management, 12*(1), 133–141.

Global Digital Report. (2019). *We Are Social*. Available at: https://wearesocial.com/global-digital-report-2019.

Gorlin, D. (2019). Tri trenda, kotorye pomogut transformirovat 'biznes v cifru. *E-xecutive.ru*, 2209(5). Available at: https://www.e-xecutive.ru/management/itforbusiness/1990156-tri-trenda-kotorye-pomogut-transformirovat-biznes-v-tsifru.

Hays. (2019). *The DNA of a Marketing Leader*. Available at: https://www.hays.co.uk/job/marketing-jobs/dna-of-a-marketing-leader.

Koptelov, A. (2016). Gotov li vash biznes k cifrovoj transformacii? *E-xecutive.ru*, 7330(5). Available at: https://www.e-xecutive.ru/management/itforbusiness/1985479-gotov-li-vash-biznes-k-tsifrovoi-transformatsii.

Mediascope News. (2019, April 17). *The Audience of RuNet has Grown by 7% in the Last 3 Years*. https://mediascope.net/news/1035826/.

Omiyale, W. (2016). *Big Data in a Post-digital Age. 2016 Q3-Q4 GRIT Report, SVP, Confirmit, Sharing His Thoughts on the Current State of the Market Research Industry*. https://www.greenbook.org/marketing-research/GRIT-Commentary-Big-Data-in-a-Post-Digital-Age-1020398.

Pemberton, C. (2019). *8 Top Findings in Gartner CMO Spend Survey 2018–19*. https://www.gartner.com/en/marketing/insights/articles/8-top-findings-in-gartner-cmo-spend-survey-2018-19.

Sahno, O. (2019). *E-commerce v 2019 godu: klyuchevye fakty, kotorye nel'zya ignorirovat'*. https://rb.ru/opinion/e-commerce-2019/.

Smirnov, A. (2019). 5 oshibok uvlechennyh cifrovoj transformaciej. *E-xecutive.ru*, 6395(56). Available at: https://www.e-xecutive.ru/management/itforbusiness/1989903-5-oshibok-uvlechennyh-tsifrovoi-transformatsiei?utm_campaign=1605.

Torres, R., Sidorova, A., & Jones, M. (2018). Enabling Firm Performance through Business Intelligence and Analytics: A Dynamic Capabilities Perspective. *Information & Management, 55*(7), 822–839.

Valenduc, G., & Vendramin, P. (2016). *Work in the Digital Economy: Sorting the Old from the New* (ETUI Working Paper 2016: 03).

World Economic Forum. (2016). *The Future of Job—Employment, Skills and Workforce Strategy for the Fourth Industrial Revolution*. Available at: http://www3.weforum.org/docs/WEF_Future_of_Jobs.pdf.

CHAPTER 3

EU Digital Policy as a Tool for Navigating the Fourth Industrial Revolution

Olga Butorina

Introduction

The digital single market strategy supported by the EU leaders in June 2015 was a further step in the long-term strategy of economic integration. Firstly, the Rome Treaty of 1957 proclaimed the goal of creating a common market for goods in the European Economic Community; then the Single European Act of 1986 enshrined the objective of an Internal Market with the four freedoms of movement of goods, services, capital, and labour. Any single (or common) market adheres to the principle of non-discrimination, which ensures equal market access for companies of member states. Providing various efficiency gains it thus contributes to the better allocation of resources and productivity growth—an internal dimension of any common market. However, regional integration projects always have an external dimension, since improving the quality of the

O. Butorina (✉)
Institute of Europe, Russian Academy of Sciences, Moscow, Russian Federation
e-mail: butorina@ieras.ru

N. Konina (ed.), *Digital Strategies in a Global Market*,
https://doi.org/10.1007/978-3-030-58267-8_3

domestic market sets the scene for the improvement of a region's international competitiveness, as well as for the strengthening of its position in the global economy.

In the 1950s, the Dutch economist Jan Tinbergen distinguished between negative and positive integration. Negative integration was defined as the removal of barriers to trade, including customs duties, though this leads to favourable consequences. Positive integration begins constructively, being aimed at creating new elements and new economic qualities; an example of positive integration is the introduction of a common customs tariff (Tinbergen 1954).

This division has become generally accepted in the academic literature on regional integration. In these terms, any common market proceeds from the idea of negative integration, since its task is to create an internal economic space without frontiers. If this can be done, then steps are taken towards positive integration.

As for the international dimension of a common market, this can both work towards trade liberalization and towards creating a new quality of the global environment from its very beginning. Here, the division into negative and positive integration can be carried out with a certain degree of conventionality. The EU traditionally promotes a liberal agenda, upholding the principles of free trade and fair competition at the international level (with a few exceptions, the largest of which remains its Common Agricultural Policy).

Regarding its digital policy, it has only taken a few years for the EU to have moved from tasks of a predominantly internal nature—when negative and positive integration was a response to external challenges—to global tasks.

Methodology

This chapter analyses the EU official programmes, statements, and expert reports prepared by the request of the EU institutions. The advantage of this method is that it makes outlining the range of tasks possible. Its disadvantage is that it inhibits tracing the way these tasks are implemented; this opportunity, however, may arise soon. To assess the EU's place in the digital technology market, the author selected two key segments for which there is representative statistics data from international organizations—the World Bank and UNCTAD—as well as from the Eurostat. These segments included information and communication technology (ICT) goods and services and digitally deliverable services.

Results

A Digital Single Market

The first important document in this area is "A Digital Single Market Strategy for Europe" presented by the European Commission in May 2015. The name itself contains an unambiguous reference to the 1986 Single European Act, and its goal to create the Single European Market, a legacy which is recognized by many scholars (Mărcuţ 2017: 3, Kondratieva 2019).

This suggests that the new programme primarily aims to transform and improve the European digital goods and services markets. The need to take special actions was explained by external factors and the changing nature of modern production processes:

> The global economy is rapidly becoming digital. Information and Communications Technology (ICT) is no longer a specific sector but the foundation of all modern innovative economic systems. The Internet and digital technologies are transforming the lives we lead, the way we work - as individuals, in business, and our communities as they become more integrated across all sectors of our economy and society.

The document outlined two interrelated external goals the Digital Single Market aims for: (1) maintaining and strengthening its position as a "world leader" in the digital economy; (2) creating favourable market conditions for the European companies to grow globally. It was noted that the fragmentation of the digital goods and services market does not allow EU companies to fully realize their potential on the global stage (European Commission 2015).

The document had a special section on the international dimension. According to the official position, building a full-fledged Digital Single Market will help companies to grow beyond the EU and make it an even more attractive place for foreign investment. The EU has announced its goal to create an open digital market based on the reciprocity of its trading partners; the European Commission explicitly stated that it would put pressure on partners to adhere to the principle of openness of the digital market while "effectively respecting intellectual property rights".

The openness of the global digital market meant the removal of any existing barriers to digital commerce. The authors of the document piqued the interests of European companies whose performance was hindered by these barriers. The phrase that the EU was "the world's first exporter of digital services" alluded to the scale of the damage.

To solve this problem, two means have been proposed. The first is to actively influence the developing international environment during its formation. The EU should continue to develop an "ambitious digital trade and investment policy" which, in fact, uses the potential of the EU as a normative power, allowing them to set those global ideas about the norm that met the European Union's interests and values. Besides, the EU intended to engage in the traditional long-running practice of bilateral free trade agreements, which it signs with its international trade partners (European Commission 2015).

In 2018, the European Commission announced a plan for the digitalization of its activities, designed for the period until 2022. The subject of the document predetermined its internal orientation, which is why it contains very few references to the global aspects of the EU's digital policy. For example, the introduction identifies digitalization as one of the four main medium-term challenges the European Union is facing, along with globalization, climate change, and demographic shifts. One of the desired results of the Commission's digitalization should be its increased ability to meet the requirements of today's globalized world, with a digital information space and real-time data flow (European Commission 2018). The Commission's digitalization, as expected, could increase its efficiency and effectiveness, which in turn could have a positive impact on the markets, namely, to "create international growth opportunities for all types of innovative companies, even the smallest start-ups" (European Commission 2018).

Another noteworthy document is the Domestic Market and Consumer Protection study, published in January 2019, which was conducted at the request of the European Parliament through its Committee on Internal Market and Consumer Protection. Its authors were three experts from the Bruegel think tank who specialize in economic issues (Marcus et al. 2019).

The report provides a standard argument in favour of a single market—the digital market specifically. It is expected that this will allow all EU citizens, regardless of their country of residence, to make electronic orders for physical and virtual goods and services, as well as provide access to e-government services. Considerable hopes are placed on the economies of scale: "The resulting Single Market gains could be expected to result in lower prices, greater choice, and enhanced convenience for consumers, scale economies, and the enhanced competitiveness of the EU in comparison with its global trading partners" (Marcus et al. 2019). That means that the removal of internal barriers (negative integration) is interpreted as a preliminary—and indispensable—condition for increasing the global competitiveness of the European Union.

Strengthening the international position of European companies also depends on the technological factor: namely, on the comprehensive digitalization of society and the economy. This includes numerous advanced technologies: fast broadband and mobile (5G) communication services, artificial intelligence, robotics, big data, machine learning, the Internet of Things, cloud computing, and possibly blockchain. Experts noted the EU's non-competitiveness in the global audiovisual market (e-books, films, etc.) and called for wide-ranging industrial policy measures to strengthen the global competitiveness of the European audiovisual sector (Marcus et al. 2019).

A separate topic of the report was fair competition in the global digital service market. In this respect, the authors identified two main risk sources.

The first is the excessive concentration of business in the hands of large international platforms such as Google, Facebook, Uber, Apple, and Amazon. As is noted in the report, fake news has cast a slur on their reputation in recent years, but has also created situations that jeopardized the rules of free competition. Their actions also gave rise to serious concern about fair treatment of taxation and related state aid issues.

The second source—both of risky problems and of solutions—is the advanced technologies themselves. On the one hand, automatic online pricing algorithms can spontaneously collude with one another, which violates the free-market-pricing principle. On the other hand, automated tools—based on artificial intelligence, machine learning, and big data methods—can help the timely detection of collusion. They can be very useful in order to reasonably separate cases when price convergence occurs naturally, and therefore is permitted from situations where such convergence is the result of collusion (Marcus et al. 2019).

This implies the need to strengthen the EU competition policy and "to protect EU interests from encroachment by third countries" which tend to freely interpret the established rules of mutually beneficial multilateral cooperation. At the same time, experts advocated a cautious and balanced approach to the competition law, because "EU prosperity depends on global acceptance of a liberal economic order that is now under threat".

They warned against Europe being seen as applying tools in a self-serving way. In sum, future moves should have an internal goal—to promote the competitiveness of European industry, rather than to target global competitors. The report also raised the issue of cooperation with OECD partners on fair taxation of digital platforms (Marcus et al. 2019).

Striving for Digital Leadership

In autumn 2019, the new European Commission, headed by Ursula von der Leyen, started its work. Mission letters sent by the President to Cabinet Members shed light on the Commission's strategic objectives. The Executive Vice President responsible for the digital policy is Margrethe Vestager, a Danish politician and an economist by training. In the previous Junker Commission (2014–2019) she was responsible for the Competition dossier. The instruction she received contained a very ambitious goal: the European Union had to focus on maintaining digital leadership in the areas where it could be seen, and on reducing the backlog in other areas, relying on new generation technologies.

In order to achieve digital leadership, the European Union focuses on making markets work better, and on helping the industrial sector of EU countries, so that it can more easily adapt to new conditions such as globalization, climate change, and digitalization (von der Leyen 2019). The letter developed and clarified earlier calls to use the EU's regulatory power to formulate the international rules of the game. During the first 100 days of the new Commission's mandate, it set out to develop common EU approaches to artificial intelligence, to update liability and safety rules for digital platforms, and to find common ground with external partners in digital taxation. It called to intensify cooperation with the competent authorities of other countries who are responsible for compliance in their areas with the rules of international competition.

February 19, 2020, The European Commission published the message "Shaping Europe's Digital Future", which identifies priorities in this area. At the same time, two more documents were issued: the White Paper on Artificial Intelligence and the European Data Strategy (European Commission 2020c).

One distinct application for ensuring the EU's technological sovereignty was the main novelty in the Shaping Europe's Digital Future strategy. It refers to the integrity and resilience of data infrastructure, networks, and communications. The European Union should actively develop its technological potential in order to reduce dependency on other parts of the globe for the most crucial technologies. The idea, which was already introduced in the report to the European Parliament, that technological sovereignty is not directed against any of the global partners, but instead aims to realize the interests of the EU and support the European social model, is repeated there (European Commission 2020a).

The principle of a European Open Digital Space is postulated again, but here in close connection with its normative claims. The EU space is declared open to anyone willing to play according to EU rules and to comply with its standards. The EU aims to "truly influence how digital solutions are developed and used on a global scale". Judging by the document, the EU has advanced in developing its approach to the competition rules in the market of digital goods and services.

More specifics have emerged regarding the European Union's leverage of its regulatory power. The Commission intends to promote EU rules through association and trade agreements with third countries, as well as through agreements within international organizations—these include the UN, OECD, the International Organization for Standardization, and the G20.

As well as in other areas, the EU intends to apply its regulatory power primarily to the groups of countries with which it is building closer and preferential relations. These are the states applying for EU membership, as well as the countries with which the EU is pursuing its neighbourhood and development policy. Particular attention is paid to Africa, where it is envisaged to create a single African Digital Market, with the financial and technological assistance of the EU.

The EU intends to continue developing global standards for advanced technology. To ensure free competition, the European Commission will address unjustified restrictions for European companies in third countries, enforce EU legislation and international rules in the digital sector and, if necessary, propose new rules in order to limit the distortive effects of foreign subsidies in the internal market.

What are the objective prerequisites for the EU to become a leading force in shaping the rules of the game in the global digital market? Answering this question requires looking at statistical data.

The world exports of ICT goods (including computers and peripheral equipment, communication equipment, consumer electronic equipment and electronic components) in 2018 was $2.2 trillion. EU-27 (without the UK) amounted to $306 billion and imports for $430 billion. In other words, the EU global market share of ICT goods was equal to 14% in exports and to 17% in imports. While exports from the countries and territories of developing Asia reached $1.6 trillion, or 72% of global exports. The biggest exporters were China, China Hong Kong, Korea, Singapore, and China Taiwan.

According to the World Bank, in 2017, the global export of ICT services (balance of payments statistics) amounted to $536 billion. Of these, $277 billion (52%) were accounted for by EU-28 countries. These figures are consistent with the UNCTAD statistics, which estimates global exports of ICT services in 2018 at $568 billion, of which 306 billion (54%) came from EU member states.

The global market for digitally deliverable services is much larger.[1] World exports of digitally deliverable services in 2018 were $2.9 trillion (50% of total trade in services), with the EU-28 accounting for 49%, the United Sates for 15%, and China for 4%. However, these figures need some reconsideration. Firstly, the United Kingdom, the world's fifth largest economy, formally withdrew from the European Union on 31 January 2020. Its exports of digitally deliverable services totalled $267 billion, or 9% of global exports.

Furthermore, trading among EU countries traditionally accounts for a significant part of the total EU trade. According to Eurostat, in 2018, in its exports of ICT services, 52% of the EU countries' exports went to member states, and the remaining 48% to extra-EU trade partners. If this ratio is also applicable to the total EU digitally deliverable services, the true figure of its global share may stand for not more than 20–25%.

Another risk factor is the extremely uneven distribution of EU digital service exports across its member states. Suffice it to say, almost 18% of the global ICT service market (taking into account both the EU's internal and external trade) is provided by Ireland; another 7% by Germany; countries such as France, the Netherlands, Belgium, Spain, and Sweden have shares ranging from 2 to 4%. This suggests that Ireland and Germany will be most active in shaping the external dimension of the EU's digital

[1] According to UNCTAD's definition digitally deliverable transactions include all cross-border transactions that are delivered remotely over ICT networks—i.e. over voice or data networks, including internet, in an electronically downloadable format. While digitally ordered transactions refer to the sale or purchase of a good or service, conducted over computer networks. E-commerce is defined as something that is ordered digitally but delivered physically or digitally.

policy. In exports of digitally deliverable services five countries (Germany, Ireland, the Netherlands, France, and Luxembourg) account for 2/3 of the total EU amount.

Conclusions

In its digital policy, the European Union combines the objectives of negative and positive integration. It is consistently moving from solving internal problems (creating a single market for digital goods and services) to deploying a global agenda and strives to play a leading role in establishing international norms and rules for a new digital era. However, the EU shares on international markets of digital goods and services do not suffice for its dominant position. The growing importance of Asian countries in these areas allow us to expect a difficult negotiation process at the level of international forums.

References

European Commission. (2015). *A Digital Single Market Strategy for Europe. Communication from the Commission to the European Parliament, the Council, the European Economic and Social Committee and the Committee of the Regions*. Brussels, 6.5.2015 COM (2015) 192 final.

European Commission. (2018). *European Commission of Digital Strategy. A Digitally Transformed, User-Focused and Data-Driven Commission*. Brussels 11/21/2018 C (2018) 7118 final.

European Commission. (2020a). *Communication from the Commission to the European Parliament, the Council, the European Economic and Social Committee and the Committee of the Regions. A European Strategy for Data*. Brussels, 19.2.2020 COM (2020) 66 final.

European Commission. (2020b). *Shaping Europe's Digital Future*.

European Commission. (2020c). *White Paper on Artificial Intelligence—A European Approach to Excellence and Trust*. Brussels, 19.2.2020 COM (2020) 65 final.

Kondratieva, N. B. (2019). Cifrovizacija edinogo rynka ES. In Al. A. Gromyko & V. P. Fedorov (Eds.), *Evropa mezhdu treh okeanov* (pp. 379–395). Moscow: IE Ran.

Marcus, S. J., Petropoulos, G., & Yeung, T. (2019, January). *Contribution to Growth: The European Digital Single Market Delivering Economic Benefits for Citizens and Businesses* (CEPS Special Report).

Mărcuţ, M. (2017). *Crystalizing the EU Digital Policy. An Exploration into the Digital Single Market*. New York: Springer.

Tinbergen, J. (1954). *International Economic Integration*. Amsterdam: Elsevier.
von der Leyen, U. (2019, December 1). *Mission Letter—Margrethe Vestager, Executive Vice-President for a Europe Fit for the Digital Age*. Brussels.

CHAPTER 4

Institutionalization of the Fourth Industrial Revolution in National Economics and on Global Market: Different Paths to Success

Vladimir Osipov and Ante Rončević

Introduction

The problems implementing the Fourth Industrial Revolution encompass not only national economies, but also the global market. There are two main paradigms of institutional policy: the state and the initiator. The initiator of the achievements of the Fourth Industrial Revolution plays a role according to its benefits and goals. The state, as an initiator, pursues a top-down policy by imposing formal limitations and stimulating

V. Osipov (✉)
Moscow State Institute of International Relations (MGIMO University), Moscow, Russia
e-mail: vs.ossipov@inno.mgimo.ru

A. Rončević
University North, Varaždin, Croatia
e-mail: aroncevic@unin.hr

N. Konina (ed.), *Digital Strategies in a Global Market*,
https://doi.org/10.1007/978-3-030-58267-8_4

economic activity, all for modernization in accordance with the principles of the Fourth Industrial Revolution. If the idea of the Fourth Industrial Revolution on the level of the national economy is initiated by SMEs and independent large corporations, then a down-top policy is implemented, and the state may turn out to be a weak actor which should adapt to the changing conditions. Top-down policies are implemented mostly in Natural States, and down-top policies characterize the Open Access Order. Since the Fourth Industrial Revolution is associated with high technologies and the development of the Internet of Things, the leading role in the global market is played by developed countries, which are creating an institutional image of the new global market.

Methods and Materials

The main goal of the research is to define the paths of institutional policy of the Fourth Industrial Revolution in both Natural States and Open Access Order; this is done through applying the methodology of Douglass North and assessing its impact to global market. Briefly, the main idea of North and his colleagues (North et al. 2009) consist of how to characterize and classify states, in accordance with access to legal violation. If this access is guaranteed for all people, and they can seek and find protection against illegal wrongdoing, it means that the state is Open Access Order. If access to legal violation can only be sought by elites, this state is Natural. From this point of view, Open Access Order is a freer society for entrepreneurship, as business initiatives are supported, protected and encouraged. The State in Open Access Order is led by business initiatives.

The other way of statehood is Natural States. These are mostly state initiatives in economic actions, and business is led by state initiatives.

For this institutional analysis, the general theory of systems and the system-structural approach based on it were used to describe the goals, economic activity, and initiators of Fourth Industrial Revolution.

Potentially most important, the methodology of Schwab and Davis (2018)—a very specific approach for the Fourth Industrial Revolution implementation—was used in this research. The world-famous WEF-leader described the main points of Fourth Industrial Revolution as a set of breakthroughs of blockchain, artificial intelligence, additive materials, Internet of Things, digital-, bio-, neuro-, geo-, space- technologies, and both virtual and augmented reality. Thanks to the methodology of Schwab, it is possible to evaluate the implementation of the Fourth Industrial Revolution in national economics by its sectors.

Literature Review

Researchers from different countries have been discussing two basic groups of problems and tasks facing the Fourth Industrial Revolution in their papers. Some of them write about applied and technical tasks, and in this area we note research of Coetzer (2018). A significant global group of researchers made their contribution to the development of the Fourth Industrial Revolution in the concrete sectors of national economies: in the Czech Republic (Koren and Kordos 2019; Sojkova and Kocourek 2017), in South Africa (Dekeda and Adonis 2019; Pillay et al. 2018), in the United Kingdom (Flynn et al. 2017), in Germany (Galetska et al. 2019), in Japan (Iwamoto et al. 2019), in Slovakia (Jaskova and Kordos 2020), in the Philippines (Kim et al. 2019), in Australia (Kim and Heo 2018), in the Russian Federation (Lenchuk 2018; Galushkin et al. 2019; Skryl 2017), in Romania (Pirvu et al. 2017), in India (Safar et al. 2020), in Malaysia (Sohimi et al. 2019; Sumari et al. 2017), in Iran (Ziaei Nafchi and Mohelska 2018) and in Nigeria (Owoseni and Twinomurinzi 2020).

Very interesting research has been conducted as comparative analyses of different national economies, also globally, including:

The Czech Republic and Poland (Basl et al. 2017), Korea, China, the USA, Germany and Japan (Min et al. 2019), Brazil and Canada (Ottonicar et al. 2019), in the EU (Grzelakowski 2019; Huckova et al. 2018).

A further significant contribution to fully developing the agenda of the Fourth Industrial Revolution, global market development, geopolitics and new world order were made by Machado et al. (2020), Bonciu (2017, 2019), and Efremov et al. (2019).

Results

In order to determine the processes of institutional policy in connection with the Fourth Industrial Revolution, it is imperative to turn to the methods of implementing its main achievements in economic activity across different national jurisdictions. As is well known, small and medium enterprises are more developed in terms of the Fourth Industrial Revolution than larger enterprises; this is due to SME mobility, the speed of decision-making and how economic resources (and more efficient ones) are allocated. Large enterprises, in the context of our research, are those under the influence of the state: not only regarding the juridical status of large enterprises, but also the unofficial influence of the state and its apparatus on the economic activity of large enterprises. Our model (Fig. 4.1) lays out the two main groups of influencers in terms of the Fourth Industrial Revolution: governmental bodies (state and large enterprises, state-owned corporations etc.) and economic actors (SME, private enterprises not under the state's influence).

Open Access Order follows economic actors in terms of the Fourth Industrial Revolution, as economic actors are always in search of innovations (new products, new materials, new technologies, new organizations and new markets). The State—as the guarantor of private property,

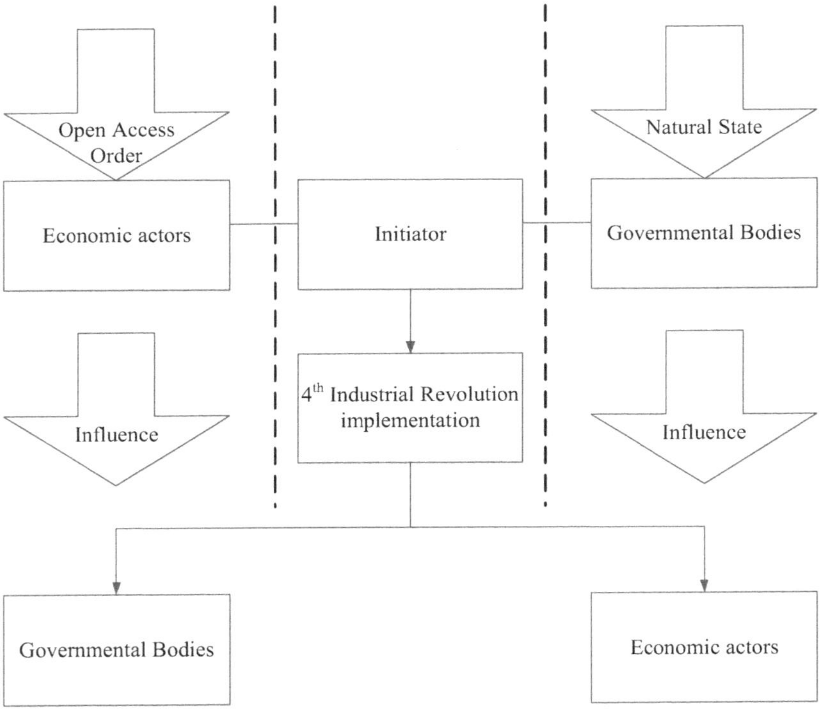

Fig. 4.1 Open Access Order and Natural States in terms of the Fourth Industrial Revolution (*Source* Created by the authors)

anti-monopolization policies, and low transaction costs—creates an institutional field for economic activity. Within the framework of New Public Administration, the State tries to adopt business culture and instruments in its activity. This means that the State is passive, but enterprises (first and foremost SME) are active. Open Access Order pursues a down-top path to embed the institutions of the 4th Industrial Policy. North and his coauthors refer to the United States, the United Kingdom, France, The Netherlands and—more commonly—all liberal Western Europe states.

The other way this is visible is in Nature States, where government plays the role of initiator in terms of the Fourth Industrial Revolution. Post-Soviet Republics, and South American and African states, were named as Natural States by North and his colleagues.

By looking at the data in Table 4.1, it is clear that developed countries constitute 76% of the export of digitally deliverable services in absolute volume, whereas developing and transition economies constitute only 24%. This means that developed countries (mostly Western liberal countries) have a more effective system for producing digital goods. A slightly better situation can be seen in the percentage of digitally deliverable exports in services: developed countries have 56%, developing countries 38% and transition countries only 28.7%. This structure shows that Western liberal countries are oriented on post-industrial economics, where digital technologies, and the Fourth Industrial Revolution's achievements in general, occupy an essential place.

It must be noted that Natural States are mostly developing and transition countries, occupying only a modest export position in digitally deliverable services. In contrast to them, Open Access Orders are mostly

Table 4.1 International trade in digitally deliverable services, export in 2018

US dollars at current prices in millions		*in percentage (%)*
World	2,931,400	100.00
Developing economies	659,870	22.51
Transition economies	39,430	1.35
Developed economies	2,232,100	76.14
Percentage of total trade in services		
World	50.2	–
Developing economies	38.0	–
Transition economies	28.7	–
Developed economies	56.2	–

Source UNCTAD; https://unctadstat.unctad.org

developed countries of the liberal Western world, and their position in the export of digitally deliverable services is very strong. It is very difficult to imagine many changes in this trend.

For a more detailed comparative analysis of the situation with the implementation of the Fourth Industrial Revolution's achievements, Table 4.2 ranks states in high-technology exports. Only 70 countries, from more than 200 globally, are presented, according to their volume and their place in the high-technology sector.

The absolute leader, by volume of high-technology exports, is China. The volume of Chinese high-technology exports is 3.5 times bigger than the second best exporter, Germany. The leading ten countries in this field are all developed countries; however, Eastern Europe countries (such as Czech Republic, Poland and Hungary) occupy relatively high positions, although Post-Soviet countries hold very poor positions in high-technology exports according to US$. It is important to note that the trends of a number of people, and the established state of institutions, play a role in the creation and development of high technologies. Developed countries show a trend for established institutions, whereas developing and transition countries are dependent on number of people. Small developing and transition countries show the poorest positions in high-technology exports by US$.

However, ranking states in high-technology exports by their percentage of manufactured exports reveals very interesting tendencies. Malaysia, not China, leads the world, with 52.8%; second place is held by Singapore and third place by the Republic of Korea. Their export-oriented economies show good results, and prove tehri chosen institutional policies and economic strategies to be successful. Kazakhstan, Latvia and Czech Republic show the success of export-oriented strategy in the Post-Soviet and ex-Socialist space. The middling positions of the countries N11-27 can be explained by their ambivalent strategy not only to exporting high technological goods, but also in using this inside their national economic spheres to reach a higher level of human well-being. Almost all the less successful countries in this regard show some uncertainty towards their economic development strategy. It is impossible to clearly define the export orientation of their national economics, but it cannot be said that these countries have reached a developed position, instead remaining developing or transitive (Ranks N28-70). Fifteen of these countries are Post-Soviet or ex-Socialist states.

Table 4.2 Ranks of states in high-technology exports (current US$ and % of manufactured exports) in 2018

No.	*Country*	*Current US$*	*Country*	*% of manufactured exports*
1	China	731,890,595,214	Malaysia	52.8
2	Germany	210,082,307,180	Singapore	51.7
3	Korea, Rep.	192,789,656,676	Korea, Rep.	36.3
4	United States	156,365,524,736	China	31.4
5	Singapore	155,446,548,683	Andorra	28.5
6	France	117,814,412,441	France	25.9
7	Japan	111,020,443,595	Ireland	24.7
8	Malaysia	90,395,903,009	Iceland	23.5
9	Netherlands	85,690,573,245	Thailand	23.3
10	United Kingdom	76,926,541,023	Israel	22.8
11	Mexico	74,886,123,830	Netherlands	22.7
12	Thailand	44,795,081,987	United Kingdom	22.6
13	Belgium	36,817,017,951	Kazakhstan	22.0
14	Ireland	36,493,794,777	Norway	21.2
15	Czech Republic	36,128,837,160	Mexico	21.1
16	Italy	32,581,025,234	Latvia	20.3
17	Canada	31,036,316,910	Czech Republic	19.6
18	Switzerland	30,136,242,614	United States	18.9
19	Poland	22,236,772,391	Costa Rica	18.5
20	India	20,273,090,235	Japan	17.3
21	Hungary	18,065,921,731	Hungary	16.9
22	Sweden	17,441,832,214	Estonia	16.8
23	Spain	16,982,244,849	Germany	15.8
24	Austria	16,687,499,480	Canada	15.8
25	Israel	12,971,903,000	Sweden	14.4
26	Brazil	11,096,280,497	Denmark	13.9
27	Russian Federation	10,183,007,833	Switzerland	13.4
28	Denmark	9,587,875,363	Brazil	13.0
29	Slovak Republic	8,971,242,840	Greece	12.8
30	Romania	6,637,140,086	Lithuania	12.1
31	Indonesia	6,389,604,745	Austria	11.6
32	Finland	4,515,414,673	Russian Federation	11.0
33	Norway	4,294,542,879	Slovak Republic	10.6
34	Turkey	3,116,828,012	Poland	10.6
35	Portugal	2,978,219,490	Belgium	10.4
36	Lithuania	2,516,321,413	Bulgaria	10.3

(continued)

Table 4.2 (continued)

No.	*Country*	*Current US$*	*Country*	*% of manufactured exports*
37	South Africa	2,239,945,787	Romania	10.1
38	Slovenia	2,089,386,354	New Zealand	9.7
39	Estonia	2,065,396,343	Paraguay	9.7
40	Bulgaria	2,012,779,716	India	9.0
41	Latvia	1,881,856,793	Finland	8.9
42	Kazakhstan	1,762,977,653	Croatia	8.9
43	Greece	1,754,801,996	Ghana	8.3
44	Ukraine	1,247,555,874	Kyrgyz Republic	8.1
45	Costa Rica	1,148,831,708	Indonesia	8.0
46	Croatia	1,011,939,688	Italy	7.5
47	Luxembourg	858,269,925	Colombia	7.3
48	Belarus	716,991,900	Spain	7.2
49	Chile	680,276,777	Armenia	7.1
50	New Zealand	606,940,905	Luxembourg	7.0
51	Colombia	606,299,077	Tanzania	6.9
52	El Salvador	277,848,583	Slovenia	6.8
53	Peru	210,478,636	Chile	6.4
54	Tanzania	186,258,425	El Salvador	6.1
55	Iceland	143,430,802	Ukraine	5.4
56	Egypt, Arab Rep.	125,216,606	South Africa	5.3
57	Paraguay	102,336,648	Ecuador	5.3
58	Ecuador	68,401,030	Portugal	5.3
59	Kenya	54,899,302	Mongolia	5.0
60	Ghana	50,006,668	Bolivia	4.9
61	Nigeria	41,631,961	Peru	4.6
62	Kyrgyz Republic	40,023,711	Azerbaijan	4.0
63	Armenia	36,293,330	Belarus	4.0
64	Andorra	33,913,480	Kenya	3.6
65	Georgia	26,950,274	Georgia	3.3
66	Azerbaijan	21,177,989	Moldova	2.5
67	Bolivia	19,560,046	Turkey	2.3
68	Moldova	18,944,087	Nigeria	1.9
69	Uzbekistan	12,428,993	Egypt, Arab Rep.	0.9
70	Mongolia	6,763,250	Uzbekistan	0.5

Source WorldBank data; www.worldbank.org

After privatization and the breakdown of technological chains in Post-Soviet countries, their governments decided to move to a new development strategy through state-owned corporations, which are formed by consolidating industry assets which were, previously, legally independent (the Russian Federation, Ukraine, Kazakhstan, Kyrgyz Republic, Armenia, Uzbekistan and Georgia). State-owned corporations also occupy a significant place in the national economies of the United States, Canada, India, Brazil, Greece, Chile, South Africa, Ecuador and Turkey. If federal government corporations in the USA, as agents, play a role in implementing government policy in certain areas of public goods production, state-owned corporations in other countries operate within specific markets, such as energy.

The Russian Federation has experience in establishing state-owned corporations for restoring its technological chains and organizing its production process, as happened after the privatization and turbulence of shock therapy. State-owned corporations, as budget actors, play the role of sector management agents. Of course, budget investments (instead of private) are a step away from a market economy, but without strong links and nets between economic actors, it is impossible to restore any economy. This dichotomy partially justifies the creation of state-owned corporations as new and strong actors within economic activity. On the other hand, as has been seen, it is better to settled upon the problem of the monopolistic position of state-owned corporations in some sectors, as this solves the task of duality in subordination and the issue of weaker control by the state (Silverstrov et al. 2019). In this case, the Russian Federation has tried to reach breakthroughs in terms of the Fourth Industrial Revolution by dint of state-owned corporations; however, almost all others Post-Soviet countries simply use state-owned corporations and government corporations to produce public goods or to manage a specific energy sector.

The government has significant resources, access to an extensive infrastructure and a huge amount of data. However, as leaders in this field show, the state is not capable of creating digital solutions.

The structural analysis shows that governmental bodies and state-owned corporations concentrate on budget financing and political goals. Political goals are a priority as top management depends on governmental decisions. Independent economic actors instead concentrate on satisfying consumer needs; its competitive bent makes its stronger in this activity.

The special "greenhouse" conditions of such economic activity make state-owned corporations weak in competitive strikes, especially on the global market. Their bureaucratic corporate culture does not allow for the competitiveness essential for high class professionals, as independent economic actors offer better conditions for jobs, according to innovative corporate culture.

Independent economic actors understand that innovations and venture investment are a high-risk activity, and losses here are accepted as a possible outcome. Losses in state-owned corporations are regarded as the inefficient spending of budget funds which can be prosecuted for fraud.

Therefore, the different roles played by state-owned corporations in developed or in developing and transition countries are based on the different essences of Open Access Order and Natural States.

The results of this research allow us to assert our three main positions. Firstly, Natural States pursue a top-down policy to embed institutions in terms of the Fourth Industrial Revolution. For success, their initiatives are founded upon state-owned corporations and governmental bodies. Secondly, Open Access Order goes radically the other way—a down-top path. This position lets Open Access Order, due to its competitive advantages and value co-creation, take the initiative towards economic actors such as SME, large corporations and digital platforms, according to the terms of the Fourth Industrial Revolution. Thirdly, a state's institutional policy, which cannot of itself choose the path a development strategy will take, can be corrected to orient itself on exporting, otherwise the internal use of its digital goods make national economics more competitive.

Discussions

On the basis of the results of the research, we can offer another institutional path, which will reap competitive rewards for developing and transition countries.

Collaboration between state-owned corporations or governmental bodies and independent large corporations such as SME is an important—and feasible—path a driver of economic development can take. The practice of collaboration between a government and independent economic actors has long been widespread across the global market, and there are different mechanisms to instigate it, such as a public–private partnership. Large companies and SME could be contractors for such a dialogue between governmental bodies and state-owned corporations; the case of Singapore demonstrates this, as here, such a collaboration proved to be one of the paths for improving the both the state's functioning and the population's well-being. One case in point is the Smart Nation & Digital Government Office (SNDGO) initiative, launched in 2017 to reform public services: the government acts as a customer, and digital products are created by digital platforms and innovative SME. Another case is Estonia, whose digital state is one of the most developed in the world. Digital platforms and SME offered a number of various solutions for governmental bodies to develop state services its residents could use to take part in the elections, to sign and register deals, to pay taxes, to receive a birth certificate and even to validate or achieve citizenship.

In the Russian Federation, the decisions taken by technology companies in the corporate and public sectors are still poorly represented—this is one of the factors that impedes the country's digitalization process. An important task now is to transfer the economy to digital tracks as quickly as possible: this is what government and business structures all over the world need to rely on. Digital and IT industries should be able to promptly propose solutions to respond to any changes, and the state should be ready to implement these solutions. The competitiveness of national economies on the global market depends on the speed of digitalization.

Conclusions

Institutional, comparative and structural analysis allowed us to describe and explain the tendencies of institutional policy in terms of the Fourth Industrial Revolution in Open Access Order and Natural States, according to the classifications of Douglass North and his colleagues. The experiences of the Fourth Industrial Revolution initiatives that have already been implemented in national economies show that institutional traps have been avoided; this allows those countries that embark on a later path to succeed.

References

Basl, J., Sasiadek, M., Petr, D., Gerhard, C., & Vaclav, O. (2017). Comparison of Industry 4.0 Application Rate in Selected Polish and Czech Companies. *Idimt-2017—Digitalization in Management, Society and Economy, 46*, 401–410.

Bonciu, F. (2017). The Race Towards the Future: Geopolitics Versus Technology. Implications for Romania. *Romanian Journal of European Affairs, 17*(1), 75–84.

Bonciu, F. (2019). Impact of the 4th Industrial Revolution on the World Order. *Romanian Journal of European Affairs, 19*(2), 51–62.

Coetzer, J. (2018). *Application of HCI Design Principles in overcoming Information Illiteracy: Case of a M-Health Application for a Rural Community in South Africa*. 2018 International Conference on Intelligent and Innovative Computing Applications (Iconic) (pp. 64–70).

Dekeda, B., & Adonis, M. (2019). *The Case for Integration of Renewables in Rail Freight Yards in South Africa*. Proceedings of the 2019 Twenty Seventh International Conference on the Domestic Use of Energy (Due) (pp. 156–162).

Efremov, V., Vladimirova, I. V. B., Lackovic, A., & Pavelin, G. (2019). *Globalization of the World Economy: Features of the Current Stage*. Economic and Social Development (ESD) (pp. 27–36).

Flynn, J., Dance, S., Schaefer, D., Gao, J., ElSouri, M., & Keates, S. (2017). Industry 4.0 and Its Potential Impact on Employment Demographics in the UK (Proceedings Paper). *Advances in Manufacturing Technology XXXI, 6*, 239–244.

Galetska, T., Topishko, N., & Topishko, I. (2019). Corporate Social Activities in Germany: The Experience of Companies. *Baltic Journal of Economic Studies, 5*(3), 17–24.

Galushkin, A. A., Nazarov, A. G., Sabyna, E. N., & Skryl, T. V. (2019). The Institutional Model of Formation and Development of Industry 4.0 in the Conditions of Knowledge Economy's Formation. *Studies in Systems, Decision and Control, 169*, 219–226.

Grzelakowski, A. (2019). Assessment of the Current State of the EU Inland Shipping Development and Its Perspectives from the Policy and Transport Market Point of View. *Scientific Journals of the Maritime University of Szczecin-Zeszyty Naukowe Akademii Morskiej W Szczecinie, 58*(130), 74–83.

Huckova, R., Sokol, P., Rozenfeldova, L., Duic, D., & Petrasevic, T. (2018). *4th Industrial Revolution and Challenges for European Law*. EU Law in Context—Adjustment to Membership and Challenges of the Enlargement (pp. 201–215).

Iwamoto, T., Kocaoglu, D., Anderson, T., Kozanoglu, D., Niwa, K., & Steenhuis, H. (2019). *Development of the HRTech Market in Japan*. 2019 Portland International Conference on Management of Engineering and Technology.

Jaskova, D., & Kordos, M. (2020). *Labour Market Changes in the Regions of Slovakia in the Context of Industry 4.0*. Vplyv Industry 4.0 Na Tvorbu Pracovnych Miest 2019 (pp. 183–191).

Kim, J., Torneo, A. R., & Yang, S. B. (2019). Philippine Readiness for the 4th Industrial Revolution: A Case Study. *Asia-Pacific Social Science Review, 19*(1), 139–153.

Kim, S., & Heo, C. (2018). Analysis of Mineral Resource Exploration and Strategy in Australia (Review). *Economic and Environmental Geology, 51*(3), 291–307.

Koren, V., & Kordos, M. (2019). *The Readiness of the Labour Market in the Czech Republic for Industry 4.0.* Vplyv Industry 4.0 Na Tvorbu Pracovnych Miest (pp. 101–113).

Lenchuk, E. (2018). Russia's Industrial Policy: Shifting Towards the New Industrialization. *Zhurnal Novaya Ekonomicheskaya Assotsiatsiya-Journal of the New Economic Association, 3,* 138–145.

Machado, C. G., Winroth, M. P., & Ribeiro da Silva, E. H. D. (2020). Sustainable Manufacturing in Industry 4.0: An Emerging Research Agenda. *International Journal of Production Research, 58*(5), 1462–1484.

Min, Y., Lee, S., & Aoshima, Y. (2019). A Comparative Study on Industrial Spillover Effects Among Korea, China, the USA, Germany and Japan. *Industrial Management & Data Systems, 119*(3), 454–472.

North, D. C., Wallis, J. J., & Weingast, B. R. (2009). *Violence and Social Orders. A Conceptual Framework for Interpreting Recorded Human History.* Cambridge: Cambridge University Press.

Ottonicar, S., Valentim, M., & Mosconi, E. (2019). Public Policy Applied in Industry 4.0: A Comparative Study Between Brazil and Canada Focusing on Information Literacy. *Revista Ibero-Americana De Ciencia Da Informacao, 12*(2), 558–584.

Owoseni, A., & Twinomurinzi, H. (2020). *Evaluating Mobile App Usage by Service Sector Micro and Small Enterprises in Nigeria: An Abductive Approach.* Information Technology For Development.

Pillay, N., Maharaj, B., & van Eeden, G. (2018). *AI in Engineering and Computer Science Education in Preparation for the 4th Industrial Revolution: A South African Perspective.* 2018 World Engineering Education Forum—Global Engineering Deans Council.

Pirvu, B., Zamfirescu, C., Kifor, C., Naito, M., Carausu, C., Topala, P., et al. (2017). *Smart Factory in the Context of 4th Industrial Revolution: Challenges and Opportunities for Romania.* Modtech International Conference—Modern Technologies in Industrial Engineering V (p. 227).

Safar, L., Sopko, J., Dancakova, D., & Woschank, M. (2020). Industry 4.0-Awareness in South India (Article). *Sustainability, 12*(8).

Schwab, K., & Davis, N. (2018). *Shaping the Fourth Industrial Revolution.* Cologne: World Economic Forum.

Silverstrov, S. N., Osipov, V. S., & Zeldner, A. G. (2019). The Role of State Corporations in Redesign of Sectoral Supply Chain Management. *International Journal of Supply Chain Management, 8*(5), 314–324.

Skryl, T. V. (2017). A Paradigm Shift in Russia's Industrial Policy: From a Raw Model to Innovative Technological Growth Points. *International Journal of Ecological Economics and Statistics, 38*(2), 49–58.

Sohimi, N., Affandi, H., Rasul, M., Yasin, R., Nordin, N., & Adam, S. (2019). Malaysian Industrial Collaborations for Skills Development in 4th Industrial Revolution. *Journal of Technical Education and Training, 11*(3), 63–72.

Sojkova, L., & Kocourek, A. (2017). *Is the Czech Republic Preparing for Society 4.0?* Proceedings of the 13th International Conference: Liberec Economic Forum 2017 (pp. 125–135).

Sumari, P., Idris, Z., & Abdullah, J. (2017). We Must Invest in Applied Knowledge of Computational Neurosciences and Neuroinformatics as an Important Future in Malaysia: The Malaysian Brain Mapping Project (Editorial Material). *Malaysian Journal of Medical Sciences, 24*(1), 1–9.

Ziaei Nafchi, M., & Mohelska, H. (2018). *Industry 4.0 and Labor Market in Iran as a Developing Country*. Hradec Economic Days, Pt Ii (Vol. 8, pp. 550–561).

CHAPTER 5

The Impact of the Fourth Industrial Revolution on Network Business Models

Tatiana Skryl and Marina Gregorić

Introduction

The importance of industrial development within the economy is increasing every year. The state approaches this question relatively thoroughly, and carefully searches for the methods for the most effective formation of innovative network in the country. This is connected to the fact that, under modern conditions, the body of a national economy is more and more determined by the country's internal economic potential of its regions, their innovativeness, and their ability to modernize.

Within managing the territory of a country, strong inter-regional misalignment of production locations, the absence of the state, and corporate coordination of location issues demonstrate that issues of spatial development are becoming very urgent. Moreover, it is important to assess factors that influence regional innovativeness and search for

T. Skryl (✉)
Plekhanov Russian University of Economics, Moscow, Russia

M. Gregorić
University North, Koprivnica, Croatia

N. Konina (ed.), *Digital Strategies in a Global Market*,
https://doi.org/10.1007/978-3-030-58267-8_5

mechanisms and instruments of their innovative industrialization, which helps to achieve balance regionally and increase innovativeness across the country's, both of which are fundamental in modern geopolitical realities.

Each stage of socio-economic and social development transforms the conditions of industrial modernization, including self-organization, in accordance with the new challenges and tasks around the spatial development of business and society as a whole.

The spatial organization of innovative activity is connected, first of all, with territorially outlined flows of resources in industrial development (production, labour, financial, infrastructural, etc.) and their management. This is directed at maintaining interaction between subjects of innovative activity and the system instigating innovative relations; this makes particular productive forces attractive in economic activity, increasing the competitiveness and the optimum spatial organization of economic subjects and their functioning.

Building a modern spatial network for industrial development requires acknowledging particular features of regional spatial systems; these include structurality, dynamism, density, spatial organization, proportionality, balance, adjustment, production specialization, consistency, continuity of development, separability, spatial self-development, and the mutual conditionality of objects (the interaction between which is the way of their existence), and the allocation of spatial structures (on the distribution of elements and connection thereof). However, it is impossible not to also consider such features of the innovative space as variety, differentiation, and the discrete properties of space.

During the industrial revolution, the efficiency of the innovative activity's network organization comes through the construction of the corresponding organizational-economic mechanism for the transformation of the innovative space; this requires learning lessons from previous experience of its implementation. The functioning and development of innovation spaces is a continuous process, accompanied by a cycle of conditions, resources, factors, and products.

Federal State Statistics Service (Rosstat) data show that, despite the measures taken by the government, the industrial activity of the Russian national economy is still at a low level. Thus, the share of organizations that carried out technological innovations in 2017 was 9.3%, while the share of innovative products across the total volume of shipped products was 7.9%. For comparison, the values of these indicators in 2007 were 9.3

and 5.0%, respectively. It can be observed that there have been no quantitative or qualitative changes in the structure of domestically produced goods.

This suggests that there is a need for new institutional support into industrial development, in order to improve the efficiency of the innovation process through a significant reduction in the costs of innovation.

In modern practice, the weakness of the institutional environment, and a lack of strategic certainty, shortens the planning horizon for the majority of decision-makers, and gives state policy a predominantly short-term reactive character. It is under these conditions that the government should act as a driver of instigating modernization in the industrial sector of the national economy, as this is directly aimed at developing the country's economic potential, ensuring the production of competitive industrial products, and developing its non-resource exports. It is important to note that current trends of economic growth in Russia should also be inclusive. By analysing the various options for industrial policy implemented earlier in Russia and abroad, the most effective option is that which emphasizes the removal of various institutional barriers to doing business. At present, this mechanism is fixed within the framework of the development of the cluster.

Methodology

Any economic activity usually creates a unified complex dynamic system; intensive production, transport and cultural links are created in particular places and at particular times. This process of industrial localizing is commonly referred to as agglomeration: one of the stages of urbanization. In order to distinguish different types of agglomerations, a simple classification scheme that distinguishes the advantages of one from another can be given as an example. This classification leads to four main types of agglomerations (see Fig. 5.1).

The first type of agglomeration is cities. In this agglomeration, general production of regional or city specification is located. Urban or regional production includes all firms and industries in one concentrated location. Their location is primarily due to the reduction of transport costs and the efficiency of large-scale operations. This fact is the reason for the emergence of larger production belts and megacities. Common urban agglomerations have a wide range of economic activities. Bigger cities, especially capitals, have, among other things, political and market power,

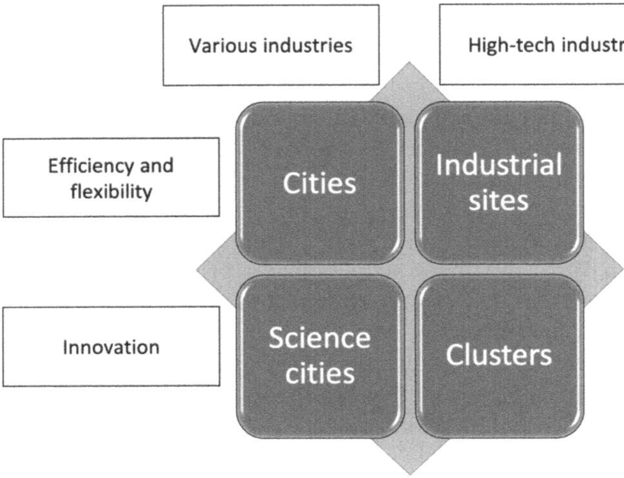

Fig. 5.1 Four types of agglomerations (*Source* Created by the authors on the base of Malmberg et al. [1996])

and therefore prove attractive sites to large corporations for the location of their headquarters.

The second type of agglomeration includes economic activities related to firms engaged in high-tech industries, resulting in the creation of industrial zones. Such areas represent the basis for flexible production systems that can meet the needs of volatile markets (Stroiteleva et al. 2019).

In both cases, agglomeration effects are achieved through processes whereby linkages between firms, institutions, and infrastructure within the same geographical area generate economies of scale, the development of common labour markets and pools of specialized skills, enhanced interaction between local suppliers and customers, and common infrastructure. An agglomeration economy is considered to emerge when such linkages either reduce costs or increase the income—or both—of firms involved in local exchanges.

Where the first two types of agglomeration refer to flexibility and efficiency, the other two types are centres of knowledge creation and implementation.

Science cities, the third agglomeration, are specialized hubs for knowledge creation and innovation in a region without respecting sectoral boundaries. Instead of specialization or spatial concentration in related industries, emphasis is placed on the regional diversity of skills and competencies, where interactions (often unplanned) between different actors can lead to new ideas, innovation projects, products, services, and technologies.

The fourth type of agglomeration is clusters. In contrast to science cities, a cluster generates new ideas and innovative technologies in high-tech industries. The cluster itself consists of interrelated and interdependent enterprises, specialized suppliers, support services, and relevant institutional actors in the high-tech field.

Significant progress has been made in recent years in cluster research. Existing research methods can be improved by developing common definitions and key variables used in this area. Scientists have not reached consensus on a number of critical issues concerning the value and functioning of clusters. While some studies showed that firms were growing in their innovativeness by placing R&D in clusters, others argued that adverse selection worked within clusters and as such working within clusters harmed the most innovative firms and delivered the least value. There is, therefore, still no clear answer as to whether changes in innovation, at the enterprise level within clusters, are linked to network linkages or agglomeration.

Many economists point out that industrial activity should be grouped geographically, and that it is cluster activity that affects economic performance (Stepnov et al. 2019). The more similar the activities of firms in a cluster, the more likely it is that relevant and valuable knowledge will be transferred from one enterprise to another. At the micro-level of the enterprise, this will manifest itself as benefits and costs. The flow of knowledge through training is valuable to the target firm and will be considered as a direct benefit, while knowledge outflow is likely to be accumulated by competitors and will mean costs. Over time, a particular firm will realize that, while knowledge outflows today may benefit its competitors, it is this effect that improves its own potential future knowledge inflows. Thus, from the perspective of the cluster as a whole, both knowledge inflows (to the main enterprise) and knowledge outflows (to its competitors) are positive results.

Standard definitions of economic clusters were first defined by the US federal government in 1949. Later, Krugman conducted studies of economic clusters, and showed that an economy of scale exists when production is close to the concentration of its demand, while at the same time the size of demand depends on the cost of access to goods; thus, consumers and producers should, as a rule, be close to each other (Krugman 2003). He found that the density of economic clusters depends on the cost of transportation, economies of scale, and the relative size of production in a given economy.

Porter presented in-depth theoretical and practical evidence that geographic, cultural, and institutional closeness improves the quality of information flows within a cluster (Porter 1998). He noted that, although existing reasons for combining production (such as the cost of transmitting codified information) had declined over time, new reasons had emerged, such as the difficulty of transmitting implicit knowledge over long distances. He noted that the economic and innovative effectiveness of clusters in the United States differed markedly (Porter 1998). He also provided evidence that the interaction of different clusters leads to successful regional economic outcomes.

Despite the significant progress made in cluster research, much remains to be proven; this field remains subjective. Scientists differ in their opinions on key findings. There are many definitions for the same terms, and performance indicators vary greatly from study to study.

Formal definitions of industrial clusters are quite simple. Existing research confirms that a cluster is a group of enterprises belonging to the same or related industries, located in the same or close geographical points. However, the approaches to the definition of industrial clusters are objectively different.

Baptista and Swan define a cluster as a region with a high level of total employment, and observe the growth of clusters as a measure of a particular geographical area's innovation (Baptista and Swann 1998). Porter has developed a comprehensive definition of clustering based on employment and wages in the private sector, as well as patents created by the economic area (Delgado et al. 2014). Bell defined the city as a cluster and designated any firm working within the city as belonging to this cluster (Bell 2005). Lee claims that the cluster is based on a group of firms in a particular industry (including suppliers and/or users) (Lee 2000). Zucker defines clusters as geographical areas, united universities, where outstanding scientists work (Zucker 1988). Agrawal and Cockburn show that the presence of a large, local, R&D-intensive firm increases the cluster's ability to transform local university research into commercially valuable innovations (Agrawal et al. 2010).

The next question to ask is whether, in practice, the geographical proximity of research team members always facilitates innovation. Many research papers have shown face-to-face teams are more likely to create new technologies that are successfully commercialized, while geographically dispersed R&D teams generate more commercially valuable and highly effective innovations.

For example, studies have shown that communication between engineers drops dramatically when engineering jobs are more than 30 m apart (Osipov 2020). In addition, long-distance communication often forces mental workers to rely on other modes of communication, such as email and telephone, which are more dependent on codified forms of knowledge. However, there is also evidence that these harmful effects of geographical dispersion can be minimized by developing teamwork and socialization among members of different units within the enterprise. Conversely, the labour market for researchers is geographically dispersed. Researchers may move to new cities, universities, or research schools, but at the same time may maintain research relationships with colleagues in their alma mater (Torkunov 2019).

Results and Discussion

As mentioned above, the literature has long suggested that agglomeration of industries does not offer many advantages. Some studies show an increase in innovative patent activity by firms within a cluster; others do not find any increase in innovation. There are two potential reasons why clusters may not be linked to innovation.

Firstly, any observed increase in secondary flows of information may be due to formal market mechanisms, such as contracts or equity participation between firms, rather than to any special effects of geographical proximity. In addition, studies suggest that the best knowledge coming from clusters is protected by legal mechanisms; only the least valuable knowledge is freely available. Others argue that clustering increases competition for resources based on R&D, suppressing innovation (Ustyuzhanina 2016).

Finally, others argue that firms within clusters also participate simultaneously in global information networks. Thus, it is difficult to separate the advantages of local and global network participation. Recent research shows that information flows are quite strong between the prior location of the inventor and the place where he or she moves, suggesting that social relations and networks play an important role in information flows between clusters (Sengul et al. 2012).

A literature review on the effectiveness of industrial clusters highlights two main issues. First, state policy, in the field of forming industrial clusters, must ask if clustering is conducive to innovation and productivity growth. The second question is the issue of strategic management: today there is no consensus on how the presence of clusters should influence the strategy of an enterprise, so the conditions under which an enterprise should decide to place its innovation activities within a cluster are up for debate.

Recently, empirical research in economics and economic geography has focused on the first question: public policy.

The literature on strategic management is divided between the lemon markets, which claims that only the lowest enterprises are located in clusters while top corporations place their areas in large agglomeration centres. This, however, runs contrary to the traditional opinion established by Porter, according to which the location of a cluster brings more benefits than costs.

To solve this contradiction, the following solution is proposed, in which the decisive factor is the consideration of the type of competition in this branch (Allen 2017). For this analysis we will take the branches with the perfect competition and oligopolistic ones.

In an industry with a completely competitive market, a cluster has a geographically concentrated contribution of labour and professional competences amongst its innovation activity, which should attract firms. However, the incentive for firms to place their innovation activities within a cluster depends on the structure of the industry in which the firm competes. In a highly competitive market environment, there are a relatively large number of small firms, each of which has a relatively small market share and therefore small profits. Thus, these firms likely have nothing to lose from an unintentional outflow of information and even more to lose from inflows due to the strong interconnectedness within a cluster. This seems to be dominated by the public benefit aspect of knowledge generation, with local information flows considered to be generally positive for both the firms themselves and the local region.

In the oligopolistic production structure, a relatively small number of large players have a relatively larger share of valuable information. Thus, knowledge leakage from one firm to a competitor can have a significant impact on the balance of power within a cluster consisting of fewer large firms. Close interconnectedness and interdependence in oligopolistic firms' clusters jeopardizes their own information and knowledge assets, exposing themselves to unintentional external flows of available knowledge and competencies. As a result, these firms will decide not to place themselves in a cluster if they cannot find a way to avoid unintentional information and knowledge leaks.

Thus, before selecting locations for their R&D activities, the enterprise needs to consider the competitive environment of the markets in which they will interact, as well as the structure of the cluster. Larger R&D-intensive firms, clustered in industrial clusters with other larger competitors, can participate in games with high rates of knowledge-sharing, which can damage the competitive position of the industry. Smaller firms in more competitive markets are more likely to participate in knowledge-sharing, which adds value to the industry.

Since the literature uses disparate performance indicators to assess the innovation activity of clusters, there is a lack of clarity on which aspects influence the performance of firms (Sengul et al. 2019). New research suggests multidimensional relationships between location variables, firm profitability, firm value, knowledge chain building, firm growth, and innovation.

The R&D strategy of firms in relation to economic clusters is influenced by two contradictory forces. Enterprises undertaking R&D activities within economic clusters can benefit from specialized resources and implicit knowledge about a particular product. However, the risks of knowledge leakage can lead to an unfavourable scenario in which clusters can attract other inefficient firms that have much to gain and little to lose (Tolbert and Zucker 1996). In addition, there is disagreement over the issue of measuring performance within economic clusters.

Firms may compete to gain access to the valuable knowledge needed to develop commercially viable technologies. Much of this knowledge will be owned by the business.

There is a large amount of literature that emphasizes the importance of clusters in high-tech industries (Agrawal et al. 2014). Thus, firms that use high levels of knowledge in their innovation activities compete for access to regional knowledge located in geographical centres of excellence. These firms create a presence in knowledge-intensive regions so that they can interact with locally embedded R&D experts. Let us compare the number of clusters in EU and Russia (Table 5.1).

The line of reasoning underlines the importance of industrial clusters, where research work, which involves knowledge generation, can be carried out by collective research scientists. The most competitive firms seek to place some of their important R&D within industrial clusters. Firms are placing their resources in new geographic areas to gain access to locally embedded industry expertise. By interacting with R&D workers at the heart of innovative inventions, firms can gain a competitive advantage by applying this new knowledge on a smaller scale.

Table 5.1 The number of clusters in EU and Russia by 2020

Industry	*European Union*	*Russian Federation*
Aerospace Vehicles and Defence	38	6
Agriculture	55	4
Apparel	60	1
Automotive	82	3
Biopharmaceuticals	60	9
Business Services	74	0
Coal Mining	17	0
Communication Equipment and Services	62	2
Construction Products and Services	64	10
Distribution and Electronic Commerce	76	0
Downstream Chemical Products	72	7
Downstream Metal Products	65	15
Education and Knowledge Creation	75	0
Electric Power Generation	51	6
Environmental Services	54	4
Financial Services	59	1
Fishing	51	1
Food Processing	63	3
Forestry	48	5
Furniture Production	76	2
Hospitality and Tourism	76	8
Information Technologies	76	13
Jewellery and Precious Metals	30	1
Medical Devices	67	5
Oil and Gas Production	46	3
Production Technology and Heavy Industry	71	4
Transportation and Logistics	72	0

Data source European Cluster Collaboration and Russian Cluster Observatory

The work of the industrial cluster and the strategy for implementing R&D of enterprises differs sharply in terms of comparing their strengths and weaknesses. On the one hand, firms can enhance their competitive advantage by spreading their knowledge, using multiple centres of excellence, and coordinating information on a geographical scale. For example, Canon's industrial cluster is integrated into a science cluster along the east coast of the United States, thousands of miles from its R&D headquarters in its home country of Japan; on the other hand, the enterprise could lose control over management, risking losing ownership of the R&D results.

Clusters are particularly important for multinational enterprises, which by their very nature are networked firms. They can use their networks to effectively connect to a range of local clusters to assimilate and integrate knowledge. Nevertheless, knowledge flows are almost always two-way. Thus, multinationals can also serve as conduits between clusters, so that their network knowledge contributes to the effectiveness of all clusters in which they operate.

Conclusion

The global innovation system consists of knowledge transfer processes that are spatially limited. These can only be accessed through physical presence and through processes that involve the transfer of such knowledge over distances. Research firms are an essential part of the global innovation system, as they include both processes of knowledge generation. Firms embedded in industrial clusters—functioning as integral parts of these clusters—access, filter, and generate knowledge. The internal networks of firms in a cluster are global enablers, and knowledge flows between firms in each cluster are an essential part of the content of the flow.

This conclusion acknowledges the nature of innovation in a cluster. Thus, the internal innovation system of multinational corporations and the cluster innovation system influence each other. It becomes clear that the knowledge strategy of firms underpinning their competitive advantage is based on optimized knowledge transfer and integration functions. These functions are determined by the inclusion of the firm in the cluster structure in which it decides to locate its activities.

Complex innovations require the creation of business models capable of attracting and uniting specialists of different professions into temporary teams. Such teams are formed to solve specific complex tasks (project implementation) requiring the interaction of specialists in different spheres of activity. After solving a task (project implementation), the team is disbanded. Then, other teams are formed to solve other tasks.

As intercompany relationships develop and become more complex, rigid forms of integration based on ownership control and a pyramid of subordination are being replaced by soft, network-based forms of integration based on mutual benefits of cooperation.

The development of information and communication technologies, as a result of the industrial revolution 4.0, provided an additional impetus to intensify the formation of network business models. This process has created the possibility not only to quickly exchange information, but also to separate production from offices, to divide the production process into components, and localize these in different parts of the world. As the basis of the result, the network forms of production replace traditional linear-functional and divisional forms; the cluster loses regional boundaries and becomes international.

References

Agrawal, A., Cockburn, I., Galasso, A., & Oettl, A. (2014). Why Are Some Regions More Innovative Than Others? The Role of Small Firms in the Presence of Large Labs. *Journal of Urban Economics, 81*(1), 149–165.

Agrawal, A., Cockburn, I., & Rosell, C. (2010). Not Invented Here: Innovation in Company Towns. *Journal of Urban Economics, 67*(1), 78–89.

Allen, R. (2017). *The Industrial Revolution: A Very Short Introduction*. Oxford: Oxford University Press.

Baptista, R., & Swann, P. (1998). Do Firms in Clusters Innovate More? *Research Policy, 27*(5), 525–540.

Bell, D. (2005). Ethics and Evil: Frameworks for Twenty-First Century Culture. *The Antioch Review, 74–75*(4–1), 1044–1058.

Delgado, M., Porter, M., & Stern, S. (2014). Clusters, Convergence, and Economic Performance. *Research Policy, 43*(10), 1785–1799.

Krugman, P. (2003). *The Great Unraveling*. New York: W. W. Norton.

Lee, K. Y. (2000). *From Third World to First:: The Singapore Story—1965–2000. Memoirs of Lee Kuan Yew*. New York: HarperCollins.

Malmberg, A., Solvell, O., & Zander, I. (1996), Spatial Clustering, Local Accumulation of Knowledge and Firm Competitiveness. *Geografiska annaler, 78*B(2), 85–97.

Osipov, V. S. (2020), *Digital Future: Economic Growth, Social Adaptation, and Technological Perspectives*. Advances in Intelligent Systems and Computing. 1100 AISC (pp. 272–292).

Porter, M. (1998). *On Competition*. Boston: Harvard Business School.

Sengul, M., Costa, A. A., & Gimeno, J. (2019). The Allocation of Capital Within Firms. *Academy of Management Annals, 13*(1), 43–83.

Sengul, M., Gimeno, J., & Dial, J. (2012). Strategic Delegation: A Review, Theoretical Integration, and Research Agenda. *Journal of Management, 4*(23), 25–31.

Stepnov, I. M., Kovalchuk, J. A., & Gorchakova, E. A. (2019). On Assessing the Efficiency of Intracluster Interaction for Industrial Enterprises. *Studies on Russian Economic Development, 30*(3), 346–354. https://doi.org/10.1134/S107570071903016X.

Stroiteleva, T. G., Kalinicheva, E. Y., Vukovich, G. G., & Osipov, V. S. (2019). Peculiarities and Problems of Formation of Industry 4.0 in Modern Russia. *Studies in Systems, Decision and Control., 169*, 145–153.

Tolbert, P. S., & Zucker, L. G. (1996). The Institutionalization of Institutional Theory. In S. Clegg, C. Hardy, & W. Nord (Eds.), *Handbook of Organization Studies* (pp. 175–190). London: Sage.

Torkunov, A. V. (2019). University as a Part of National Economy, *Voprosy Ekonomiki* (12), 111–122. https://doi.org/10.32609/0042-8736-2019-12-111-122.

Ustyuzhanina, E. (2016). The Eurasian Union and Global Value Chains. *European Politics and Society, 17*, 35–45.

Zucker, L. G. (1988). Where Do Institutional Patterns Come From? Organizations as Actors in Social Systems. In L. G. Zucker (Ed.), *Institutional Patterns and Organizations: Culture and Environment* (pp. 23–49). Cambridge, MA: Ballinger.

CHAPTER 6

Strategies for Creating Value Chains in the Digital Economy

Alina Ignatieva and Pavel Trifonov

Introduction

The system of international trade is currently experiencing a transformation, shaping approaches toward the development of new products and the structure of supply chain management processes. Global value chains play a key role in the contemporary global economy, especially attracting global players to the idea of value chains and, consequently, to transforming the structure of global trade, providing the opportunity to integrate more and more companies into them on both an industrial and on the country's level. For Russia, the choice of, and the rationale behind, the strategy of involvement in global value chains is an extremely important goal, yet it is becoming harder to achieve, due to growing competition and the digital transformation of economic processes.

A. Ignatieva
Moscow State Institute of International Relations (MGIMO), Moscow, Russia

P. Trifonov (✉)
Financial University Under the Government of Russia, Moscow, Russia

N. Konina (ed.), *Digital Strategies in a Global Market*,
https://doi.org/10.1007/978-3-030-58267-8_6

Assembly and manufacturing centers in value chains have localized in certain developing countries (outside countries with TNC headquarters), thanks to the effect of such factors as falling labor costs (primarily on the Southeast Asian markets), the development of informational and logistical technologies, tightening environmental protection regulation for the production process, and higher prices for electricity and a number of raw materials. According to the latest OECD statistics, more than 60% of the aggregate international trade turnover can be accrued to the GVC system.

International trade is accompanied by the ongoing multilateral exchange of intermediary commodities, services, ideas, human resources, investments, and information. More and more often, this exchange is conducted abroad and not within a single economy. These processes form the "twenty-first-century trade" which is based on the link between trade, investments and services (Moiseychev and Meshkova 2015).

Thanks to involvement in GVC, the economies of a number of countries are currently undergoing rapid development (Table 6.1) and are transitioning to a new development level, allowing for higher added value and the implementation of more technologies and know-how into the "agriculture," "manufacturing" and "services" industries.

While some researchers focus mainly on the role of technological and IT changes in shaping and transforming global networks, certain analytics showcase instead that the "Industry 4.0" technology interacts with the GVC infrastructure.

Table 6.1 High-tech exports rate to the total manufacturing volume

Country	*2000*	*2010*	*2015*	*2016*	*Growth rate 2016/2010 (%)*
China	19.0	27.5	25.6	25.2	133
Germany	18.6	15.3	16.7	16.9	91
France	24.6	24.9	26.8	26.7	108
Great Britain	32.4	21.0	20.8	21.8	67
India	6.3	7.2	7.5	7.1	114
Japan	28.7	18.0	16.8	16.2	57
South Korea	35.1	29.5	26.8	26.6	76
OECD countries	24.4	16.9	17.8	17.4	72
Russia	16.1	9.1	13.8	10.7	67
The USA	33.8	20.0	19.0	20.0	59

Source Developed by the authors on the base of World Bank DATA [WWW Document] https://data.worldbank.org/ (accessed 15 November 2019)

An example of this can be seen through the results of this interaction with a number of "Industry 4.0" areas.

More and more products are equipped with sensors designed to collect and process data and to then transfer it to the recipient. Manufacturing equipment and transport equipped with sensors is able to provide live data. This allows the extent of wear of the equipment to be determined, and storage levels to be monitored, in order to develop the required system of facilities planning, as well as to assess the consumption level of individual product types. As such, the Internet of Things (IoT) will increase the extent of integration among those involved in global value chains, and will have an effect on a decreased need for intermediary distribution channels (Porter and Heppelmann 2014). Moreover, this "IoT" technology will be able to solve the issue of geographically dispersed value chains, dividing distribution and information channels. Thanks to IoT, each article of goods will receive a unique identification number, connecting it to information channels (its origin, use, and purpose) circulating in GVC channels.

The need to coordinate and synchronize distribution and information channels will, with time, become obsolete; this will lead to significant advantages emerging, which could raise the efficiency of production and sales management systems, especially for transnational channels within GVC. Therefore, the main purpose of IoT for GVC is the reduction of transactional costs arising in international manufacturing and the lowering of barriers in the way of implementing international divisions of labor mechanisms in the "global factory." However, upon active usage of the "Internet of Things" technology, cyber-security risks will arise—risks of systematic breakdowns in the activity of organizations, or of equipment malfunctioning. Each of the millions of built-in sensors and communication devices is a potential entry point for cyber-offenders (hackers). This must be taken into account while developing an information channels management strategy: potential risks are to be analyzed, the probability of such risks is to be assessed, and measures to minimize them are to be developed.

Managers in company managers have, over many years, made managerial decisions based on only a limited array of sources for data. Such traditional managerial sources generally include production reports, internal accounts, and reports of the results of marketing research. Nowadays data are generated from lots of sources, particularly sensory data from intellectual products and data from search engines and social networks (e.g., Google, Facebook, Twitter), allowing companies to access new sources of valuable information along with access to means of improving computing capacity and allowing data storage costs to be reduced (Davenport et al. 2012). Use of the "Big data and analytics" (BDA) technology features a prospect-oriented approach, collects data (both new and existing), and forms pattern sources for determining events and possibilities. The role of traditional information technologies, in turn, is more outdated, and regards the process of collecting data on anomalies and alerting management thereof. The effect of BDA may manifest itself in monitoring new tendencies and opportunities on foreign markets without the need to assume material liability on a local level. Departments responsible for the distribution of goods in corporation branch offices will be able to efficiently optimize not only their sales, but also the manufacturing and distribution of goods, all around the world. However, there are two major risks of implementing this technology: (1) higher expenses for hiring and training staff in order to manage these systems (Davenport et al. 2012; McAfee and Brynjolfsson 2012; Constantiou and Kallinikos 2015); (2) breaches of numerous people's confidentiality (clients, employees) due to a widespread use of big data. In order to regulate this process, a certain (transnational) management regime will be necessary. Intrusion into private lives, and the violation of moral and ethical social values, may very well limit a business' opportunity to maximize commercial profit with BDA. This is to be taken into consideration upon effecting strategies.

The first industrial robots are believed to have appeared in the 1960s; they emerged in factories in countries with higher cost of labor than other countries. This approach allowed the USA, Japan, and a number of European countries to begin the technical revamp of their manufacturing facilities, in order to optimize prime cost of products and to raise their quality, as well as to further develop sustainable positions in GVC by developing the innovational technology sphere and producing high-tech products (Sirkin et al. 2015). Robotic technologies became widespread in a number of industry sectors. This is due to the following reasons:

- Costs of both hardware and software fell by more than 20% in the past decade, while the capacity of robotic systems is steadily increasing by approximately 5% a year.
- The technological capabilities of many traditional robotic systems were limited in terms of potential operations spectrum, being of a stationary character. Currently, industrial robots are becoming more and more versatile and mobile, becoming capable of performing harder tasks and working in less structured environments. Modern

robots also possess informational communications with other manufacturing systems thanks to IoT.

- Due to cost reductions, robotic systems were introduced into small and medium-sized businesses.

These tendencies brought a few changes into the structure of modern GVC, favoring developing countries in search of lower production costs (Buckley and Strange 2015). These changes were mitigated thanks to a combination of market liberalization and restructuring the economy in many countries, as well as through the liberalization of international trade and investments, financial deregulation and the integration of global capital markets, technological achievements (namely, in IT and transportation), and an improvement of contract performances and intellectual property protection in many countries (Strange and Zucchella 2017). Modern GVC are physically "divided/split" into many value chains, with more labor-intensive production taking place in developing countries. This resulted in the fragmentation of international production, with intermediary commodity trade amounting to more than 60% of world exports.

Methodology

For the purposes of classifying types of GVC, identifying strategic techniques for the creation thereof, and selecting assessment criteria expert, evaluation was utilized in the course of the research. Namely, experts in the field of international trade were surveyed, and academic publications and analytics from leading consulting firms, as well as international organizations publishing GVC statistics, were analyzed. Based on data usage on the performance indicators of the import/export of goods, foreign value added in GVC, and volumes of foreign direct investments, the main types of GVC were identified, factors affecting GVC development were formulated, and opportunities for integrating Russian businesses into international GVC systems were determined.

A key feature of the current state of GVC is the slowing down of GVC growth. Foreign value added indicators (hereinafter FVA) in imported goods and services included in the country's exports structure reached their peak in 2010–2012, after two decades of uninterrupted growth.

From 1990 to 2010, the share of FVA in total export volume grew continually, facilitating the growth of world trade. The increase was gradual: 7 percentage points per every 20 years. In the last decade, the growth of GVC has stopped, with the FVA share having dropped to 30% in 2017. This decline in the FVA share can be explained through a recent slowing down of economic globalization rates and the tendencies of attracting foreign investments into the economy (FDI).

The FVA share for other developing economies is lower than 15%. The lowest rate was recorded at 9%, seen in countries with slow economic growth (underdeveloped countries). This is due to these countries' policies being isolationist, or their role being limited to the provision of natural resources. As a result, these countries secure investments into other countries' exports: they are integrated inversely into GVC (inverse vertical integration strategy). They have restricted access to GVC, which is dependent on the exports of other countries (World Investment Report 2018: Investment and New Industrial Policies) (Table 6.2).

Upon analysis of a number of studies (Yeung and Coe 2014), several factor groups of the market force may be identified forming the main profile of GVC and their strategy profile:

1. Optimizing of the costs-capabilities ratio (e.g., labor, technology, know-how, and capital);
2. Sustaining market development (e.g., coverage and access, dominance, time of market entry, client behavior and preferences);
3. Financial discipline (access to finance, pressure on investors and shareholders).

Table 6.2 GVC classification based on the role of managing entities

Type of chain/indicators	*Driving force*	*Leading stages*	*Industries*	*Manufacturers' owners*	*Networks*
Manufacturer-regulated GVC (vertical, upwards (direct) and downwards (inverse))	Production capital	R&D and manufacturing	Automobile, aviation, pharmaceutical, electronics	TNC	Based on investment
Customer-regulated GVC (horizontal)	Trade capital	Design and marketing	FMCG production	Local companies from developing countries	Based on trade

Source Created by the authors

These three-factor groups, along with various combinations thereof, are a necessary cause-effect condition for the development of special strategies. They are basically independent variables for any researcher to use to explain the character of GVC organization, their management form with various consequences for industrial changes, and territorial development in mind. The majority of academic sources stress the rationale behind cost reduction in managing value chains controlled by purchasers and the importance of technological leadership in value chains controlled by manufacturers. Only few studies analyzed the "costs-capabilities ratio" parameter as a dynamic concept, with a number of studies analyzing "market development" and "the quality of financial organization" in their analysis of global manufacturing in various industries and sectors.

A number of authors identify the characteristic strategies of involvement in Global Value Chains for businesses operating in the field of international economic transactions (Moiseycheva and Meshkova 2015):

1. A strategy of integrating into the global GVC system and working under the auspices of large TNCs, having developed a starter plan of action, gaining profit, and securing a position in the selected segment (particularly for organizations with limited resources).
2. A strategy of the "takeover" of the best positions in GVC, requiring a more active intellectual input, e.g., in the area of R&D, logistics, marketing, services.
3. A strategy of entering into the global market with completely unique new products (provided the company has the knowledge and a high innovational potential).
4. A strategy of focusing on one particular function, with subsequent perfection and optimization thereof (provided that the product has a single technical and technological competence, in the form of a competitive advantage).
5. A strategy of accumulating potential for developing new functions and transitioning into more profitable segments of GVC.

Each of the described strategies depends on the level of competition, the market potential of those involved in GVC, the level of technological development, including analysis of the technological future's uncertainty (Kovalchuk and Stepnov 2019), the extent of political support, the ability to use organizational and economic factors and models in the selection, and the development of value chains creation strategies.

One of the key factors affecting the competitiveness of the manufacturing industry is investment in fixed assets. Attention is drawn to the decline in the innovative potential of the Russian economy, which was determined by the share of innovative goods and services in the total volume of gross value added.

Table 6.3 shows the dynamics of the ratio of investment in fixed assets to gross value added produced in the manufacturing sectors (chemical production, production of machinery and equipment, and others) in the above time interval—this is an indicator of investment potential.

The calculation was performed using the following formula:

Ki = Ifa/V,

Ki-ratio of investment potential (by deflator)

Ifa—investments in fixed assets by type of economic activity

V-GDP of the corresponding sub-sector (by deflator)

The calculation is shown in Table 6.3.

It is worth noting the volatile nature of the dynamics of the share of investment in gross value added. Thus, since 2011 to date, there has been a decrease in this share from 21.18 to 11.88% for the economy as a whole,

Table 6.3 Ratio of investment potential of the Russian economy, %

The manufacturing sector	*2011*	*2012*	*2013*	*2014*	*2015*	*2016*	*2017*	*2018*
Economy, investment potential	21,18	19,93	18,30	16,40	13,14	12,62	12,50	11,88
Manufacturing, investment potential	20,32	19,61	19,86	18,61	14,75	13,50	13,23	12,67
Food, beverages and tobacco, investment potential	18,44	16,02	14,89	14,74	11,39	9,86	10,78	10,20
Textiles and clothing	8,63	8,01	8,04	10,71	4,77	3,72	4,70	4,39
Chemicals	24,42	26,59	26,82	19,32	14,98	15,47	21,71	21,67
Machinery and transport equipment	22,04	20,18	25,45	25,51	24,61	20,84	15,85	17,08
Other manufacturing	20,16	19,71	19,61	18,53	14,54	13,25	12,12	11,17
Dispersion, %	18,73	14,30	15,74	12,05	19,57	19,13	19,04	21,03

Source Developed by the authors on the base of World bank DATA [WWW Document] https://data.worldbank.org/ (accessed 15 November 2019)

in the manufacturing industry by 8%, in mechanical engineering by 5%, in chemical production—by 3%.

In most sub-sectors, as well as in the economy as a whole, there is a drop in the value of the indicator in the period under review, with the exception of "chemical production," which is characterized by a monotonous drop in volatility with a deep minimum in 2015. At the same time, it should be noted that in General, the share of investment in the manufacturing industry does not change over the specified period due to the redistribution between groups of industries from the medium-tech to the low-tech level. It should be noted that the share of investment is falling markedly in the leading industry of mechanical engineering. The reason for the decrease in this share of investment is the fact that the main sources of financing are the company's own funds.

The analysis of these results shows that the differentiation of the investment potential value remains at the level above 2.5%. This indicates that the distribution of investment by manufacturing sector exacerbates structural problems in the OP. In practice, the production of industrial goods is mainly limited to 3–4 industries.

The main purpose is to promote technological re-equipment of production. However, the data in Table 6.3 shows that this problem has not been solved. Indeed, the age of fixed assets in the period from 2014 to 2017 remains almost unchanged and remains at the level of 16 years, with some trend to increase.

And its value increases from 2014 to 2107 from 15 to 16 years, this indicates that low-tech equipment is used. At the same time, it should be noted that in the world practice, the age of moral aging for machine—building products is 6–8 years. Thus, the industrial policy of the state should be aimed at a sharp reduction in the age of production capacity used.

Another important factor determining the competitiveness of production in OP is the investment of enterprises in long-term development, which involves technological re-equipment of production.

The share of technologies that are more than 6 years old is high. from 2014 to 2018, it increased from 51 to 58%. The age of moral aging is 6–8 years.

Results

Export diversification is a part of a dynamic process of economic growth and economy diversification. For many countries, dependent on commodity products, the expansion of their export basket, as a result of increasing manufacturing volumes, is a sign of value added, and a successful structural transformation. Between 1995 and 2017, export of manufactured goods rose from 65 to 74% to the total export volume. However, this increase mainly reflected the acceleration of growth and structural changes in many developing countries.

Current global economic trends show that the world may be entering a "slow equilibrium" period, characterized by a slow-down of growth and a decrease in trade, foreign direct investment, and capital flows. It was back in 2018 that international organizations repeatedly revised their global economic prospects downwards. In its March 2019 monthly report, the World Bank announced that the global trade of goods lost its momentum in 2017. On an annual basis, the increase in container shipments was 5% as of February 2018, and fell to 2% in February 2019. In a similar manner, the annual growth of new export orders fell to negative levels in February 2019. As for FDI flows, the overall value fell by almost 20% from 1.46 trillion dollars in 2017 to 1.2 trillion dollars in 2018, which is proportionate to the value of FDI right after the global financial crisis of 2009.

Growing environmental issues also cast doubt on the viability of an economic policy some developing countries could re-employ, aimed at repeating the explosive growth of commodity exports of agriculture or manufacturing.

Over the course of a country's international trade, the goods and services produced on the basis of their comparative or competitive character are exported.

The widespread introduction of the "Industry 4.0" technology has the potential to transform the placement and organization of manufacturing plants all across the world, as well as to further broaden the meaning of the terms "goods" and "services" in their traditional sense. Businesses with high levels of automatization will see the substitution of under-qualified personnel; however, the demand for highly qualified personnel will increase (e.g., software developers, mechatronic engineers, data analytics specialists). Live integrated connection through GVC will reduce the need for optimizing unfinished production volumes. Effective interaction of businesses between "B2B" and "B2C" business models will also occur, which will serve to develop existing products.

New business models, based on GVC transition from centralized to decentralized value chains, will appear, whereby manufacturers of consumer goods will be able to utilize a "hybrid" approach to localizing sales of goods and their accessibility for selected market segments and will be able to develop a fully personalized model with consumers, efficiently taking the company's manufacturing activity upon themselves.

Clients will be taking part in GVC more and more actively, acting as suppliers of key information and services, drafting reviews of the goods. Company-client relations will be re-formatted in many respects, as BDA provides client testing and synchronization opportunities, which would allow for a more flexible approach for optimizing development, launch, and adaptation costs.

A further growth of digital technologies and internet platforms for the distribution of goods (e.g., Amazon, Alibaba) will create an opportunity for smaller firms to enter global markets.

Finally, new national and supranational institutional mechanisms will appear, reflecting and regulating the emerging complicated reality.

The growing link between machines, goods, parts, and people will require new technology and regulation, as well as international standards to determine the interaction procedure of these elements in the digital factory of the future. New "data protection" laws will also need to be adopted, and/or self-regulation of the industry will have to be enhanced, in order to protect the private lives of people and to impose restrictions on data access.

Reconfiguring GVC and changing the relations of authority between those involved therein will lead to conflicts of interest in terms of where the goods are manufactured and where value is created; this will become a matter of legal regulation, including taxation and customs issues arising from distribution channels regulation (De Backer and Miroudot 2013).

The strategy of Russian businesses for entering GVC or creating new GVC will be determined by the following factors (Ponte et al. 2011):

- The level of political and economic relations with Eurasian partners;
- The success of national projects designed to stimulate the growth of manufacturing, particularly the high-tech segment of the economy;
- The quality of investment policy and the efficiency of utilizing financial instruments;

- The extent to which Digital Economy technologies are developed, including "Industry 4.0";
- Securing stability in the policy of macroeconomic regulation of the economy.

Conclusions/Recommendations

In the course of Russia's integration into GVC, in terms of raising the efficiency of economic relations, there is a need for precise action coordination at each and every stage of the functioning of value chains. This emphasizes the need for the development of an organizational management mechanism, which would be able to:

- Analyze international transactions in global value chains;
- Track and analyze the full spectrum of logistical processes, starting from the inception of the concept and moving to the end consumer, including after-sale servicing;
- Track connections between suppliers;
- Track flows of capital of the largest transnational corporations;
- Successfully affect the selected strategies of integrating into GVC with the affordable expenses of all available resources in mind;

Everything mentioned above signifies the necessity to build various organizational management structures in order to control the interaction between TNC and GVC more efficiently, as well as to draft up contracts in a more thorough manner (should manufacturing abroad be conducted on a contractual basis). In this regard, a major role is played by the precise personalization of power and liability in persons involved in the process of creating and controlling global value chains. This will allow the efficiency of economic relations in GVC to rise and, therefore, result in the increase of gross value added.

References

Baum, C., & Wee, D. (2015). *Manufacturing's Next Act*. Philadelphia: McKinsey & Company.

Berthon, P., Pitt, L., Kietzmann, J., & McCarthy, I. P. (2015). CGIP: Managing Consumer-Generated Intellectual Property. *California Management Review, 57*(4), 43–62.

Brown, L. R. (1981). *Building a Sustainable Society*. New York: W. W. Norton.

Buckley, P. J., & Strange, R. (2015). The Governance of the Global Factory: Location and Control of World Economic Activity. *Academy of Management Perspectives, 29*(2), 237–249.

Choi, H., Kim, S., & Jung, T. (2019). The Role of Innovation in Upgrading in Global Value Chains. *Global Economic Review, 48*(3), 273–283.

Constantiou, I. D., & Kallinikos, J. (2015). New Games, New Rules: Big Data and the Changing Context of Strategy. *Journal of Information Tecnology* [WWW Document] https://journals.sagepub.com/doi/abs/10.1057/jit.2014.17. Accessed 17 November 2019.

Davenport, T. H., Barth, P., & Bean, R. (2012). How "Big Data" Is a different. *MIT Sloan Management Review, 54*(1), 21–25.

Davey, M. (2014). Entrepreneurship in the Informal Economy. *The International Journal of Entrepreneurship and Innovation, 15*(4), 287–288.

De Backer, K., & Miroudot, S. (2013). *Mapping Global Value Chains* (OECD Trade Policy Papers, No. 159). Paris: OECD Publishing.

Hamilton, G. G., Petrovic, M., & Senauer, B. (Eds.). (2011). *The Market Makers: How Retailers Are Reshaping the Global Economy*. Oxford: Oxford University Press.

Kovalchuk, J., & Stepnov, I. (2019). Research of the Technological Future's Uncertainty. *MGIMO Review of International Relations, 12*(6), 214–224. https://doi.org/10.24833/2071-8160-2019-6-69-214-224.

McAfee, A., & Brynjolfsson, E. (2012). Big Data: The Management Revolution. *Harvard Business Review, 1210*(10), 1–9.

Moiseychev, E., & Meshkova, T. (2015, June 3). *Russia in Global Chains of Value Creation: In Search of Effective Strategies* (Working paper, Bridgesnetwork).

Ponte, S., Gibbon, P., & Vestergaard, J. (2011). Governing Through Standards: An Introduction. In S. Ponte, P. Gibbon, & J. Vestergaard (Eds.), *Governing Through Standards: Origins, Drivers and Limitations*. Basingstoke: Palgrave Macmillan.

Porter, M. E., & Heppelmann, J. E. (2014). How Smart, Connected Products Are Transforming Competition. *Harvard Business Review, 92*(11), 1–23.

Rogatnykh, E. (2016). Global Value Chains and Their Impact on the Development of the National Economy. *World and National Economy, 39*(4), 7–15.

Sirkin, H., Zinser, M., & Rose, R. (2015). *The Robotics Revolution: The Next Great Leap in Manufacturing*. BCG Perspective. Available at https://www.bcgperspectives.com/content/articles/lean-manufacturing-innovation-robotics-revolution-next-great-leap-manufacturing.

Strange, R., & Zucchella, A. (2017). Industry 4.0, Global Value Chains and International Business. *Multinational Business Review, 25*(3), 174–184.

Yeung, H. W., & Coe, N. M. (2014). Toward a Dynamic Theory of Global Production Networks. *Economic Geography, 91*(1), 29–58.

World Bank DATA. (2018). Available at https://data.worldbank.org/.

World Investment Report. (2018). *Investment and New Industrial Policies*. Available at https://unctad.org/en/PublicationsLibrary/wir2018_en.pdf.

CHAPTER 7

Sourcing and Digital Strategies Performance of Big Companies in Key Global Markets

Dmitry Stapran and Igor Stepnov

Introduction

Issues of sourcing and forming effective development structures are directly related to the competitiveness of individual companies as well as to the competitiveness of the national economy in general. Building business processes based on sourcing management creates more effective business models, and promotes the development of the outsourcing services markets—from traditional (legal, financial, logistics, information technology services) to very complex (oil and gas service, trading and distribution, contract production, R & D, etc.). These strategies turn

D. Stapran (✉)
PwC Russia, Moscow, Russia

I. Stepnov
Moscow State Institute of International Relations (MGIMO University), Moscow, Russia
e-mail: stepnoff@inbox.ru

Financial University under the Government of the Russian Federation, Moscow, Russia

N. Konina (ed.), *Digital Strategies in a Global Market*,
https://doi.org/10.1007/978-3-030-58267-8_7

small and medium-sized companies into sourcing partners. The latter act in the zone of significant economic risks and at the same time become the innovative platform, "a breeding ground" that helps the Russian economy make a new leap forward in its development.

The notion of competitiveness has been evolving for a long time, having passed from a resource-based view to dynamic capabilities. It is the key advantage that sourcing can focus on. Products are no longer competitive; only companies that provide products as a service win. The economy is instead increasingly aspiring to a service model. However, due to the slow nature of adaptation to different conditions in different markets, vertically integrated companies are unable to take advantage of the strategic benefits of sourcing. It is for this reason, for instance, that Russian retailers lose to international retailers in foreign markets and even start on their home ground.

It is difficult to overestimate the relevance of studying sourcing as a tool for improving the efficiency of businesses. At the same time, it is important to determine the dynamics of the development of sourcing, drawing important lessons from the history of its formation in Russia. It is necessary to identify the factors determining the managerial process of making a decision to either implement a business process in-house or to transfer (contract) it to an outside company, as well as to model the mechanism for solving outsourcing tasks.

Methodology

We developed our original methodological model of the "five forces of sourcing" to analyze the periodization of sourcing in the Russian economy (Fig. 7.1).

Transaction costs indisputably play a crucial role in the case of sourcing. Originally formulated by R. Coase (1937) and later developed by K. J. Arrow (1969) and O. E. Williamson (1990), the theory of transaction costs takes an act of economic interaction as the unit (a deal, such as a transaction that can be made both within the firm and with another company). The expenses and losses associated with such an interaction are transaction costs. Ideally, if the organization of the production of goods or services is cheaper with an outsourcing partner, outsourcing should be chosen. Companies attain competitiveness by doing something better than other firms; according to M. Porter (2008), a company can do something cheaper than others (price advantage), or its product can have unique qualities (differentiation). The choice of a particular

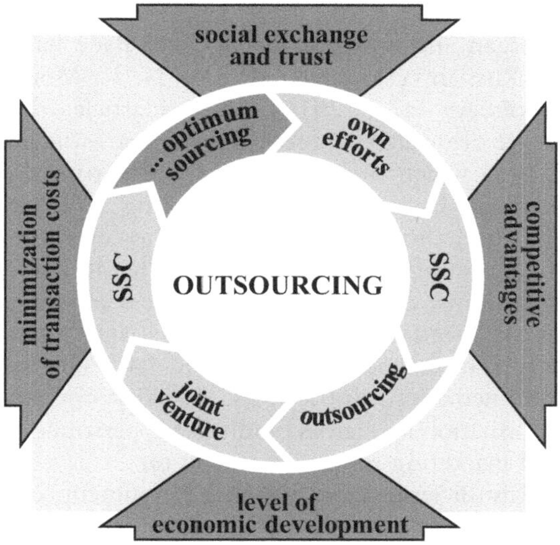

Fig. 7.1 Model of the "five forces of sourcing" (*Source* Created by D. Stapran)

model of competitive advantage determines the operating model (value chain—a set of business processes with the help of which a company gains profits). Business processes that help achieve competitive advantage become the main processes, which should be the focus of the business. As the resources of the company are limited, the rest of the value chain processes, as a rule, must be outsourced. Competitive advantage used to be a more stable resource, whereas now, on the contrary, the speed of change calls for the need to constantly adapt to have dynamic capabilities (Teece et al. 1997). Thus, our first force is "transaction costs," and our second force are "competitive advantages."

"Trust and social exchange" is our third force. As the intangible benefits of interactions between businessmen sometimes mean more than profit, these are very important components of sourcing. While assessing future or current sourcing relationships, a businessman compares the amount of money and effort invested in theses relationship with another businessman with alternatives. Greater confidence and engagement, compared to alternatives, ensure that investments into relationships that businesses have already made will endure, and that opportunistic behavior will be avoided. At the same time, a lack of trust destroys even the most profitable relations. The theory of trust and social exchange was developed by P. M. Blau (1974), H. Thorelli (1986), and later by R. Morgan and S. Hunt (1994); this issue has also been partially studied by Russian researchers, such as N. K. Moiseeva and O. N. Malyutina (Moiseeva et al. 2010). In this article, the three factors mentioned above are called "forces" which, just as in physics, affect the "sourcing cycle," which in business is the company's choice of the method for sourcing its value chain (insourcing, outsourcing). In the situation of the developing Russian economy, however, these forces demonstrate their influence differently compared to the developed economies. The Russian institutions that simplify the process of doing business are underdeveloped: affordable financing (bank loans, venture funds, etc.), protection of private property (judicial and law enforcement systems), transaction intermediaries (distributors, logistics operators, retail networks, etc.), information mediators (audit firms, personnel agencies, available statistics, and marketing research), and so on.

Insufficient institutional development creates "institutional voids" (Khanna et al. 2010). Such "voids" increase the transaction costs of both national and foreign enterprises operating in the Russian market. Information asymmetry breeds mistrust between economic actors and intensifies the role of trust and social exchange, limiting it to a narrow "trusted circle" (for instance, acquaintances, friends, and relatives). Another result of "institutional voids" is the low level of competition and the overconcentration of capital in most sectors of economy, including the oil and gas industry which somewhat reduces the influence of such "forces" as competitive advantage. For this reason, we consider the "level of economic development" to be the independent fourth "force." In terms of its level of development, the Russian economy is very similar to other economies of BRICS countries, as well as Argentina, Turkey, Mexico, Kazakhstan, among others.

Finally, sourcing relationships can be characterized as dynamic rather than static. What was outsourced can be returned to the company, structured as an daughter company or affiliate to create a shared service center, then outsourced again and take up any other form. This is not a linear process but a "sourcing cycle" on which the five-force model is based. The direction of the movement of the "sourcing cycle"—toward outsourcing, or toward in-house processes—is determined by four external forces: transaction costs, competitive advantage, trust and social exchange, and the level of economic development. The opposite is also true—depending on the "sourcing cycle" phase, transaction costs can increase, competitive advantage can decrease, trust can rise or fall. Thus, the "sourcing cycle" is the fifth independent "force" forming the completed methodological model of the "five forces" developed by the authors.

Results

Four **main stages can be distinguished of the development of sourcing relations in Russia**:

1. stabilization;
2. activization;
3. uncertainty;
4. development.

It is worth mentioning that even in the Soviet economy sourcing relations already existed. The development of Soviet industry was facilitated by manufacturing outsourcing, which was then called "the socialist cooperation" (Shabanov 2013). Manufacturers of components and assemblies were assigned to the parent enterprise, while orders for scientific developments were placed in leading research institutes throughout the Soviet Union.

At the same time, in the USSR there also existed outsourcing of business processes. In the 1960s and 1980s, when computer needs exceeded available resources, so-called shared computing centers were created, which provided access to the computer resources of outside organizations. There were about 30 centers like this in the Soviet Union.

The collapse of the Soviet Union disrupted the existing sourcing links but did not lead to the rapid formation of new ones. For this reason, it is more correct to call the first stage of the development of sourcing in Russia the "stabilization" period. It was not, however, a period of stability. According to the leading Russian economists, this period was characterized by "a large-scale macroeconomic economic crisis..., which led to the collapse of the budget and monetary systems, to exceptionally high inflation rates, to a drop in production" (Gaidar 2003). In terms of phenomena significant for sourcing, this period was characterized by the following factors.

Firstly, privatization. Regarding outsourcing, the new private owners of enterprises were focused primarily on maximizing profits, which was achievable by means of reorienting the marketing from domestic to foreign markets (the oil and gas sector, metallurgy, coal, and other types of industry). New owners used the competitive advantage of low manufacturing costs for producing raw materials, taking into account the sharp devaluation of the ruble in Russia. New owners were also not familiar with the outsourcing culture, instead having experience in the functioning of vertically integrated structures of the Soviet industrial period. Admittedly, in the 1990s, the market for outsourcing services (services, logistics, finance, etc.) was extremely poorly developed.

Secondly, institutional voids. This transformation took place in a weak state. Almost all institutions of state power were severely damaged. Sometimes, one key area of business activity in the post-Soviet economy was identifying institutional voids and filling them, albeit often chaotically. The absence of state institutions repeatedly increased the firms' transaction costs. They were forced to integrate particular areas of activity—rail transport, port infrastructure, their own financial structures (banks, insurance companies), and others—into the value chain. Thus, the trend of the Soviet economy toward vertical integration—and at least maintaining, if not expanding, the "boundaries of firms"—only intensified. At this stage, the development of sourcing in general and outsourcing in a some sense seemed less urgent; instead, businesses were preoccupied by the need for "survival" under the new conditions. Besides, it must not be forgotten that this was also the period of the strengthening of the activities of organized crime, the so-called "redistribution" of property, and other criminal "features" of the 1990s. In general, organized crime syndicates could also be considered a certain means to fill those institutional voids that appeared after the strong state dissolved. The remnants of this phenomenon can still be observed in the form of the significant role played by the security system in the economy nowadays.

Thirdly, the period of stabilization was characterized by the transformation of existing cooperative links. Many of these were severed or broken due to the emergence of customs borders and other barriers between used-to-be parts of the centralized USSR—the new CIS countries. Earlier, united in single value chains, companies, being forced to survive and being transferred to the hands of private owners, began to demonstrate opportunistic behavior. Information asymmetry strengthened their desire to protect their own interests. This inevitably led to the businesses losing confidence in each other. In addition, the common values that had united firms, such as ideals of the socialist economy, ceased to exist. Disagreements were reinforced by the existence of new national values inside independent CIS states, which only increased distrust and the tendency to break relations. Connections were preserved only where their instantaneous destruction was impossible (a single energy, railway, pipeline, and other systems).

A good illustration of the depth of institutional voids is the example of McDonalds entering the Russian market in the early 1990s. In the US, McDonalds outsources most of its operations, focusing only on its competitive advantage—fast customer service with inexpensive food of an consistent quality. Moreover, now, the basis of this business is effective franchise management: in practice McDonalds does not manage fast food restaurants in principle. In Russia, at the time this company entered the market, however, there were neither intermediaries on whom it could rely on, nor franchise partners. Its traditional partners in Europe refused to enter the Russian market due to regulatory difficulties and other problems.

However, the company did not abandon its plans and decided to fill the institutional voids itself. McDonalds encountered an absence of outsourcing partners in distribution and logistics. The agricultural standards were incompatible with the policy of the company. There were no qualified managers to work with suppliers in the labor market.

In response to institutional voids, McDonalds had to go for one of the deepest vertical integrations in its history.

To do so, the company built its own production complex in Moscow–with an area of 100 thousand square meters–to produce meat, ketchup, mustard, and a number of other goods. The company imported livestock from Holland, potatoes from the USA, and attracted specialists from Canada to train Russian farmers in modern farming methods. McDonalds also provided funding to improve agricultural practices. In addition, the company financed its suppliers in advance to ensure they had sufficient working capital to purchase modern equipment.

The company also invested in the creation of its own logistic capacities for the transportation of goods: a fleet of trucks.

In order to overcome the lack of human resources, McDonalds sent 50 foreign specialists to Russia, and also organized mass internships in Canada for Russian specialists for several months.

The result of the chosen strategy was McDonalds having an 80% share in the fast food market of Russia by 2008. At the same time, such a strategy, of course, increased McDonalds' transaction costs, and diverted significant financial and human resources; the company's total investment in Russia amounted to $250 million by 2008 (Khanna et al. 2010).

The above example generally illustrates what transaction costs those companies operating in the young Russian economy during its initial formation had to bear. Naturally, the effective use of sourcing to achieve strategic competitive advantages was out of the question.

The second stage led to **intensifying** efforts of these companies in the use of sourcing tools. A number of factors contributed to this.

Firstly, the 1998 currency crisis, like any crisis, contributed to the "cleansing" of the market; ineffective insourcing structures collapsed through bankruptcy, mergers and acquisitions, etc. Concentration on the competitive advantages of the "five forces" model began to have a greater impact, since many companies realized that it was impossible to perform all processes equally effectively–it was necessary to concentrate on the main ones instead.

Secondly, the political and economic situation began to stabilize: the internal Russian conflict in the North Caucasus had ended, and the prospects for business development had become more predictable. However, along with the political stabilization and development of the economy, rising living standards and wages in Russia production costs began to go up. This increased the influence of the transactional cost factor in economics and business practices; economic actors were looking for optimal forms within the "sourcing cycle." Outsourcing became one of such tools.

Thirdly, a lot of firms providing outsourcing services appeared in the economy. The number of businesses in the Russian economy rose from its initial figure of 1.2 million in 1994, and stabilized at the level of 5 million by 2004–2005. As a result, confidence in the market–which now was able to provide services at the request of private and public organizations—grew.

Fourthly, in the 1990s, sourcing globally acquired the status of a tool for structuring the "boundaries of firms," and in this capacity it began to gain popularity in Russia.

By the beginning of the activation period, the main financial and industrial groups (FIG) had already been established. During privatization or collateral auctions, holdings appeared–such as Lukoil, Yukos, Surgutneftegaz, Sidanko, Sibneft, Norilsk Nickel, Severstal, NLMK, or aluminum plants—which would later be included in the RusAl group.

Svyazinvest, Gazprom, Avtovaz, and Aeroflot received their majority or minority private shareholders. At that very time, the formation of the FIG could be observed in China, Vietnam, South Korea, and a number of countries in Eastern Europe.

Relationships of trust and cooperation developed, and in this arena, FIG survival statistics are important. According to domestic researchers, of the nine private FIGs created in the 1990s only two survived—Oneximbank and Alfa Bank. Obviously, in general, the campaign to create private FIGs in the 90s failed (Khanin 2012). It influenced sourcing practices as well.

In this situation, one of the safe sourcing options was the creation of shared service centers (SSCs), the number of which increased significantly in the early 2000s. The first attempts to transfer support activities into specialized intra-company units were made by the Russian oil companies. These were followed by other industrial manufacturers, as well as by companies from other industries (Rostelecom, Severstal, Tele2, Ak Bars, RusAl, etc.).

At the same time, Russian companies quickly went from creating JSCs to outsourcing, as JSCs served an intermediate form of sourcing (Fig. 7.2).

In fact, most of these decisions were made between 2000 and 2006, which is a rather short period for the formation of a fully fledged outsourcing industry.

Simultaneously, many companies continued down the opposite trend—the construction of vertically integrated structures. This was natural due to the small "shadow of the future"—the perceived expectancy of mutually beneficial relationships between businessmen–as noted by Robert Axelrod (Axelrod 1984). This trend continued, particularly, in the real estate—the industry that suffered most of all during the crisis of 2008–2009. Real estate investors (whether commercial or residential) integrated

Fig. 7.2 The way from the operations method to outsourcing (*Source* Created by D. Stapran)

the maximum number of elements—from cement factories and reinforced concrete structures facilities, to construction companies and sales offices—into value chains.

During this period of development, the trend in the public sector went against the trend for privatization as was popular in the 1990s. The strengthened state took the path of uniting the remaining state-owned companies into industrial clusters. The government proclaimed the policy of building "national champions"—state holdings in various industries, though they could be perceived as clones of Soviet vertically integrated enterprises.

The United Shipbuilding Company, the United Aviation Corporation, Rosatom, Rusnano, Rostekhnologii, and others appeared in the Russian economic arena from 2006 to 2008. They replenished the list of previously formed state-owned super companies—Rosneft, Gazprom, Sberbank, VTB, Svyazinvest, Aeroflot, Russian Railways, Transneft, and others.

"National champions" immediately showed a desire to use economies of scale (which, according to our observation, is the main "curse of outsourcing") and integrate into its boundaries a significant number of elements of the value chain. For example, Rostekhnologii had Novincombank as its base bank as it was in the same "boundaries of the company." The same happened in the case of service, repairs, sales, and other enterprises. Aeroflot owned a part of Sheremetyevo Airport, Transneft owned ports, Rosneft owned terminals and pipelines. The presence of logistics assets in the structure of state-owned companies was almost universal.

The aforementioned features of the activities of public and private companies are clearly explained in terms of insufficient trust to sourcing partners. At the same time we should admit the objective presence of "institutional voids." The banking sector remained an example of such voids. Foreign automobile concerns entering the Russian market adapted to market shortcomings by expanding the "boundaries of firms" by means of creating financial companies for lending to purchasing their own cars (Toyota Bank and others serve as examples). Foreign retail chains also faced institutional voids; during the period of the Russian economy's active growth, this deficit was observed in everything—in warehouse and trading areas, means of transporting goods, and so on. Some companies, such as Metro Cash and Carry or Ashan, invited their outsourcing suppliers in logistics—FM Logistics and other companies—to enter the Russian market together with their prime customers. The latter assessed the improvements in the institutional environment in the Russian economy and agreed. This is noticeably different from the situation in the early 1990s described above, when McDonalds entered the Russian market and foreign companies considered its institutional voids to be too large to follow their client.

During this period, one example of the "sourcing cycle" can also be observed on the scale of the country's economy—the example of state participation in the economy, when the privatization period was replaced by the period of strengthening state property.

As indicated, the current stage of the development of sourcing ended with a structural correction in the market in the form of the economic crisis of 2008–2009, in the course of which vertically integrated structures turned out to be less adaptive to changing realities and were therefore mainly affected.

Moreover, it was closer to the completion of this stage that important processes began to unfold in a number of industry markets, which increased the sourcing options of economic actors. Among these are the liquidation of RAO "UES of Russia" and the creation of a competitive electricity market; the outsourcing of support functions (repairs, engineering, etc.); the privatization of the Russian Railways carriage fleet and the creation of a competitive transportation market; the privatization of a significant number of sea and aviation ports; and the beginning of a new round of cautious privatization in the form of "people's IPOs." The crisis, however, has seriously affected this trend in the economy.

The next step is best described by the term "**uncertainty**," as it is characterized by contradictory trends. On the one hand, difficulties in the economy continued to stimulate both public and private businessmen to look for ways to reduce transaction costs, including the opposite tendency to return businesses from outsourcing to insourcing (sourcing cycle). Some examples of the reverse sourcing cycle can be seen in the electric power industry (when energy companies massively returned engineering and repairs to the companies), the oil and gas industry (when Rosneft purchased back previously outsourced oilfield service companies), logistics, IT (almost every "national champion" created its own IT company), and other industries. This tendency was promoted by a number of factors, primarily the strengthening of the role of the state in the economy. The share of the public sector increased after the crisis: according to some estimates, it decreased from 33 to 31% in 2003–2007, but by 2016 it had increased to 40–50%. Some vivid examples were the purchase of Bashneft by Rosneft, the purchase of Magnit by VTB, the purchase of Tele 2 by Rostelecom, and other transactions of this kind by quasi-state structures. This created a general atmosphere of distrust, both among society and in the economy, regarding privatization (a phenomenon largely similar to outsourcing) and business in general.

Secondly, public companies, having a motivation different from private companies, are not inclined to actively use an instrument such as outsourcing in their activities. Moreover, in some industries, like the electric power industry, the use of this tool is sometimes interpreted by law enforcement agencies as an illegal activity.

Recently, the policy of strengthening the role of the state in the economy has only intensified. For example, the policy of cleansing the banking sector of unscrupulous players led to a critical share of the state in the banking system—up to 70%, a 10% increase in 2016. At the same time, among the 10 largest banks in Russia, only 3 are private, and their assets make up only about 10% of the assets of all the ten banks.

In addition to the banking sector, the state also retained its participation in other large Russian holdings, such as Gazprom, Rosneft, Russian Railways, Transneft, Russian Networks, RusHydro, Inter RAO, Rostekhnologii, Sberbank, VTB, and others.

Private companies also turned to be concentrated in the hands of powerful businessmen, often called "oligarchs." This structure of the economy, according to Williamson, is not optimal in terms of transaction costs. He speaks about "the danger of oligarchies, which are inevitable but evil, a retreat from the ideal that needs to be carefully analyzed and the damage from which needs to be minimized" (Williamson 2013).

Therefore, during the period of uncertainty, large commercial holdings were finally formed. In total, the 100 largest companies employ about 2.5 million people, and their revenue in 2018 amounted to 25 trillion rubles. In general in Russia, during the period of "uncertainty," a rather concentrated economic structure arose, in which, in particular, the 643 largest Russian companies accounted for 77% of GDP in 2014, the top 5 companies accounted for 88% of corporate profit, and the top 50 largest taxpaying companies provided 47% of all corporate taxes in Russia in 2016 (Shapovalov 2015; Moiseev and Tkacheev 2017).

From a macroeconomic point of view, there was a global cyclical crisis of overproduction in 2014, coming on top of the slowdown in economic growth which began in 2012.

From the point of view of companies' sourcing strategies, the features mentioned had several consequences.

Firstly, the concentration of capital still justified economies of scale. One vivid example was the development of the largest Russian logistics operator from the logistics division of NLMK. Other examples are the creation of inner telecom operators by Russian Railways, or Sberbank.

Secondly, the strength of the negotiating power—from the point of view of game theory—did not promote trust between customers among the largest companies and their outsourcing partners, since the tendency for opportunism among the former remained quite high (DeSteno 2014).

Thirdly, a generally wary attitude toward outsourcing remained. This is evidenced by the "renaissance" of the interest in creating SSCs among large companies—in 2017–2018 such projects were launched in Inter RAO, FGC, and others.

Fourthly, it was during the period of "uncertainty" that the "sourcing cycle" at the microeconomic level was most clear, as evidenced, in particular, by the example of Rosneft that reintegrated back oilfield services, logistics, IT and other formerly outsourced operations.

Simultaneously, a number of outsourcing directions, on the contrary, began to develop very actively in the 2010s. This is mainly in the area of outsourcing information technology and logistic services. The number of high-quality and independent intermediaries emerged, both in the field of professional services and in the field of production.

Outsourcing and other sourcing options were especially developed at the level of small and medium-sized enterprises (SME). SMEs rarely have significant bargaining power in regard to each other. In this connection, they are forced to cooperate. As business conditions have become more predictable, the "shadow of the future" has increased, and the tendency to build long-term sourcing cooperative links has intensified (Axelrod 1984).

Furthermore, SMEs operate in competitive markets. Consequently, competitive advantages and transaction costs become much stronger factors for them.

After 2018, in Russia, a new stage in the **development** of outsourcing should be expected. This can lead to an increase in the role of outsourcing in the economy—up to 24% of GDP by 2021—and can lead to stagnation (Fig. 7.3). The implementation of one particular scenario will depend on a number of variables.

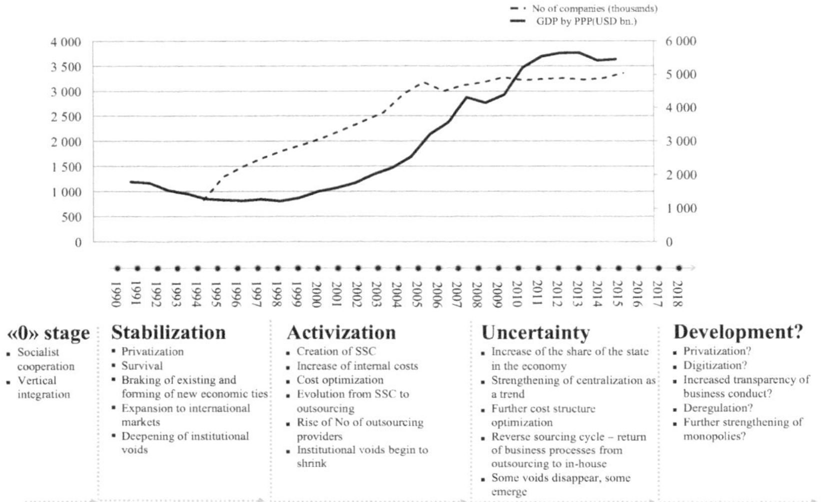

Fig. 7.3 Stages of outsourcing development in the Russian economy (*Source* Created by D. Stapran)

The main variable seems to be the level of Institutional voids. The Russian economy has already made some significant progress in overcoming them, but they continue to occur. The elimination of voids in the markets of labor, goods, and capital, and the growth in the number of independent and qualified intermediaries, will increase the attractiveness of various sourcing options not only for SMEs but also for large companies. Moreover, all the prerequisites have developed for this—the relations in the economy have become predictable, and the "shadow of the future" has increased enough. In a number of industry markets, prerequisites for creating "ecosystems" are emerging. The agricultural market, the telecommunications market, and the retail market serve as examples of an effective "co-opetition," where companies alternately change the roles of competitors to complementors in order to achieve certain goals (Brandenburger and Nalebuff 2019).

Economic sanctions, however, create, rather than eliminate, institutional voids, as they hinder the creation of cooperative links with potential foreign outsourcing providers. One example of this is the forced refusal to form an oilfield service company in Russia on the basis of an alliance of the foreign Schlumberger and EDC.

The state of institutional voids can be greatly influenced by the targeted actions of the state. According to Porter, "state policy can restrict or encourage the entry of new players both directly and indirectly—raising or removing entry barriers. Examples include the encouragement or prohibition of foreign investment in certain industries or enterprises, licensing, protection of intellectual property (patents), support or deterrence of the trade union activity, bankruptcy regulation, etc." (Porter 2008). Intensification of reforms in the economy will inevitably lead to a decrease in regulation and barriers that will positively affect the development of outsourcing and increase sourcing options. This will also be facilitated by the accelerated privatization of state property and a decrease in the state's share in the commercial segment of the Russian economy. Private enterprises and businessmen, as has been repeatedly noted, have different motives and tend to more actively practice outsourcing and experiment with configurations of outsourcing relations. The development of competition in different markets will also contribute to the greater development of sourcing practices, as achieving strategic advantages will become even more important.

The actions of the state to increase the transparency of doing business—first of all, tax transactions—will be no less important. It will also lead (and is already leading) to an abdication of outsourcing by the companies using outsourcing transactions for tax and other optimization purposes. Some of the functions of companies that they did not formally plan to outsource on account of these very tax optimizations can now be transferred to outside professional service providers. The fact that this is possible is proved by the practice of General Electric, which has transferred all its accounting and tax accounting around the world, including in Russia, to the international audit and consulting company PwC.

More transparent rules of the game in the banking market will play the same role. Despite the increase of the state's share in the banking system, this led to a certain cleansing of the market from sourcing practices when banks and depositors' funds, as well as pension funds, were used to finance private projects by the owners of these financial organizations. A clear signal from the Central Bank and the law enforcement system about the inadmissibility of such practices will lead to the lack of a motive for including financial organizations into the perimeter of firms and holdings. Consequently, they will become more reliable, consistent and predictable players, and will be trusted more, according to Morgan and Hunt.

At the same time, the pace of digitalization and robotization of a number of processes will become an important variable. On the one hand, this will lead to the situation when the entire direction of outsourcing services (primarily associated with a large share of staff costs in the prime cost) will become obsolete; at the same time, the high cost of digitalization and robotization, as well as a relatively small share of outsourcing services squeezed by them, will not significantly affect the dynamics of sourcing. On the other hand, the development of technologies will change the technological continuity of processes, which, according to Williamson, determines the "boundaries of the firm" at a particular time; such a technological continuity can be exemplified by industrial energy storage technologies, which can revolutionize the power industry and transform the existing value chains.

On the whole, the prospects for the development of sourcing practices in Russia seem very encouraging. This has been confirmed by the experience over the last three decades, when sourcing relations in the Russian economy—although being of a cyclical character, often returning to the starting point—were gradually moving toward the development as a spiral.

Conclusions/Recommendations

The research has examined some regularities of the development of outsourcing as part of the sourcing processes for individual firms, industry segments, and the Russian economy in general, over a thirty-year period; from this it possible to establish the periods of the development of outsourcing, identify individual stages, give qualitative characteristics to each of the stages, and confirm the hypothesis about the presence of "sourcing cycles."

The study of the history of the formation and development of sourcing in Russia shows that this phenomenon has gone through its formation period and is now used by many companies. In the late 1990s and early 2000s, large Russian businessmen—owners of privatized businesses—began to transfer secondary or ancillary activities to independent subsidiary and dependent companies. This was done by businessmen in the oil, gas, coal, steel, automotive, and energy industries, among others.

At the initial stage in industrial markets such as logistics, processing, repairs, operation, maintenance, construction, protection, and others, there were not enough players, the conditions for competition were not there, and confidence had not been accumulated. In the economy there were significant "institutional voids" that Russian firms sought to fill with the help of vertical integration. That is why even new lines of business, such as retail, included support elements of the value chain into the perimeter of company activities. At the same time there were exceptions: some industries were originally built according to the model of outsourcing service providers. These were, for example, information technology and consulting.

As competition developed, the number of outsourcing companies and successful outsourcing "cases" grew, and client businessmen gradually began to outsource some activities. This happened with logistics, the oilfield service business, repairs in the energy industry, and others. The cyclical crises in the Russian economy in 1998, 2008 and 2014 also played a significant role in stimulating the development of outsourcing.

Today, companies' sourcing strategies are rapidly developing. However, the growth or stagnation of sourcing in general—and outsourcing in particular—will depend on a number of variables. One of them—perhaps the most important one–will be public policy and the pace of the elimination of "institutional voids" in the Russian economy. In addition, the reduction of the role of the state in the economy, deregulation in certain industry markets, and digitalization (as an element in creating more transparent and trust-based "rules of the game") will influence the development of sourcing relations.

References

Arrow, K. J. (1969). *The Organization of Economic Activity: Issues Pertinent to the Choice of Market versus Non-Market Allocations* (pp. 1–6). Washington, DC: Joint Economic Committee of Congress. http://citeseerx.ist.psu.edu/viewdoc/download?doi=10.1.1.324.971&rep=rep1&type=pdf.

Axelrod, R. (1984). *The Evolution of Cooperation*. New York: Basic Books.

Blau, P. M. (1974). *On the Nature of Organizations*. New York: Wiley.

Brandenburger, A. M., & Nalebuff, B. J. (2019). *Co-opetition*. New York: Currency Doubleday.

Coase, R. (1937). Nature of the Firm. *Economica, 4*(16), 386–405.

DeSteno, D. (2014, March). Who Can You Trust? *Harvard Business Review* (Boston), pp. 1–5.

Gaidar, E. T., et al. (2003). *Transition Economy. Essays on Economic Policy in Post-Communist Russia. 1998–2002*. Moscow: Delo.

Khanin, G. I. (2012). Economic History of Russia in Modern Times. *Terra Economicus, 10*(Special issue).

Khanna, T., Palepu, K. G., & Bullock, R. J. (2010). *Winning in Emerging Markets: A Road Map for Strategy and Execution*. Boston: Harvard Business Press.

Moiseev, I., & Tkachev, I. (2017, August 15). Research of RBC: The Largest Taxpayers of Russia. *RBC Gazeta*.

Moiseeva, N. K., Malyutina, O. N., & Moskvina, I. A. (2010). *Outsourcing in the Development of Business Partnerships*. Moscow: Finance and Statistics.

Morgan, R., & Hunt, S. (1994). The Commitment-Trust Theory of Relationship Marketing. *Journal of Marketing, 58*(3), 20–38. https://doi.org/10.2307/1252308.

Porter, M. E. (2008). *The Five Competitive Forces That Shape Strategy*. Boston: Harvard Business Review.

Shabanov, A. (2013). How Did Outsourcing Develop? Background. *UCMS Group Russia*. http://blog.ucmsgroup.ru/how-did-outsourcing-develop-history-of-the-question/.

Shapovalov, A. (2015, November 13). Norm in Unprofitability. *Kommersant*.

Teece, D., Pisano, G., & Shuen, A. (1997). Dynamic Capabilities and Strategic Management. *Strategic Management Journal, 7*(187), 509–533. https://doi.org/10.1002/(sici)1097-0266(199708)18:73.0.co;2-z.

Thorelli, H. (1986). Networks: Between Markets and Hierarchies. *Strategic Management Journal, 7*(1), 37–51. https://doi.org/10.1002/smj.4250070105 17.

Williamson, O. E. (1990). Transaction Cost Economics. In R. S. Willig (Ed.), *Handbook of Industrial Organization* (pp. 135–182). Amsterdam, New York, Oxford, and Tokyo: North Holland.

Williamson, O. E. (2013). *The Transaction Cost Economics Project: The Theory and Practice of the Governance of Contractual Relations*. Northampton: Edward Elgar Publishing Inc.

CHAPTER 8

Technologies of the Fourth Industrial Revolution as a Driver of Advancing in Digital Operations Management

Julia Kovalchuk

Introduction

The digital transformation of business processes, high and progressive production technologies, the intellectualization of services, and increasing digital literacy of employees are al integral parts of the modern economy. Changes in technologies and processes within the framework of the fourth industrial revolution (Schwab 2017)—or even the fifth industrial revolution (Marsh 2013), which is currently underway and fully corresponds to the upward phase of the sixth wave of Kondratyev's large cycles—affect not only the designed elements but also the production process itself, which requires substantial modernization not only of the production process itself but also of its organizing principles.

J. Kovalchuk (✉)
Moscow State Institute of International Relations (MGIMO University), Moscow, Russia
e-mail: fm-science@inbox.ru

Moscow Aviation Institute (National Research University), Moscow, Russia

N. Konina (ed.), *Digital Strategies in a Global Market*,
https://doi.org/10.1007/978-3-030-58267-8_8

Practice shows that technological and design innovations constitute a significant component of investment in the development of industrial enterprises. At the same time, it has long been considered that improving the manufacturing process management is the least capital-intensive factor of development. This view has thus far proved to be incorrect, since a radical restructuring of production processes is required not only due to technical re-equipment but also in terms of their adjustment to fundamentally new means of decision support, including the latest information systems and the Internet of Things.

Methodology

The evolution of industrial equipment (especially in terms of increasing labour productivity) is inextricably linked with the achievements of production design; we accordingly argue that the current changes in organizational forms and methods should be correlated with new technologies that relate to the digital economy and new forms of production design, for example:

Industrie 4.0 (Industry 4.0—Digital Enterprise);
Manufacturing 4.0 (Production 4.0);
Industrial Internet;
Connected Enterprise;
SMART Manufacturing;
Smart Factory, etc.

Ignoring manual labour—the primary production technology—then the evolution of production technology over the past hundred years and the level of production technology that developed countries have reached can be represented through the chart in Fig. 8.1. At the same time, objectively, the development of technologies was carried out to increase labour productivity and production flexibility, tasks which are still relevant today. For example, about 50 industrial robots that are capable of replacing whole shifts of highly qualified employees in productivity have been established at the Russian enterprises of the United Aircraft Corporation (Zhishkevich 2018), but these tasks also limited by the potential increase in unemployment (due to the release of labour) and changes in professional competencies (due to the need to master new skills on more

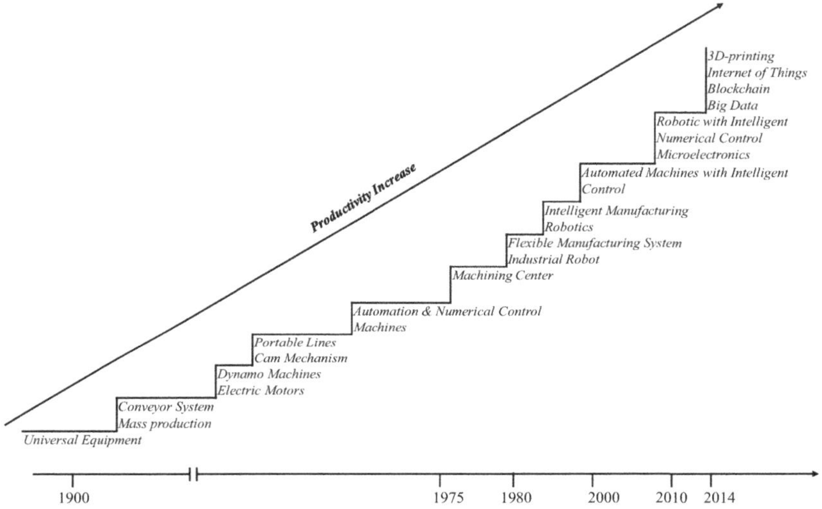

Fig. 8.1 The evolution of manufacturing equipment and machinery (*Source* Created by the author)

advanced equipment). Thus, according to a study by Aston University, on average, approximately 2.5 positions in work are freed after introducing 1 robot (the range is generally from 0.8 to 6.2 workplaces) (Mahdawi 2017). In fairness, we note that introducing 1 robot creates 0.8 jobs in the robotics manufacturing industry itself or its maintenance.

However, the integration of information technologies in the industry, within the framework of digital transformation, makes it necessary to analyze trends in the implementation of automated control systems for industrial enterprises (Fig. 8.2); these systems currently link many functions that are necessary not only for the production process but also for related activities.

In fact, information technology makes it possible to maximize a product's competitiveness by (1) increasing the degree of satisfaction of customer needs not only with the functional properties of the product, but also with the level of service, repair, and product modernization; (2) cost reduction, particularly time costs (time of designing, creating, and testing the prototype) and material costs (for creating and using the product).

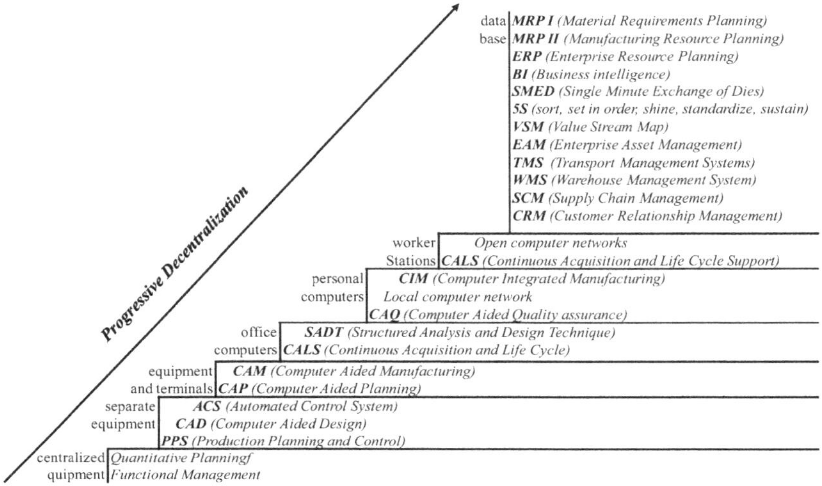

Fig. 8.2 Trends in information technology used in production management (*Source* Created by the author)

Thus, in the context of the digital economy, although integrating production capacities and information technologies can create new products for the prospective buyers' temporary needs, special attention must be paid to the speed of achieving competitive advantages, along with the search for reducing production costs. This solution helps to reduce delays when releasing a new or a modified product, and solutions may even outstrip future customer needs.

Results

Since the period of large-scale industrialization began, the concept of operations management has transformed, due to changes in the market and a shift in customer needs (Fig. 8.3). It has shifted from focusing on efficiency to focusing on quality, flexibility, innovation, and, ultimately, on shortening the development time for new products.

As a consequence, competition-based primarily on time should be considered, as this is a decisive factor in accelerating the development and organization of creating new or modified products. If, earlier, the main benefits from the rational operations management included low costs,

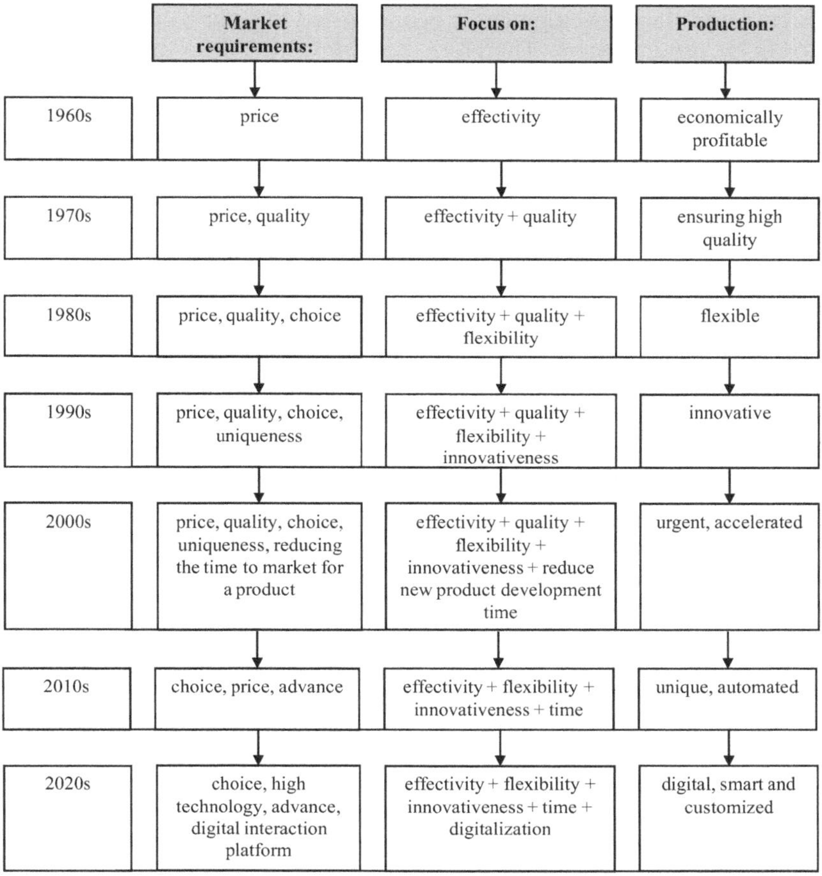

Fig. 8.3 The determinants of classical and digital operations management (*Source* Created by the author)

today, when consumer demands are growing, time is instead the main factor in obtaining competitive advantages. This is due to a change in the concept of modern products.

The introduction of the new technologies of the fourth industrial revolution has already significantly adjustmented understanding of the products' very conceptual physical essence, as products become complex systems, and their development is being carried out not by engineers, but mostly by programmers. Therefore, according to Porter and Hepelman (2015), "smart" products connect various elements, technologies, and capabilities, which can then be described as related products; these are: (1) physical components, including electronics; (2) intelligent components (sensors, microprocessors, data storage devices, software, embedded operating systems, digital interface); (3) the connection of nodes (ports, antennas, protocols, and networks that provide interaction between the product and some cloud run on running on remote servers, containing the product of an external operating system). The functionality of all these components is, in the product image, supported through specific connections (the technology stack), which serve as a platform for storing and analyzing data, launching applications, and protecting access to the products and data coming into and out of them; in other words, it is a gateway for exchanging data between the product and the user, combining data from business systems, external sources, and other related products.

Therefore, a delay in the release of a new or modified product is fraught with the loss of competitive advantages and a decrease in the performance of an industrial enterprise. This means that, in the current conditions, it is important to be ahead of the future needs of consumers, as well as the actions of competitors, in order to be effective.

Similarly, in operations management, there is a growing need for orientation; ensuring the competitiveness of an industrial enterprise and its products requires the active involvement of digital technologies into production, which cannot be done as successfully without orienting operational management. Moreover, another advance found through temporal relations, since, by viewing the manufacturing process management as a combination of elements of the production process in time and space, it is impossible to be ahead in space for objective reasons.

To ensure product manufacturing- the requirements for which were determined by their consumers (who in turn are subject to environmental influences)—the concept of early manufacturing process management was created in the early 2000s; this represented a manufacturing process management that can provide rapid changes in production engineering and can speed up production to the due date in accordance with market requirements (Kovalchuk and Stepnov 2017). Advanced operations management can still be effectively applied if conditions for a quick response, and anticipation of changes in both external and internal environments, are provided.

When using advanced operations management, it becomes necessary to adhere to special principles, the degree of implementation of which depends on the time and money spent to prepare and create a new product. These principles include:

- *cost-effectiveness*; this involves achieving the desired result in a given time interval with minimal labour or resources (material and financial);
- *synergy*; this assumes that, as a whole, the total result of an enterprise's activities is better than the sum of its performance indicators for its product divisions when using the same technologies, equipment, R&D results, etc.;
- *continuity*; here, there is a relationship between existing and new phenomena and processes within the framework of the advanced manufacturing management, when the new retains some necessary elements and properties of the old;
- *the legitimacy of the alternatives*; this assumes that, within the framework of the leading manufacturing process, there are some prototypes of a new or improved product, types of equipment, and manufacturing technology, of which there will only be those necessary for the mass production of the selected new product by the time the production process starts;
- *learnability*; within the framework of advanced production management, as well as the framework of new methods of production management, new knowledge and experience can be analyzed and perceived from an external environment, and new methods of production design can be created on the basis of existing ones;
- *the susceptibility of production to advance*; this involves the use of a diagnostic mechanism within advanced production management to constantly monitor changes in the external and internal environment of the production system, adequately anticipate them, and promptly implement the corresponding changes;
- *production adaptability*; the manufacturing process will purposefully adapt to changes in the external and internal environment by changing its quantitative and qualitative characteristics;
- *impact on the external environment*; this implies there is the ability to anticipate and shape external changes after applying new technical capabilities and creative approaches;

- *production flexibility*; this similarly implies there is the ability to perceive innovations, adapt to changing operating conditions, and switch to the release of a new product in a limited time using minimal resources;
- *production mobility*; the elements production must move in time and space, and be used in necessary combinations, to optimize advanced operations management;
- *integrating participants in the advanced manufacture process*; when designing and producing a new or improved product which needs feedback from both developers and manufacturers, as well as consumers, interdependent flexible joint actions should be employed;
- *capacity sufficiency*; all units involved in the advanced manufacturing process ought to have the corresponding capabilities and relatively equal throughput;
- *guaranteed work performance*; the advanced manufacturing process implies the performance of the specified amount of work within the required time frame; it should be of appropriate quality and established cost, with the involvement of highly qualified specialists;
- *innovative support;* all elements of the advanced manufacturing process should be innovative;
- *sufficiency and increased motivation of employees*; as part of the advanced manufacturing process, this requires the constant activation of designing and manufacturing a new or improved product;
- *continuous improvement*; the problems of an industrial enterprise—identified and analyzed during diagnostics—become the base for eliminating them when changing the production system, thereby determining the direction of the advanced manufacturing process.

Under modern conditions, the advanced manufacturing process does not change the above basic principles, but is instead supplemented by the essential provisions for modern approaches that accompany digital transformation in the industry.

For example, for operational planning and production design, the so-called Novocherkassk system, which was created in the USSR back in the early 1960s, was used for a long time with extreme efficiency. It was created at the Novocherkassk Electric Locomotive Plant, and became the prototype for modern ERP systems in the lean production format (Piterkin 2013). The distinctive advantage that made the Novocherkassk system widely used in Soviet and further Russian industrial enterprises are its abilities to organize production to a predetermined quantity and "just in time" (note that the famous Kanban was still in the blueprint stage when it was created), subject to the criterion of minimizing production costs. These advantages can be enhanced by adopting modern tools, including digital technologies and automated control systems, in order to increase the efficiency of organizational processes and implement advanced operations management, namely:

1. The formation of backlogs (in the most simplified version representing work in progress) as compensation for lead times when sending parts (assemblies) to assembly. The backlogs are to be calculated by the normative method and be stored in the central warehouse if the enterprise is big and shops are in different rooms (or buildings). In this case, the parts should be as standardized as possible. As an alternative to creating backlogs in the digital economy, 3D printing should be considered, having the real potential of reducing production costs and reducing production time. In general, 3D printing (using methods of layer-by-layer deposition, electron beam or laser sintering, metal sintering or laser sintering) has become more effective in contrast to cutting and milling machines producing parts by removing existing layers; therefore 3D printing does not imply material waste, and maximum manufacturing accuracy is achieved (Perry 2018). It is worth mentioning that plastic, metal, and composite materials can be used.
2. Mass production in the digital economy will be transformed—the future lies in small-scale production—so it is necessary to rebuild the production design system for using a multi-line production method or conveyor assembly. For example, the automotive industry is actively implementing the concept of "Industrial Internet of things" (IIoT), which makes it possible to use a method of shop management through collecting and analysing the data received from equipment during production processes, as well as to record online the actual performance of the machine and compare it with the planned performance. Such an instant report will allows for identifying and anticipating malfunctions or inefficient operations (both for processes and equipment), as well as for comparing enterprises' production indicators, assembly lines, or equipment, which will make production processes as efficient as possible (Park 2019).

3. Business models and production scenarios can be adapted to customers' parameters, since it is important to maintain the products' competitiveness through management, interact with customers at the design stage, reduce the lead time from several weeks to several hours, and also fulfil single orders at the mass-production price. All this is possible when using digital technologies that will not only help to cooperate with customers (i.e. when delivering products), but also control the number of products in stock, the volume of products not yet manufactured, and the delivery of parts to production. One of the solutions used by companies today is the creation of a new enterprise that manufactures products for individual orders with a batch size of one product and a unit cost lower than that of old products. This means the formation of a distributed network of additive production, in which products are manufactured directly in logistics centres equipped with the necessary digital solutions. An integrated digital platform enables fast production scaling. Using a web configurator with countless customization options, the client can order a product that fully meets their requirements, and placing the production next to the end, the customer can reduce the cost of delivery and speed up the execution of the order (World Economic Forum, McKinsey & Company 2019). The effectiveness of such business models is manifested in a significant reduction in the launch of a new product on the market (up to 75%), and a reduction of up to 60% of capital binding in inventories.
4. Assembly process management is effective within the MES system (Manufacturing Execution System), which is a production process management system as a special application software, designed to solve problems of synchronization, coordination, analysis, and the optimization of output within a specific production. For example, the Russian KAMAZ company currently produces up to 800 complete sets and 4 thousand different versions of their car annually, so, due to the need to optimize all business processes, including the choice of technical solutions, designing a variable model of the modular car, and adjusting the route maps of the technological process, issues around manufacturing process for individual customer requests are relevant. In this regard, digital technologies should be integrated into the MES system used, namely: (a) the use of digital doubles for modelling cars at the request of potential buyers; (b) the use of digital models simulating real conditions

for testing structural components and vehicles in the format of a "digital prototype" or a "digital double"; (c) identifying workers when starting work on equipment, issuing an electronic task and instructions for performing operations in strict accordance with the technological process, and confirming the completion of operations while filling out an electronic passport for work in progress and then for the finished product (Malyasev 2019); (d) mobile messaging allows defects to be checked and offers the possibility of stopping the conveyor to prevent a huge number of defects; (e) organizing digital security through a video surveillance system and photo capture.

5. Making a production programme in the digital economy and order-based production requires real-time updating (as an order is received and recorded by the automated control system). For multi-product companies, order processing and further production may be associated with the need to process large amounts of data, and its collection and analysis have a direct impact on the correctness of decisions. In this regard, progress in artificial intelligence, neural networks, and cognitive modelling is extremely relevant.
6. Regarding the enterprise's capacity foor production, when increasing volumes of orders at the maximum level of utilization, and facing objective financial problems (for example, the inability to invest in its expansion), solving the problems associated with increasing production volumes can be considered as organizational: technologically improving production processes through the unification of parts, which allows the number of readjustments of equipment to be reduced, and also instigates the search for opportunities to increase processing speed on existing equipment without compromising stability. For example, the plants of the Russian Cordiant holding, which unites the Yaroslavl Tire Plant (PJSC Omskshina), increased its equipment productivity by eliminating tolerances for the size of semi-finished products (which had been several millimetres), then unified individual components, without compromising the consumer characteristics of the finished pneumatic tires. All this made it possible to reduce the assortment of side wings and sidewalls and, as a result, the number of readjustments on the manufacture units (Tryaskov 2019).
7. In addition to implementing EAM (Enterprise Asset Management) and CMMS (Computerized Maintenance Management System), it is necessary to consider applying predictive analytics methods by

installing sensors on equipment when equipment failure can be predicted and one can get messages (or orders) for repairs before the equipment malfunctions or a problem arises, as well as unplanned outages.

8. Increasing competition for customers, and the ever-growing need for a quick change of product generations, entails the development of rapid modifications and design changes, as well as the introduction of new product models on the market. This requires not just the use of automated manufacturing control systems, but also their combinations—for example, developing a process map in the VSM (Value Stream Map) system, which allows one to determine the optimal location of equipment and ways of transporting resources in the production process when eliminating those areas that restrict production parts, or discrepancy in cycle time, or cycle time for redistribution to reduce equipment downtime. Then comes solving the problems of increasing equipment efficiency through optimization in the SMED (Single Minute Exchange of Dies) system, which provides quick equipment readjustment. In case of the Cordiant holding, the use of the SMED technique reduced the downtime for cutting the textile cord by 12%, even though the total idle line, due to the number of recharges, amounted to more than 30% of the work shift fund; readjustment of assembly lines with a change in tire size decreased by 10%, which allowed 20 thousand additional tires to be produced per year (Tryaskov 2019).

Current digitalization trends, which are actively penetrating enterprises and are associated with the technological manifestations of the fourth industrial revolution (Schwab 2018), are objectively transforming not only industrial enterprises themselves, but also the whole industries (especially high-tech ones); however, each enterprise perceives changes differently (Ross 2017). There are certain difficulties in these processes since these transformations cannot be integrated technologically and organizationally into the business processes of industrial enterprises. Thus, engineering, traditionally oriented towards technological advances in the industry (starting from the advent of the steam engine, metal-cutting, or mechanical looms to increase labour productivity), under modern conditions becomes:

- an industry platform for using new opportunities for automation and robotization, an adaptation of technologies and organizational systems of smart manufacturing (SMART Manufacturing based on Industrie 4.0) with the integration of physical, intangible and digital assets, and intellectual capital and information interaction with partners in the value chain;
- a global network that allows business processes to be combined, based on information exchange in product supply chains (including blockchain) as authentication of raw materials' origin, components, and assemblies, of finished products, and of information flows through digital platforms, which are a business model which creates value by facilitating exchange between two or more interdependent groups of participants;
- the sphere of economics for testing on-demand economy business models (that is, "on-demand or on-order economics", when it is not about selling goods and services but accessing them precisely when it is necessary, and getting orders online while they are executed offline), and the "sharing economy" (i.e. when the proposal is formed and implemented to use free or extra things and resources), which creates new opportunities for adapting and individualizing products, creating consumer chains, and forming information platforms that combine supply and demand and disrupt existing production structures, changing existing approaches to interaction, including financing of various kinds and from different sources;
- the distribution sector of the manufacturing of specialized products, and the provision of specialized services (niche industries), taking into account the development trends of customized products with the possibility for attracting designers and engineers, the interactive exchange of ideas, and developments based on 3D-design and 3D printing technologies.

The development of info-communication technologies—not only those currently taking place but also those predicted—significantly changes the nature of the relationship between suppliers, manufacturers, and consumers, or sellers and buyers. At the same time, modern business models—given the limitlessness and relative security of information exchange—are designed taking into account the digital platforms as a technological solution to their participant's coordinating and interacting.

An analysis of actually functioning digital platforms makes it possible to highlight their typology: for example, (1) a platform-company, when the digital platform became the reason for the company's formation; (2) a platform for an open interface that provides for user interaction and exchange in a particular industry; (3) a platform of intra-value chains for coordinating the companies working jointly at the final product, including production in a cluster.

Today, even a new version of capitalism should be singled out: "digital capitalism". An entrepreneur makes profit through cooperation; development of the digital economy implies spreading digital cooperation on a platform principle. Consequently, whereas, more than two centuries ago, workers were assigned to factories due to specialization in the classic version of Marx's theory, now, the platform allows: (a) including manufacturing and service sectors; (b) cutting transaction costs using a single information environment and information technology infrastructure; (c) taking the opportunities for part-time employment, which makes it possible to create reserves for saving standard costs and ensure the growth of labour productivity while reducing unproductive time losses.

Take industrial enterprises into account, introducing digital transformation technologies changes participation in value chains based on the use of additional elements. For example, blockchain is an expensive technology, but blockchain makes it possible to improve the supply chain and verify the authenticity of products, providing true transparency, responsibility, and efficiency, which did not exist before. At the same time, though, blockchain is not perfect, as there are some vulnerabilities and disadvantages to this technology. These are primarily related not to hacker attacks, but logical errors. The same is true of IoT—Internet of Things—which connects machinery, physical infrastructures, and the devices of numerous companies through cloud-based operating systems, and provides transactions, operations, and logistics, as well as data collection and analysis.

From an industrial point of view, the implementation of high technologies and the use of business and digital twins are now the most relevant trends. In high-tech industries and mechanical engineering, in which modern production technologies are actively introduced, the capabilities of digital twin technology should be used. This technology was the logical result of introducing the "digital production" concept and the Industrial Internet of Things.

Today, the "digital twins" technology is already different from the initial concept created in the early 2000s (Grieves 2014). The digital twin is considered a hybrid model (both physical and digital), combining: (a) product elements (twin-parts that are used to solve specific technical problems); (b) products (double products, which are used to reduce costs, improve ergonomics, lower maintenance and support costs, and increase the operating life) (Kaur et al. 2020); (c) a technological or production process (double processes, which are used to select technologies and search for reserves to reduce the duration of the production cycle); and (d) systems (twin systems that are used to optimize and improve the efficiency and balance of a particular system, for example, a production site, workshop, or plant). In general, a digital twin simulates a change in the state and characteristics of an object when changing the characteristics of any of its elements.

Modern industry is already using an updated technological base, with new technologies for processing materials: 3D-designing and 3D printing. These technologies are integrated into the information environment (digital platforms) to exchange ideas, information, volumes, and prices with market participants and network integration associations. Therefore, based on the principles of advancing in digital operational management, digital twins should be a virtual prototype of a real physical product, group of products, or processes tested before the actual manufacturing is launched. Overall, the main advantages of using digital twins when organizing manufacturing processes, taking into account the principle of advancement, include:

- remote and collective work on the product (structural elements, design, ergonomics) and the project for production and labour;
- designing the technological production chain, when the participants can be chosen taking into account the principles of designing Roth's matching markets (Roth 2018);
- a database when a digital twin (as an information system) allows data inheritance to create new modifications, i.e. the previous experience in the design, manufacture, and testing of new products is taken into account;
- an economic assessment of investment decisions when the prerequisites are created for significantly increasing the return on investment in R&D and equipment.

Thus, the digital twins allow the design and simulation of the value chain before the real business process, as well as the production process.

Conclusions/Recommendations

In conclusion, we note that the pace of manufacturing development is determined not only by the level of engineering and technology, but also, to a large extent, by the operations management, because within an industrial enterprise, a modern digital transformation—working ahead of consumers' expectations to design, develop, produce, and supply the necessary products more quickly—includes many areas: digital production, digital production engineering and design, digital supply chains, digital sales, a digital platform, and a digital ecosystem. Therefore, the aspects of manufacturing development and adaptability in modern industry are complementary, and constantly require better interaction between managers and technical specialists in order to make the new intellectual production more effective.

References

Grieves, M. (2014, March 24). *Digital Twin: Manufacturing Excellence Through Virtual Factory Replication* (White Paper). Florida Institute of Technology.

Kaur, M. J., Mishra, V. P., & Maheshwari, P. (2020). The Convergence of Digital Twin, IoT, and Machine Learning: Transforming Data into Action. In M. Farsi, A. Daneshkhah, A. Hosseinian-Far, & H. Jahankhani (Eds.), *Digital Twin Technologies and Smart Cities. Internet of Things (Technology, Communications and Computing)*. New York: Springer. https://doi.org/10.1007/978-3-030-18732-3_1.

Kovalchuk, J., & Stepnov, I. (2017). *About the New Industrial Production Management Concept as the Company Strategy in the Fourth Industrial Revolution*. SHS Web of Conferences, Vol. 35, Article No. 01013. https://doi.org/10.1051/shsconf/20173501013.

Mahdawi, A. (2017, June 26). What Jobs Will Still Be Around in 20 Years? Read This to Prepare Your Future. *The Guardian*. Available at: https://www.theguardian.com/us-news/2017/jun/26/jobs-future-automation-robots-skills-creative-health.

Malyasev, I. (2019). *Main Information About the MES "KAMAZ" Project*. Available at: http://www.up-pro.ru/library/information_systems/production/mes-kamaz.html (in Russian).

Marsh, P. (2013). *The New Industrial Revolution: Consumers, Globalization and the End of Mass Production*. New Haven, CT: Yale University Press.

Park, J. (2019). Advances in Future Internet and the Industrial Internet of Things. *Symmetry, 11*(2), 244. https://doi.org/10.3390/sym11020244.

Perry, A. (2018). 3D-Printed Apparel and 3D-Printer: Exploring Advantages, Concerns, and Purchases. *International Journal of Fashion Design, Technology and Education, 11*(1), 95–103. https://doi.org/10.1080/17543266.2017.1306118.

Piterkin, S. (2013). *Novocherkassk System. The Second Birth (the System of Continuous Production Planning by Rodov)*. Available at: http://www.up-pro.ru/library/production_management/planning/planirovanie-rodova.html (in Russian).

Porter, M., & Heppelmann, J. (2015, October). How Smart, Connected Products Are Transforming Companies. *Harvard Business Review*. https://hbr.org/2015/10/how-smart-connected-products-are-transforming-companies.

Ross, A. (2017). *The Industries of the Future*. New York: Simon & Schuster.

Roth, A. E. (2018). Marketplaces, Markets, and Market Design. *American Economic Review, 108*(7), 1609–1658. https://doi.org/10.1257/aer.108.7.1609.

Schwab, K. (2017). *The Fourth Industrial Revolution*. New York: Crown Business.

Schwab, K. (2018). *Shaping the Fourth Industrial Revolution*. World Economic Forum.

Tryaskov, M. (2019). *Productivity Growth at 5% Per Year Without Capital Investments: The Cordiant Experience*. Available at: http://www.up-pro.ru/library/production_management/productivity/rost-proizvoditelnosti.html (in Russian).

World Economic Forum, McKinsey & Company. (2019). *The Fourth Industrial Revolution. Targets Development of Industrial Technologies and Innovations*. Available at: http://www3.weforum.org/docs/WEF_Четвертая_промышленная%20революция.pdf (in Russian).

Zhishkevich, S. (2018, December). The Fourth Industrial Revolution in Russia: Current Programs and Projects. *Production Management, Digital Production: Today and Tomorrow of the Russian Industry* (No. 3, pp. 26–44) (in Russian).

CHAPTER 9

The Fourth Industrial Revolution and the New Paradigm of Corporate Governance

Alexander Yukhno

Introduction

Due to the significant increase in the functions performed by boards of directors, their activities are no longer limited solely to monitoring the company's past performance. Their main focus in the times of the Fourth Industrial Revolution is on increasing the responsibility its members have for the organization's future performance and strategic development. In the current period of the digital transformation, a board of directors active involvement in the issues of corporate governance and company development is becoming increasingly relevant. In this regard, it is of practical interest to study the increasing role of information and communication technology (hereinafter—ICT) and digital strategies in the company's business strategy, as well as activities of boards of directors in this context in general.

Corporate scandals in the early 2000s (Enron, Waste Management, WorldCom, etc.) reduced the level of stakeholder confidence in corporate governance systems, and determined the focus of boards of directors and

A. Yukhno (✉)
Civic Chamber of Russia, Moscow, Russia

N. Konina (ed.), *Digital Strategies in a Global Market*,
https://doi.org/10.1007/978-3-030-58267-8_9

managers on solving their internal problems and bringing financial statements under the toughened legislation. Structurally, the most important changes in corporate governance can be grouped into three main areas: changes in the field of audit and financial reporting, changes in the work of a board of directors (independent directors, strengthening the role of the audit committee, etc.) and changes in the field of financial disclosure (Clark 2005). Given that many companies have now adapted to the new conditions and rules of the game, the priorities of a board of directors began to shift towards increasing the shareholder value of companies due to their strategic development.

The digital transformation of the economy is increasing the importance of ICT for companies and changes the requirements for their activities in this area. ICT activities cover a wide range of issues, requiring both the systematic participation of various stakeholders and the development of mechanisms for creating values and managing emerging risks. ICT drives innovation and permeates all aspects of an organization's value chain, enabling it to reshape its business processes, develop a competitive strategy, and identify and meet customer preferences. This approach to understanding value significantly expands management capabilities for improving the efficiency of the existing ICT assets (Kohli and Melville 2009).

Due to the rapid rise of ICT in the organizational and business management, as well as the risks arising in this context, the strategic function of a board of directors can, in theory, expand significantly. However, it should be recognized that the current practice of corporate governance still does not pay sufficient attention to these issues. In reality, there is often a problem in transferring the supervision of ICT to the top governance level, i.e., to a board of directors. At the same time, various factors have a significant impact on the current state of affairs: sociocultural (Hofstede 2001; Auzan et al. 2019) and institutional features of states (Guriev et al. 2003), corporate culture (Aasi et al. 2017), organizational structure (Kingsford et al. 2003; Amali et al. 2018), and others. Besides, a board of directors is expected to interact more closely with the organization's management in order to discuss, review, and approve the company's strategy developed by the management.

Methods

The research is based on the analysis of the research in the field of corporate governance in the period of digital business transformation, in terms of the development and implementation of business strategies, which increasingly include the issues of ICT and digitalization. The methodological basis of the study was an empirical analysis, methods of system and comparative analysis, and expert assessments, which allowed us to identify the main trends in the use of ICT and digital strategies in the implementation of business strategies.

Results

The active development of the digital economy puts forward new requirements for boards of directors, and sets serious tasks to analyze the arising challenges and opportunities. One of its key priorities is to ensure that the company's strategy takes into account the opportunities and risks of digital transformation (Bamford et al. 2019). Thus, the Bank of Russia notes that the main functions of a board of directors currently include "assessing the impact on the company's business of new information technology, as well as the degree of materiality for the risks associated with cyber threats" (Bank of Russia 2019).

The focus of ICT has traditionally been on providing high-quality information services and improving the efficiency of business processes in organizations. They gradually began to play an increasing role in developing products, creating business models, and finding new sources of income. Today, their role is organically developing from the function of supporting the business to the function of increasing the company's efficiency, its digital transformation, and its drivers of innovation. Thus, in addition to providing regular operations, ICT functions more often include the identification of technological innovations and their quick adaptation to market-based solutions. For this reason, they are often required not only to initiate changes in business processes but also to stimulate the emergence of innovative solutions in the company's activities, as well as to become a source of competitive advantage (Nissen et al. 2018). This approach allows for a gradual change in the role of modern ICT functions from a service provider to a consultant and innovator, and is directly reflected in the processes and mechanisms of management and supervision. At the same time, it is important to ensure a common understanding of the development of ICT directions at all levels and among interested parties, to develop those internal documents that determine the procedure for implementing ICT (taking into account its development strategy), as well as for optimizing the work of the departments in order to avoid duplicating functions and to save on the resources and costs of ICT governance.

In the times of the Fourth Digital Revolution the inclusion of ICT issues in the development strategy is a natural consequence of digitalization. This step involves expanding the paradigm of corporate thinking and serious corporate changes, which may explain the lag between corporate governance practices and ongoing innovations. The authors of the 2016 "Corporate Governance Codes and Digital Leadership" report, after analyzing 15 national codes of corporate governance, came to the conclusion that—except for the revised King III Report on Governance for South Africa—the rest of the codes contained virtually no ICT provisions. In their opinion, this situation has arisen since most of them took the provisions of the G20/OECD Principles of Corporate Governance (hereinafter—the Principles) as their basis or are similar to them (De Haes, n.d.). The Principles themselves do not contain any specific provisions related to the supervision of ICT or the disclosure of information in this area, except for the use of the company's website as a channel for disclosure of material information about the company (OECD 2015).

The current version of the King IV Report on Corporate Governance for South Africa recognizes the rapid development of ICT, their potential for the development of organizations and the risks that arise in this context. The model proposed in the Report, which combines the integration of corporate governance with the supervision of ICT, is aimed on improving the efficiency of their use in order to implement the company's strategic goals and can be used as an example in practice. It should also be noted that the increasing need for a board of directors to participate in overseeing ICT issues has gradually begun to be reflected in other corporate governance codes. For example, in the 2016 Dutch Corporate Governance Code, the obligation to monitor the organization's management activities in the field of information and communication technology, including cyber risks, is assigned to the audit committee of a board of directors (European Corporate Governance Institute 2016).

In recent years, the world leading companies (Kodak, Nokia, BlackBerry, etc.) have been losing market shares due to the emergence of more innovative competitors and ongoing changes in economic sectors. According to experts, in each case, organizations had the opportunity to act ahead of the curve before they faced new realities. To do this, they needed to go through the process of so-called "strategic renewal." This update involves transforming companies' activities before the critical moment of their loss of competitiveness. In this regard, the role of a board of directors and senior management of the company in integrating the updated strategy, innovative tools, and approaches into the daily work of the organization is strengthening (Binns et al. 2014).

For a long time, the relationship between investment in ICT and the creation of competitive advantages has often been recognized as indirect, and usually has depended on the way such technologies have been implemented. This position emerged not least due to the functional approach to the company's ICT strategy (hereinafter referred to as the ICT strategy) and the need to link such investments with mechanisms for generating profit and creating value at the company-wide level (Bharadwaj 2000; Drnevich and Mcintyre 2010). Failure to understand the value of ICT investment can also be attributed to a lack of coherence between business and ICT strategies. For a long period, the prevailing view was that a company's ICT strategy should correlate with its business strategy. At the moment, due to the increasing influence of ICT on companies and major changes in this area, a mutual convergence is observed (Bharadwaj et al. 2013). As P. Drnevich and D. Croson emphasized, while investment in information technology is an integral part of the company's operations at the functional level, it also plays a significant role in the implementation of its business strategy, i.e., by increasing the companies' current non-digital capabilities and creating new values. Such investments and additional organizational capabilities change the set of strategic alternatives and opportunities to create additional value for the organization (Drnevich and Croson 2013). It appears that ICT strategies in managing data, information, software applications and ICT infrastructure have to reflect the logic of a business strategy. In turn, it is necessary to integrate approaches to improve the quality of ICT management in the context of the company's business architecture into the business strategy. As a result, the company gains significant competitive advantages and reduces potential risks (Met et al. 2020).

The emergence of new business models and the transformation of economic sectors as part of the Fourth Industrial Revolution are creating a new logic for building competitive strategies for those companies that recognize their central role in product development and service delivery (Woodard et al. 2013). P. Pavlou and O. Sawy believe that ICT creates a competitive advantage for companies in a turbulent environment through functional competencies (i.e., the ability to efficiently perform operational processes) and dynamic abilities (i.e., the ability to transform functional competencies to solve emerging problems) (Pavlou and Sawy 2006). Besides, products and services are increasingly using embedded digital technologies, which only complicates the issue of distinguishing between digital products and services from the underlying ICT infrastructure (Bharadwaj et al. 2013).

During the economy's digital transformation, taking risks becomes normal. This increases the importance of a board of directors, which should play a key role in determining its risk appetite and strategic development vector. Digitally-advanced companies are striving for new levels of competitive advantage and accepting the fact that sometimes failures can be seen as prerequisites for successful transformation. At the same time, the ability to rethink business in a digital form is largely determined by a well-thought-out digital strategy that can ensure that technologies are implemented in the way that meets the company's business goals. Based on data from 400 US companies between 1999 and 2006 S. Mithas, A. Tafti, and W. Mitchell concluded that digital strategy is not only about optimizing internal operations or responding to market competitors, but also a reaction to a competitive digital business environment (Mithas et al. 2013). Understanding the essence of such a strategy helps to reveal its relationship with other companies, industries, the external environment, and how it can be more effective in various conditions. In contrast to the ICT strategy, which is aimed at transforming technologies based on the current needs and is often isolated from the rest of the business, the digital strategy aims to apply digital technologies to business models in order to create new opportunities and transform the company's activities by seeking a balance between technology and strategy. This goes beyond the traditional functional areas (such as marketing, procurement, etc.) and various business processes with ICT support (such as order management, customer service, etc.), and relies on the exchange of information through digital platforms both inside and outside of companies, which enables the integration of multifunctional company strategies and processes through ICT capabilities (Bharadwaj et al. 2013).

A study by MIT Sloan Management Review and Deloitte notes that a company's digital strategy ultimately leads to digital maturity (Kane et al. 2015), which is a combination of two separate but related characteristics: digital intensity, and transformation management intensity. The former refers to investments in the technology initiatives aimed at changing the company's work (internal operations, changing the business model, etc.). The latter implies a focus on digital transformation in the organization, and the implementation of technological changes in practice (Westerman et al. 2017). Only 15% of respondents (out of more than 4800 business leaders, managers, and analysts from all over the world) from the companies in the early stages of digital maturity believe that they have a clear and consistent digital strategy, while among the digitally-mature organizations, this figure is more than 80% (Kane et al. 2015). The characteristics of mature digital cultures include high-risk appetite, conducting quick experiments, investing in staff development (Kane et al. 2016). The main obstacles to digital maturity are the lack of strategy and competing priorities in the company's activities presented in the table below (Table 9.1).

Developing companies are focused on integrating digital technologies into their operations in order to transform the way their businesses work. Less mature companies are focused on solving individual business problems using digital technologies, aim their strategies at improving the current operational level, but may fall into the trap of focusing on technology rather than development strategy.

The literature suggests that a digital strategy nowadays should be considered as a business strategy. Given that companies and industries are becoming increasingly digital, it has been suggested that the digital

Table 9.1 Key barriers to digital maturity

Stage of development/major barriers	*Early digital maturity*	*Evolving digital maturity*	*Digital maturity*
1	Lack of strategy	Many priorities	Many priorities
2	Many priorities	Lack of strategy	Security questions
3	Lack of understanding by company management	Inadequate technical skills	Inadequate technical skills

Source Kane et al. (2015)

strategy will gradually become a business strategy and the separation between them will disappear (Bharadwaj et al. 2013). However, it is important to understand that the development of a digital strategy is not a mandatory step just because it is actively discussed in the business environment. Taking into account its diversity and innovation, it is important to acknowledge that digital strategy is also characterized by serious risks for the company (lost investment, deviation from the current business strategy, etc.), which must be considered before deciding on its development and implementation. Besides, it is possible that, in an ever-changing context, it may negatively affect the organization's activities and mistakenly shift its priorities. In this regard, the key part in this process should be assumed by a board of directors, whose role in the period of digital transformation will continue to grow.

In practice, it is important to distinguish between the terms "digital transformation" and "digital strategy", which are sometimes used as full synonyms. Even though they are close, there are differences between them. Digital transformation leads to changes in three areas: customer experience with the company, operational processes, and business models (Bughin et al. 2019). Digital transformation requires coordination throughout the company and includes changes in corporate culture. On the other hand, digital strategy is not focused on culture, but on technology. Defining a strategy is a key element of the transformation process which ensures that technology is implemented in a way that meets the company's business goals (Liferay DXP, n.d.). In this regard, from a practical point of view, it is interesting to make proposals on the feasibility of moving to the integration of the company's digital strategy, ICT strategy, and business strategy into a single digital business strategy (Bharadwaj et al. 2013).

One of the consequences of digitalization brought by the Fourth Industrial Revolution is the increasing role of communication in various ecosystems. Innovation and ICT are radically changing approaches, enabling companies to create or destroy value in a short time frame (Andersson and van der Heyden 2017). Today, companies operate in those ecosystems that require a rapid response to changing conditions and are closely intertwined, so that digital strategies should not be analyzed independently of other ecosystems and competitors. Thus, the use of digital platforms allows companies to "break down" the traditional boundaries of industries and work in new areas that were previously determined only through digital resources (Bharadwaj et al. 2013). The exchange of knowledge and information will continue to go beyond companies. For this reason, companies need to ensure their place in the digital ecosystems which provide a close collaboration of their participants, creating mutual value. Such collaboration through wider digital ecosystems can be the core for developing effective strategies (Bankewitz et al. 2016). A board of directors must have enough competence to evaluate the strategies of existing and potential competitors and the impact of changes (economic, social, etc.) in the external environment on both the company's strategy and that of its competitors. This implies the active participation of a board of directors in creating and implementing the strategy, and allows for supervision of the company's activities in accordance with the chosen vector of development (Macavoy and Millstein 2004). Today, there is an increased number of examples of using digital resources to expand the scope of the company's business strategy: GE devices that are connected to the Internet to provide remote monitoring of the patient in real-time, Sony digital products, Nike digital products with Apple iOS support, etc. (Bharadwaj et al. 2013). Amazon, along with e-commerce and book reading equipment (Kindle), is simultaneously developing a separate area—Amazon Web Services (hereinafter—AWS). AWS is a cloud platform that provides 165 full-featured services for data centers around the world (Amazon Web Services, n.d.). In the traditional paradigm, such an approach to a business strategy could be considered illogical due to the strong differences between these business areas. For this reason, recognizing the links between them requires a broader understanding of the way digital and information and communication technologies develop and impact the company's business strategy.

Thus, thanks to the use of ICT, the boundaries between the business strategy, ICT strategy, and digital strategy are gradually blurring. A board of directors, together with senior management, should constantly encourage digital transformation and take an active part in developing and implementing the company's strategy, into which ICT issues are integrated as an important element of the overall system.

Recommendations

The analysis allows us to conclude that the active use of ICT, as well as digital strategies, significantly expands the management capabilities of companies, and sets new tasks for its board of directors. Given that in the digital age, their use is an important element in developing and implementing a company's strategy, their supervision must be located within the perimeter of the corporate governance as one of the key tasks of a board of directors.

Transformation of the activities of a board of directors itself requires a clear understanding of the measures to improve its effectiveness, and adequate measures to be taken to respond to these ongoing changes. In this regard, in order to strategically develop and minimize the risks, a board of directors is recommended to do the following:

- consider the feasibility of developing the organization's internal documents, which determine the implementation of ICT, taking into account its development strategy;
- determine the company's risk appetite and its willingness to accept risk(s) throughout the company;
- determine the main directions of digital strategy, ICT strategies, and business strategies, and consider the feasibility of combining them;
- regularly monitor the use of ICT and the implementation of the digital strategy and risk management;
- ensure close collaboration with key stakeholders in order to regularly update the organization's strategy;
- analyze the company's location and role in a particular ecosystem in order to maximize the use of emerging opportunities and implement the strategy;
- regularly raise the competence of board members so that they can understand the digitalization processes and the strategic impact they have on the organization's activities.

In the period of the Fourth Industrial Revolution, a board of directors, as the main governance body of a company, has all the opportunities to implement strategic development of a company as one of the central elements of its work. To accomplish this task, effective mechanisms for joint work between the company's bodies and careful selection of candidates for board members are required, taking into account the company's needs. The considered features of the use of ICT and digital strategies in the implementation of the company's business strategy—and the role of a board of directors in this process—have theoretical significance for creating a developed corporate governance system in Russia and abroad and can be used in practice.

References

Aasi, P., Rusu, L., & Vieru, D. (2017). The Role of Culture in IT Governance Five Focus Areas: A Literature Review. *International Journal of IT/Business Alignment and Governance, 8*(2), 42–61.

Amali, L., Hadjaratie, L., & Suhada, S. (2018). The Influence of Organizational Culture in Application of Information Technology Governance. *Journal of Information Systems Engineering and Business Intelligence, 14*(1), 1–10.

Amazon Web Services. (n.d.). *AWS Cloud Computing*. Available at: https://aws.amazon.com/what-is-aws/.

Andersson, L., & van der Heyden, L. (2017). *Directing Digitalization: Guidelines for Boards and Executives*. Available at: http://www.thisfluidworld.com/wp-content/uploads/2017/02/Corporategovernance-February-2017.pdf.

Auzan, A., Komissarov, A., & Bakhtigaraeva, A. (2019). Sociocultural Restrictions on the Commercialization of Innovations in Russia. *Economic Policy, 14*(4), 76–95.

Bamford, T., Dawkins, W., Duncan, G., Elliott, S., House, W., Le Goff, P., ... (2019). *The Digital Dilemma: Optimizing Board Composition in the Digital Era*. Available at: https://www.spencerstuart.com/research-and-insight/the-digital-dilemma.

Bank of Russia. (2019). *Information Letter No. IN-06-28 / 18 on the Guidelines for Members of the Board of Directors (Supervisory Board) of a Financial Organization, February 28*. Available at: https://www.cbr.ru/finmarket/common_inf/common_inf_let/.

Bankewitz, M., Åberg, C., & Teuchert, C. (2016). Digitalization and Boards of Directors: A New Era of Corporate Governance? *Business and Management Research, 5*(2), 58–69.

Bharadwaj, A. S. (2000). A Resource-Based Perspective on Information Technology Capability and Firm Performance: An Empirical Investigation. *MIS Quarterly, 24*(1), 169–196.

Bharadwaj, A. S., Sawy, O., Omar, A., Pavlou, P., & Venkatraman, H. (2013). Digital Business Strategy: Toward a Next Generation of Insights. *MIS Quarterly, 37*(2), 471–482.

Binns, A., Harreld, J., O'Reilly, C., & Tushman, M. (2014). The Art of Strategic Renewal. *MITS Loan Management Review, 55*(2), 21–23.

Bughin, J., Catlin, T., Hall, B., & van Zeebroeck, N. (2019). *Improving Your Digital Intelligence*. Available at: http://ilp.mit.edu/media/news_articles/smr/2019/60233.pdf.

Clark, R. C. (2005). *Corporate Governance Changes in the Wake of the Sarbanes-Oxley Act: A Morality Tale for Policymakers Too*. Available at: https://papers.ssrn.com/sol3/Delivery.cfm/SSRN_ID868673_code17037.pdf?abstractid=808244.

De Haes, S. (n.d.). *Corporate Governance Codes and Digital Leadership*. Available at: https://blog.antwerpmanagementschool.be/en/corporate-governance-codes-and-digital-leadership.

Drnevich, P., & Croson, D. (2013). Information Technology and Business-Level Strategy: Toward an Integrated Theoretical Perspective. *MIS Quarterly, 37*(2), 483–510.

Drnevich, P., & Mcintyre, D. (2010). Information Technology and Strategy: Two Camps, Four Perspectives, One Elusive Goal. *International Journal of Strategic Information Technology and Applications, 1*(2), 1–18.

Drucker, P., & Maciarello, J. (2010). *Management*. Moscow: ID Williams.

European Corporate Governance Institute. (2016). *Dutch Corporate Governance Code*. Available at: https://ecgi.global/code/dutch-corporate-governance-code-2016.

Guriev, S., Lazareva, O., Rachinsky, A., & Tsukhlo, S. (2003). *Corporate Governance in Russian Firms*. Moscow: MONF.

Han, K., & Mithas, S. (2013). Information Technology Outsourcing and Non-IT Operating Costs: An Empirical Investigation. *MIS Quarterly, 37*(1), 315–331.

Henderson, J. C., & Venkatraman, H. (1993). Strategic Alignment: Leveraging Information Technology for Transforming Organization. *IBM Systems Journal, 32*(1), 472–484.

Hofstede, G. (2001). *Culture's Consequences: Comparing Values, Behaviors, Institutions and Organizations Across Nations*. London: Sage.

Institute of Directors. (2016). *King IV Report on Corporate Governance for South Africa*. Available at: https://c.ymcdn.com/sites/iodsa.site-ym.com/resource/collection/684B68A7-B768-465C-8214E3A007F15A5A/IoDSA_King_IV_Report_-_WebVersion.pdf.

Kane, G. C., Palmer, D., Phillips, A. N., Kiron, D., & Buckley, N. (2015). *Strategy, Not Technology, Drives Digital Transformation*. Available at: http://digital.fuerstenberg-forum.de/wp-content/uploads/2014/03/57181-MIT-Deloitte-Digital2015.pdf.

Kane, G. C., Palmer, D., Phillips, A. N., Kiron, D., & Buckley, N. (2016). *Aligning the Organization for Its Digital Future*. Available at: http://marketing.mitsmr.com/offers/DL2016/58180-MITSMR-Deloitte-Digital-Business-2016.pdf. Accessed 12 November 2019.

Kingsford, R., Dunn, L., & Cooper, J. (2003). Information Systems, IT Governance and Organizational Culture. In *Proceedings of the 14th Australasian*

Conference on Information Systems Proceedings in Perth, Australia, November 26–28, 2003 (pp. 1–14).

Kohli, R., & Melville, N. (2009). Learning to Build an IT Innovation Platform. *Communications of the ACM, 52*(8), 122–126.

Liferay DXP. (n.d.). *What Is Digital Strategy*. Available at: https://www.liferay.com/resources/l/digital-strategy.

Macavoy, P. W., & Millstein, I. M. (2004). *The Recurrent Crisis in Corporate Governance*. Basingstoke: Palgrave Macmillan.

Met, I., Umut Uysal, E., & Orç, E. (2020). Blending Business Strategies with IT in Digital Era. In U. Hacioglu (Ed.), *Digital Business Strategies in Blockchain Ecosystems: Transformational Design and Future of Global Business* (pp. 317–341). New York: Springer.

Mithas, S., Tafti, A., & Mitchell, W. (2013). How a Firm's Competitive Environment and Digital Strategic Posture Influence Digital Business Strategy. *MIS Quarterly, 37*(1), 511–536.

Nissen, V., Lezina, T., & Saltan, A. (2018). The Role of IT Management in the Digital Transformation of Russian Companies. *Foresight and STI Governance, 12*(3), 53–61.

OECD. (2015). *G20 / OECD Principles of Corporate Governance*. Available at: https://www.oecd.org/daf/ca/Corporate-Governance-Principles-ENG.pdf.

Pavlou, P., & Sawy, O. (2006). From IT Leveraging Competence to Competitive Advantage in Turbulent Environments: The Case of New Product Development. *Information Systems Research, 17*(3), 198–227.

Sawy, O., & Pavlou, P. (2008). IT-Enabled Business Capabilities for Turbulent Environments. *MIS Quarterly Executive, 7*(3), 139–150.

Westerman, G., Tannou, M., Bonnet, D., Ferraris, P., & McAfee, A. (2017). *The Digital Advantage: How Digital Leaders Outperform Their Peers in Every Industry*. Available at: https://www.capgemini.com/wp-content/uploads/2017/07/The_Digital_Advantage__How_Digital_Leaders_Outperform_their_Peers_in_Every_Industry.pdf. Accessed 12 November 2019.

Woodard, C. J., Ramasubbu, N., Tschang, T., & Sambamurthy, V. (2013). Design Capital and Design Moves: The Logic of Digital Business Strategy. *MIS Quarterly, 22*(1), 537–564.

CHAPTER 10

Application of Data Mining and Machine Learning Methods to Enhance the Effectiveness of Digital Marketing Strategies

Sergey Gutnik

Introduction

In the context of the transition to the digital economy—with mobile devices, telecommunication channels, and access to global internet resources—information flow is significantly increasing. With this mind-boggling amount of data, it is important to structure and classify information, so as to eventually achieve knowledge. Complex analytical processing systems are used to extract useful information from large volumes of data; for example, machine learning methods and data mining are used to better understand customer preferences, identify targets to maximize Return on Investment in future marketing campaigns, and

S. Gutnik (✉)
Moscow State Institute of International Relations (MGIMO University), Moscow, Russia
e-mail: s.gutnik@inno.mgimo.ru

N. Konina (ed.), *Digital Strategies in a Global Market*,
https://doi.org/10.1007/978-3-030-58267-8_10

predict customer turnover and loyalty despite the quantity of gadgets they use. The work clarifies these characteristics, and conducts a benchmark study into the digital mining methods applied in business solutions and marketing strategies. The author describes the established capabilities of business analytics and the effective analytical solutions in IT sector.

The paper looks into analytical machine learning algorithms such as neural networks, and also considers the benefits of machine learning in marketing. Furthermore, the paper analyses the main stages of the evolution of digital technology in marketing strategies, and finally suggests practical guidelines for companies on how these can be used.

Methodology

Modern information technologies provide tools in marketing analysis for processing statistics, received through digital channels from different devices and services (Big Data), and for allowing relevant business information to be extracted from unstructured data (Business Intelligence (BI)).

Big Data refers to the data containing unique knowledge, which helps behavioural patterns to be recognized, whether those of individuals or systems, and also helps to discover new facts about objects of study. The characteristics that define Big Data are the "3Vs": Volume, Variety, Velocity (Maslova et al. 2017, Baesens 2014). In fact, Big Data is an ecosystem, featuring tools to process and analyse databases as well as data mining. Mathematical statistics, regression, clustering, factor analysis, game theory analysis, data mining methods, and computer modelling are technologies used in data analytics. Data analysis methods and techniques vary according to data types.

Business Intelligence (BI) tools are software that processes large amounts of business data (structured and unstructured) in order to identify patterns and derive insights to find better solutions. One of the main tasks of BI is to analyse Customer Relationship Management (CRM), particularly customer segmentation, budgeting tasks, performance management analysis, and similar areas (Kumar and Reinarts 2012). The results of the analysis are scrutinized by decision-makers to improve strategies. Behavioural scoring, customer retention prediction, marketing campaign strategies, and leading management reports are more sophisticated BI functions. Predictive analytics uses machine learning and data mining, along with traditional statistics, to solve forecasting problems.

Defining the term "Business Intelligence", the Data Warehousing Institute (TDWI), which provides in-depth education in BI, identifies that: "Business intelligence refers to the process of transforming data into knowledge, and turning knowledge into business opportunities. It is the end user who benefits from BI analytical tools, applications and data warehouse infrustructure".

Thus, BI generally refers to the following:

- the process of transforming data and information into useful knowledge and intuition to accelerate and improve decision-making;
- techniques and tools for collecting data, consolidating information, and providing access to it;
- business information received via in-depth data and consolidated information analysis.

To defining the functionalities of BI systems, three key categories can be distinguished: data integration, reporting, and data analysis.

1. Open data integration capabilities
   - BI infrastructure features an open query engine, end-to-end security, administration and portal integration, and open access to metadata. All the components must be included in the platform tools if it is to function in a unified manner.
   - Metadata management is an essential feature, which enables search, storage, utilizing large data sets, massive volumes, hierarchies, metrics, and other metadata objects.
   - Development capabilities are also provided by sophisticated BI platforms, which provide an environment to develop. They also enable users to deploy business analysis applications, by using software codes and integrating them with third-party apps and web-services; with these, users can build business process mapping, and use multifunctional BI tools to their full potential. Web Dynpro for ABAP is the SAP standard user interface technology, which provides a graphical interface to fine-tune Business Objects and other SAP Predictive Analytics solutions.
   - Interaction is also necessary. BI platform must have both data and opinion interchange tools. These capabilities can be aligned

through discussion forums and conferences. Furthermore, based on defined business rules, BI applications must create tasks to assign to particular users and track their accomplishment. In some cases, self-contained applications are required to solve the aforementioned tasks.

2. Reporting

- Reporting is one of the key features to create interactive, updated, formatted reports of a wide variety of possible views with a policy for access privilege.
- Dashboarding serves as an effective method to display reports as diagrams, histograms, tree maps, line charts, and other data visualization tools to interprete data, indicate trends, and compare the forecasts with the reality.
- Ad hoc reports allow BI-app-end users to easily build their own reports with little to no IT training. The SAP technology platform fulfils this functionality via SAP Business Objects applications, which are intended to create agile reports using additional ad hoc functions such as changing graphs, containers, texts, buttons, and tags at the click of a mouse.
- Integration with Microsoft Office applications is also important, as BI platforms are often used as intermediate tools to solve analytical tasks, and some functionalities are performed on the client's side by using Microsoft Office products, such as Excel. BI platforms must be able to export reports into different document formats and formulas, pivot tables, and provide support for updating data. Extensive functionalities also include single-cell lock and backup data storage systems.
- A search function is the most critical capability connected with metadata processing. All system objects must be categorized, and the system itself must have a convenient front-end interface for searching for required objects.

3. Data analysis

- Online Analytical Processing, such as OLAP functionality and OLAP-cubes, accelerate information processing and allow multidimensional information analysis from different viewpoints. This function is known as slicing and dicing—literally, cutting into slices and dice.

- Advanced visualization allows traditional 2-D reports with texts and bars to be converted into interactive images with charts and graphs. Visualization technology also delivers business insights through visuals, which means business processes can be easily understood.
- Modelling, forecasting, and data analysis are carried out using mathematical methods. These also allow data classification, as well as nominal and ordinal scale development. The statistical application IBM SPSS serves as an example of such an application.
- Performance scorecards are tools used to monitor the progress towards organizational goals by means of Key Performance Indicators (KPI). Performance Indicators are linked to strategic objectives for analysing information in detail. Nowadays there is a significant emphasis on interactive presentations. However, data mining and deep data analysis opportunities are becoming a growing priority trend, as is seen by the fact that IT bellwethers have entered into merger agreements for the aquisition of business intelligence software (for example, IBM's merger of the SPSS and Cognos applications). Further proof comes from the fact that the SAS Institute, a multinational developer of analytics software, has grown in revenue. Computer analysts and developers distinguish between two main categories of business analysis products: applications and tools. Applications include inquiry and report generators, whilst tools comprise of OLAP analytical processing, enterprise BI suites, and BI platforms.

BI Product Classification and Data Warehousing

BI tools are mostly divided into BI suites and BI platforms. BI suites have largely replaced inquiry and report generators. Multidimensional online analytical processing mechanisms or servers, as well as relational OLAP mechanisms, are BI tools and BI platform infrastructure. The main features of these types of applications are data warehouses, data marts and operational data stores; for example, SAP BW is one of the leading data warehousing tools. BI systems are, importantly, the last to be installed by companies. OLAP options cannot be put into practice without available OLTP infrastructure (Online Transactional Processing) or systems of other classes.

Data warehousing refers to data used for business analysis being derived from information circulating in an OLTP environment and then loaded into warehouses. Such data reflect both the current situation in general and contain historical data. Unlike relational databases, warehouses are designed to effectively process queries and analyse data. They store vast amounts of data, covering all aspects of an enterprise's performance. In order to serve narrow groups of users, a subset of data is retrieved. This structure is known as a Data Mart (DM). External data, and data from OLTP environments, are transformed via ETL processes (Extract, Transform, Load) and loaded into a data warehouse, where they are turned into multidimensional OLAP Cubes; after this, data are transformed into business information and enterprise reports, with the help of BI tools.

Query generators and reporting tools. These tools enable users to create business reports which are built on batch regulatory reporting, shadow batch system, desktop query generators, report emailing to the management, access rights differentiation, editing reports. All the functionalities are performed through a report server, email tools, event and deviation notification systems, publishing reports to a Web environment. SAP Business Objects and IBM Cognos are examples of such software. Ad hoc reports are an integral part of reporting. SAP Business Objects product range offers all the mentioned options.

OLAP or Developed Analytical Tools

One of the main uses of BI application is multidimensional data slicing. Slices, or dimensions, can include temporary or quantitative characteristics, geography, clients, products, trade subjects and objects. Key Performance Indicators and quantitative characteristics can be analysed. Users can change analysis indicators, make changes in cross-tabs, slice and dice, and ultimately see data and information in more detail according to the hierarchy this system establishes (drill down/roll-up).

These functionalities are performed through multidimensional databases provided by OLAP servers. They provide a higher standard of performance, loading data as OLAP Cubes (despite the time this requires) to carry out multidimensional analysis. Oracle Hyperion

Essbase, a traditional OLAP server, is a multidimensional DBMS platform which is used to develop analytical applications.

Relational Online Analytical Processing (ROLAP) is another potential analytical tool. However, based on Star standards, it is less effective compared to traditional OLAP or MOLAP analysis; MS Analysis Services and Oracle OLAP Services can also provide specific analytical products that are beneficial additions for relational databases.

Hybrid Online Analytical Processing (HOLAP) can also be used. An API system (Application Programming Interface) provides access to a multidimensional database, while SQL queries provide access to relational databases.

Substantially, all OLAP Tools feature Business Objects Web Intelligence, which is included in their standard confuguration.

EBIS (Enterprise BI Suites)—BI Web-portals—are interfaces used for analytical management processes. SAP Business Objects and IBM Cognos are the top suppliers of EBIS.

BI applications are defined as niche software solutions. This group is implemented to solve such tasks as sales forecasting, cost management, risk and trend analysis, or a company's performance management as a whole. Applications often integrate data from other systems: ERP, CRM, HR, and others.

Results

Today, with Data Science advancement and computer methods used in marketing, research businesses thrive on advanced digital strategies, using Data Mining, Artificial Intelligence (AI), and Machine Learning (ML) technologies.

Data Mining

Data Mining is a tool used to extract useful information from raw data to quickly build up unbiased business processes. DM involves gleaning patterns and trends through mathematical and statistical methods, such as association, sequential patterns or pattern tracking, feature selection, stratification, clustering, visualization, or regression. Such types of BI applications are widely applied and developed worldwide. For example, MTS telecom uses the IBM SPSS system to forecast calls for their call centre to improve customer satisfaction.

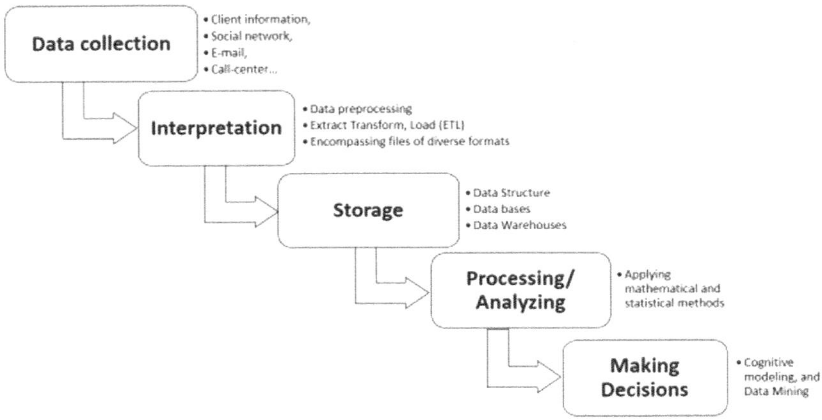

Fig. 10.1 The general steps to marketing information system process (*Source* Created by the author)

The general steps to marketing information system process are (Fig. 10.1):

- data collection;
- interpretation (involving encompassing files of diverse formats);
- storage;
- processing, applying mathematical methods;
- analysing, applying mathematical methods;
- making decisions, applying stochastic and probabilistic approaches, cognitive modelling, and Data Mining.

Predictive Analytics (PA)

Predictive Analytics is one of the most rapidly emerging BI technologies, as its essential aim is to go beyond knowing what has happened and why, and instead discover what is likely to happen and what should be done to produce the desired outcome (Abbott 2014).

Whereas traditional forecasting is mainly based on econometric approaches, Predictive Analytics anticipate trends at a macro-level. In particular, it answers the following questions:

- Which of the clients is likely to respond?
- Which advertising image is likely to attract clients?
- Are stock prices likely to drop or to rise?
- Which groups of clients are highly likely to default on a loan?

Predictive Analytics is capable of building up empirical forecasting models based on vast amounts of data in order to forecast a response. PA tasks and examples are studied in Siegel's work, where he provides 21 ways of using PA (Siegel 2013).

Both Predictive Analytics and traditional forecasting use a mathematical approach, such as regression analysis, cluster analysis, or one of the following: Association rule learning, Classification, Cluster analysis, Data fusion and data integration, Ensemble learning, Genetic algorithms, Machine learning, Natural Language Processing, Neural networks, Network analysis, Pattern recognition, Predictive modelling, Regression, Sentiment Analysis, Signal Processing, Spatial analysis, Statistics, Supervised and Unsupervised learning, Simulation, Time series analysis, or Visualization.

In order to provide PA solutions, it is important to look for contiguities; for example, the goods a client often buys may work together with other specific products, and thus cross-sell opportunities can be found. Predictive Analytics makes use of all methods of statistical analysis, machine learning, Data Mining, operation performance analysis, Artificial Intelligence, and similar technologies to find predictions influencing future events. One of the major goals of PA is to provide a predictive score for each parameter. If predictors can be found, a predictive model can be built, which is used for making better decisions. The model allows forecasting with a higher level of likelihood. The predictive model applied in marketing answers the question 'What if we offer this particular product, and what responce are we likely to receive'? It is also used to segment customers for an effective advertising campaign to boost sales.

According to a number of Data Science experts, PA is referred to Data Mining, but there is no unified approach to data analysis classification yet. This is explained by the fact that Data Science concepts are still evolving. Data Mining (extracting knowledge from databases) defines a set of methods for exploring unknown, consequential, useful, and available knowledge, interpreting it, and employing it to make decisions in different fields of human activities. The term was coined by Pyatesky-Shapiro in 1989. Data Mining methods are based on three components:

statistics, databases, and artificial intelligence (Fayyad et al. 1996); (Yang et al. 2006).

PA leaders provided a list of effective solutions (see Table 10.1), which include:

- IBM—The IBM Watson cognitive platform is a system designed to analyse human speech, interact with a human, and give personal recommendations.
- IBM Cognos Analytics, SPSS Modeler provides statistical modelling and customer behaviour forecasting.
- Microsoft—Microsoft Data System.
- Yandex—Yandex Data Factory.
- SAP—SAP Predictive Analytics Infinite Insight (KXEN).
- Google—Google Assistant, Google Now, Google Analytic and Google Data Studio are cognitive assistants, which provide data visualization and advertise performance analysis.
- Apple—Apple Siri.
- SAS Institute Analytics.
- Oracle Data Mining (ODM).
- Promt—PROMT Analyser allows users to search, extract, aggregate, structure, and analyse multilingual content from any text sources.

Cognitive technologies play a significant role in shifting from the 4 Ps marketing model (product, price, placement, promotion) to the 4 Cs model (consistency, content, convenience, contextual). "Consistency" means coordinated work across all channels, both online and offline. "Content" is responsible for providing customers and partners with all available methods to get accurate information. "Convenience" enables a customer to communicate with a service through different channels. "Contextual" is to attract a customer, taking into account their personal needs.

Nowadays PA technologies are widely used in e-commerce. Giant marketplaces and online shops possess a massive amount of customer data, which enables them to create a personalized shopping experience. Some retailers develop their own personalized product recommendation systems themselves. For example, Yandex Music, the e-commerce retail giant Amazon, and the media streaming service Netflix are among companies that have successfully created product recommendations.

Table 10.1 Leading Predictive Analytics Solutions

IBM	*SAP*	*SAS Institute*	*Microsoft*	*TIBCO*	*Oracle*	*Google*	*PROMT*	*Free software*
IBM SPSS Modeler; Cognos Analytics; IBM Watson Studio	SAP Predictive Analytics; SAP Lumira; SAP Business Objects	SAS Advanced Analytics SAS Enterprise Miner	Microsoft Data System; Microsoft Power BI Designer	TIBCO Data Science TIBCO Statistica	Oracle Data Mining (ODM) Oracle Crystal Ball	Google Analytic; Google Data Studio	PROMT Analyser	**R** (GNU project), authors: Ross Ihaka, Robert Gentleman **Python** author: Guido Van Rossum

Source Created by the author

Machine Learning. The previous chapters examine the stages through which digital technologies are applied in marketing. Big Data concepts are one important aspect thereof, involving collecting and analysing large amounts of customers' data to improve business performance. With better understanding of how data can be collected and analysed, this turned into Data Science, which implies advanced research of methods, principles, and tools to utilize information, as well as problem analysis and digital data presentation. When put in practice, Data Science and marketing research methods made it possible to use Machine Learning in business activities to develop Artificial Intelligence and Machine Learning technologies. Artificial technology methods based on Machine Learning are capable of contributing to the implementation of digital strategies in marketing processes and decision-making (Rogers 2016); (Peppers et al. 1999).

Machine Learning (ML) approaches focus on an individual consumer and adapt marketing strategies to each user (Katsov 2019). ML algorithms are taught to detect complex and less obvious patterns in data, and using these they can forecast behaviour and build systems of recommendations (Starostin 2018). Building a customer profile in traditional marketing can be used as an example of a reference, or a tool for training, to search for correlation and interrelation within a dataset. Based on a particular consumer profile, information system algorithms can identify representatives of a target audience to fit an ideal profile.

Machine Learning systems consider hundreds of parameters to accurately target advertisements (Azoev and Starostin 2012); (Butkovskaya et al. 2017). Machine Learning tools study each anonymized recipient as a set of parameters and identifications, which ML algorithms analyse. Its neural network is trained to decide which advertisement will interest which users. The training process is carried out through Machine Learning methods, comparing a particular visitor performance with data received during a training set analysis.

Based on multi-factor ranking principles and information clustering, ML algorithms take the contingent metrics of a particular visitor into account, and match them to data gathered from thousands of other visitors to identify similar behavioural patterns. The system collects and stores visitor metrics. As soon as a visitor demonstrates behaviour typical of a training set performance, they receive a product recommendation.

It should be pointed out that, besides e-commerce and marketing, recommendation systems based on Machine Learning technologies work in a variety of areas. Advances in Data Science and Machine Learning have led to the creation of a new generation of personal digital assistants, such as Apple's Siri, Amazon's Alexa, Microsoft's Cortana, or Yandex's Alice, which communicate with users and help them find business planning and management solutions.

Conclusions/Recommendations

This paper looks into up-to-date Predictive Analytics and Machine Learning technologies used to analyse data in marketing, describes solutions to their functionalities, and gives an overview of general marketing data processing. The author gives examples of top BI software solutions, and delivers perspectives on potential future trends of Business Intelligence in some digital economy sectors.

Predictive Analytics and Machine Learning enables users to create their own personalized customer experience, taking into account diverse characteristics in real time. With any relevant product, an offer can be suggested, as can a different product as a substitute in the seller's range of product lines. The analysis of technological solutions shows how digital marketing methods and tools have transformed.

References

Abbott, D. (2014). *Applied Predictive Analytics : Principles and Techniques for the Professional Data Analyst*. Indianapolis, IN: Wiley.

Azoev, G. L., & Starostin, V. S. (2012). Personalization of Product Offerings. *Marketing, 128*(6), 19–41 (in Russian).

Baesens, B. (2014). *Analytics in a Big Data World: The Essential Guide to Data Science and Its Applications*. Hoboken, NJ: Wiley.

Butkovskaya, G. V., Starostin, V. S., & Chernova, V. Y. (2017). Concept of Marketing Operational Intelligence in Advertising. *Modern Scientific Mind, 1*(13), 101–110 (in Russian).

Fayyad, U., Piatetsky-Shapiro, G., Smyth, P., & Uthurusamy, R. (Eds.). (1996). *Advances in Knowledge Discovery in Databases*. Cambridge, MA: MIT Press.

Katsov, I. (2019). *Machine Learning for Business and Marketing*. St Petersburg: Piter, Sankt Petersburg (in Russian).

Kumar, V., & Reinartz, W. (2012). *Customer Relationship Management: Concept, Strategy, and Tools*. Heidelberg: Springer-Verlag.

Maslova, L. A., Gutnik, S. A., & Chepovsky, P. V. (2017). *Business Architecture of SAP Solutions for Banking Automation of Financial and Credit Institutions*. Moscow: NOU Intuit (in Russian).

Peppers, D., Rogers, M., & Dorf, B. (1999, January–February). Is Your Company Ready for One-to-One Marketing? *Harvard Business Review*, pp. 51–160.

Rogers, D. L. (2016). *The Digital Transformation Playbook*. New York: Columbia Business School Publishing.

Siegel, E. (2013). *Predictive Analytics: The Power to Predict. Who Will Click, Buy, Lie, or Die*. Hoboken, NJ: Wiley.

Starostin, V. S. (2018). Transformation of Marketing Technologies in Machine Intelligence Era. *Vestnik universiteta, GUU, 1*(1), 28–34 (in Russian).

Yang, Q., Wu, X., Domingos, P., Elkan, C., Gehrke, J., Han, J., … (2006). 10 Challenging Problems in Data Mining Research. *International Journal of Information Technology & Decision Making, 5*(4)(Spec. Issue).

CHAPTER 11

The Evolution of Conglomerates in the Digital Era: Adapting Strategies to the Requirements of the Fourth Industrial Revolution

Natalia Konina, Irina Vladimirova, and George Stonehouse

Introduction

A new phenomenon has emerged in recent years: large global digital conglomerates are being formed. An important factor determining the balance of forces in global markets, given the exceptional dynamism and instability of both the external and internal environment, is the specificity of the digital strategy within the framework of a corporate strategy for the development of complex integrated structures, is an important factor for conglomerates to consider; this determines the balance of forces in global

N. Konina (✉)
Moscow State Institute of International Relations (MGIMO University), Moscow, Russia

I. Vladimirova
RUDN University, Moscow, Russia

G. Stonehouse
Edinburgh Napier University, Edinburgh, UK

N. Konina (ed.), *Digital Strategies in a Global Market*,
https://doi.org/10.1007/978-3-030-58267-8_11

markets, especially given the exceptional dynamism and instability of both the external and internal environment.

Although conglomerates are still quite common in emerging markets—primarily in Asia, but particularly also in India, South Korea, and China—integrated business structures of this type have proved less popular in developed countries until recently. Having emerged in the 1970s, traditional conglomerates in the West, due to their poor performance, had lost their importance by the end of the 1980s (Bowen and Wiersema 2005). Digital transformation was an urgent requirement, but in the vast majority of cases, attempts to implement digital strategies ended in failure, which seriously undermined the competitive position of firms. At the same time, traditional companies faced a new competitive challenge—aggressive high-tech firms from developing countries emerged.

Digital strategies—involving significant investments in information technology and IT outsourcing—are becoming the main elements of a business strategy, allowing firms to keep up with their competitors (Ross 2017; Stepnov et al. 2018). Companies see IT as an essential component of the most common business strategy, allowing them to gain a competitive advantage (Mithas et al. 2013). IT enhances a firm's productivity and its competitiveness by supporting other processes, resources, or capabilities. Digital strategies significantly affect the creation and development of new goods and services (Dawson et al. 2016; Hausberg et al. 2019), customer relationships (Mithas et al. 2013), and management and management functions, let alone the overall effectiveness of the company (Bereznoy 2018; Efremov and Vladimirova 2020; Konina 2018; Voigt et al. 2017). The existing literature considers digital strategies solely as a factor for improving ICT operations. The impact of digitalization on the management processes of complex integrated structures has only been considered to a lesser extent (Walton 2013; Lim 2017). In this regard, it is interesting to analyse the strategies of emerging digital conglomerates.

Methods

The authors studied the scientific literature on the problem under consideration, significantly supplemented the existing views, and finally offered their own vision of this issue. The strategies of conglomerates were considered through a historical perspective; only globalization and the characteristic features of emerging markets have been taken into account.

A systematic approach was applied, which allowed us to comprehensively scrutinize and synthesize several diverse elements that had previously been studied separately. Thus, we conducted a study on the development strategies of emerging digital conglomerates after 2010. This analysis revealed qualitative changes which aim to increase the share of services, and showed the search for new business models based upon the advantages of ecosystems.

Presently, it is hard to discern the degree of digitalization when the company's borders are blurred; this has become the most important theoretical and practical issue of integrated business structures. The study aims to analyse the strategies of emerging digital conglomerates in turbulent markets, and to determine their characteristic features.

Finally, the main conclusions are drawn by generalizing and synthesizing the data obtained.

Results and Discussion

The phenomenon of integrated corporate structures is inherent in different economies. Globalization, profound technological changes, and growing digital trends in the global economy make integrated business structures evolve and undergo significant transformations.

Large integrated business structures usually include conglomerates united by ownership, which include companies operating in various unrelated sectors. However, in recent years, many large conglomerates—such as Philips, Maersk, ON, RWE, ThyssenKrupp—have split into separate companies, being unable to ensure the effective growth of unrelated business units. The process of diversification, and the allocation of several business areas, also affected large companies, such as Siemens, DowDuPont, and GE. One characteristic feature revealed through financially assessing the conglomerate market is the so-called 'conglomerate discount' associated with the inability to efficiently manage heterogeneous and numerous production departments, and determining the fact that the conglomerate's market value is often smaller than the aggregate value of various departments. In recent decades, pressure from shareholders on conglomerate managements has increased, demanding divestment and letting companies focus on their core business. However, despite conglomerates as a form of organizing large business steadily becoming less attractive system, the trend towards their disappearance cannot be called dominant. A characteristic feature of recent times is that traditional conglomerates are trying to adapt to the requirements of the 4th Industrial Revolution; the most successful ones in this regard include diversified companies such as AB (Switzerland), Siemens (Germany), United Technologies (USA), Johnson&Johnson (USA), Comcast (USA), Walt Disney (USA), Honeywell (USA), 3M (USA), Virgin Group (UK), Hitachi (Japan), Samsung (South Korea), and LG (South Korea).

Over the past decade, against the backdrop of rapidly developing digital technologies, a group of digital TNCs with a wide diversification of businesses has formed. They can be defined as emerging global digital conglomerates. They represent a new type of network-integrated firm. Digital conglomerates span all segments of the digital markets previously shared between digital platforms, digital organizers, e-commerce companies and digital content creators, actively impinging upon the sector of new mobility, electronic devices, fintech and digital healthcare. At the same time, investors highly value their market potential, and the total market capitalization of the emerging digital conglomerates like Amazon, Apple, Facebook, Alphabet and Microsoft exceeded $4.2 trillion in December 2019 in the USA.

The authors consider the following as the key criteria for classifying companies as digital conglomerates:

1. Broad business diversification, covering various sectors of the digital economy
2. Encapsulating the most promising areas of the digital economy
3. A significant takeover of innovative firms
4. Global coverage of its operations
5. Competitive advantages associated with the accumulation and processing large amounts of consumer data (their needs and preferences)
6. High market value.

The authors include such companies as Amazon, Apple, Facebook, Alphabet, and Microsoft, as well as their Chinese competitors Alibaba, Baidu, and Tencent, as the most prominent emerging digital conglomerates. Potential digital conglomerates are yet to include the largest companies in the field of mass media and entertainment, which are increasingly switching to digital technologies, such as Yahoo, Sony, WarnerMedia, Viacom, Netflix, or Bertelsmann.

Analysis of companies' annual reports, UNCTAD data, and information from the magazines Wired, PC Magazine, PC WORLD, CNET, and Computerworld confirms that digital conglomerates depend primarily on information and communication technologies, and not on traditional approaches nor the availability of tangible assets. They use digital technology to diversify their activities and grow. The digital nature of their businesses, and the new technologies (Internet 2.0), allows them to conduct operations and bypass barriers between unrelated industries. They form an innovative corporate culture, and their success is largely due to the entrepreneurial spirit of their founders who ensured the creation and rapid development of their companies.

The study identified the following characteristics of digital conglomerates:

1. The key competencies of modern digital conglomerates are related to the platform ecosystems they created and the huge amounts of customer data generated by ecosystems. These firms have become de facto information monopolies, which is the main resource for their development. Since service sector companies are mainly focused on customer information, the information monopoly of digital conglomerates gives them a significant competitive advantage over traditional firms with insufficient data.
2. The shared consumption model allows digital conglomerates to work closely with suppliers and customers, and enrich their offerings. Their high level of knowledge and qualification of human resources, engineering skills, and terabytes of customer data, helps them achieve competitive excellence in real time.
3. Digital conglomerates are effective through the acquisition of innovative companies, and also know how to integrate these acquisitions.
4. Digital conglomerates develop and deliver comprehensive digital services that attract and retain customers.
5. Their business model is based on the low transaction costs of the Internet economy and provides a high rate of return for financing investments, growth, and acquisitions.
6. The technological leadership of such companies allows for rapid innovation, creating new types of continuous improvements in products and services. Advanced digital technologies, extensive use of business analytics and artificial intelligence allow all the customers'

preferences and desires to be tracked, reasonable segmentation (based on Dig Data) to be conducted, and innovative business processes to be applied; furthermore, it is possible to keep an eye on competitors.
7. Digital conglomerates adopt low-capital-intensive business models, leasing assets, and computing power as needed.

There was very little synergy in traditional conglomerates' activities. The business strategies of digital conglomerates are different from the 'old conglomerates': they retained their main traditional directions of strategic development, but under the influence of market changes they significantly rethought their strategies and implemented business models, and still continue to introduce new ideas. They strive to occupy all ecosystems: from hardware to content.

Apple has mastered hardware and software integration along with content availability. While the company continues to produce computers, its key focus is the release of the iPhone, which accounted for 52% of revenue in Q4 2019. However, over the past 10 years, Apple's service segment has been gaining more and more strategic value; it already provides about 20% of revenue.

Amazon has quickly evolved from an online bookstore to a major e-business portal open to third-party sellers. It has the best and most efficient logistics and, along with Internet trading, has switched to cloud computing and hardware devices such as e-readers and tablet computers. As for e-commerce, Amazon uses big data algorithms to monitor real price changes and inventory.

From the very beginning, Google's strategy was to be more than just a search engine, although this remains its main business model. The Google company has introduced a wide range of new business models, including books, software browsers, email, mobile phone software, Google Earth observation technologies, and its own social network to attract traffic to its website. Google has become a leader in Android mobile devices. It has also recently started focusing on expanding its content storage with music streaming.

Facebook places great emphasis on serving the ecosystem with new social initiatives designed to bring people together. The company imitates many other digital companies and the assorted business models they use, develops its own software, and, along with Google, dominates the highly profitable advertising business, holding more than 19% of the market.

Microsoft was forced to develop and implement an aggressive digital strategy due to the advent of downloadable open-source software, which led to the shift to cloud computing. Microsoft remains the dominant PC platform and is gaining popularity with its services (although its content still needs support). While maintaining its presence in the personal computer sector, the company expanded its offerings of enterprise software, cloud computing, computer games, and mobile computers, and attempted to create a new Windows-based ecosystem.

The study revealed the main features of the development strategies of emerging digital conglomerates:

1. Using a platform ecosystem with several levels as the basis for strategic development. Digital conglomerates operate within the framework of a platform business model, creating attractive, cost-competitive, and constantly updated customer-oriented offers. This business model is so attractive because one can use platform mechanisms to instigate exceptional opportunities to provide goods and services directly to the global market; this model guarantees access to the very active 'communication involvement' of tens of millions of users.
2. Using conventional open-source software to create a high-performance, cost-effective, scalable, and rapidly deployable technology infrastructure.
3. A reasonable combination of branded and 'open' innovative approaches. The Just-Do business model enables digital conglomerates to succeed in agile, near-continuous innovation. At the same time, they demonstrated the capacity for both gradual and breakthrough innovations, as well as great innovation opportunities in all areas of ICT business.
4. Innovative business models and innovative use of technology to change traditional business models. By releasing new offers as beta projects, users are given new choices, and in return, users provide valuable feedback, and by releasing updated and improved versions, projects can continually improve.
5. Customer focus. Digital conglomerates create new and high standards in terms of the speed, flexibility, and convenience of the

services provided. They design and deliver integrated digital engagement which attracts customers. Such an interaction is characterized by setting the client's affections as well as a high market share, the use of network effects, and being the first to enter the market.

6. Creating portfolios of digital conglomerates in various industries, with a focus on promising sectors, from food and healthcare to virtual reality and games. The main idea of this strategy is that the data available to them will provide access to the real needs of customers, and affordable digital technology will guarantee dominance in future markets. Further growth will depend on reasonable and flexible adjustments to their business models on an ongoing basis.

Conclusions and Recommendations

Conglomerates of a new type are formed based on digital technologies. Apple specializes in devices (originally computers), while Google deals with information searches, Amazon with e-commerce, and Facebook with social media. All these companies, however, are now similarly entering or influencing a wide range of markets and industries outside their core businesses. These include publications, the media, home entertainment, computing (software and hardware), advertising/marketing, telecommunications, retail, mobility, digital healthcare, fintech, and even more.

The competitive advantages of digital conglomerates are associated with economies of scale, as well as the amount and the nature of the data. With their business models and with significant data, they can identify, target, and serve a wide range of customers in different markets, enabling them to overcome industry barriers in traditional sectors and enter other industries that are not related to their core business. A general pattern has emerged in how they expand their activities. At the first stage, a technology platform or business (smartphones, search engines, social media ads, online stores) generates a large free cash flow, allowing them to invest in improving intangible assets and acquiring promising companies (primarily startups in related fast-growing areas of digital business, to generate more data at the second stage). Then, conglomerates invest in fundamental technologies to ensure the development of their digital ecosystem—in particular, computer chips or artificial intelligence systems.

New digital conglomerates, mainly those using the platform business model, are at the centre of the ecosystems they create, which allows them to receive the exclusive monopoly rents associated with the exclusive market influence. The platforms provide a special business model associated with forming a separate virtual network community; within this, a significant number of different suppliers and consumers interact instantly, freely, and with the ability to extract added value due to the network effect. For digital conglomerates, platform ecosystem management is based on their software products and information from an established community of suppliers and customers. Conglomerates that own platforms control this intellectual property and enforce the specific rules of behaviour in such ecosystems. The direct functioning of the mechanism for connecting suppliers (goods or services) and buyers is ensured by providers who use these specially developed Internet applications.

As ecosystems with a mutually reinforcing effect are created, digital conglomerates are gaining new sources of valuable information and income that are not directly related to their core business. For example, Apple now receives more revenue from its services division—which includes iCloud, Apple Pay, Apple Music, App Store, Apple TV+ , etc.—than from its traditional hardware division (MacBook). In Q4 2019, its services division accounted for 20% of revenue, while the Mac division accounted for only 11%. Meanwhile, Amazon's advertising business grew to $3.59 billion in Q3 2019 and accounted for 11.8% of the total advertising market. This allowed the company to challenge the advertising duopoly of Facebook and Google, which accounted for 36.2 and 19.3% of the online advertising market in 2019, respectively. In this market, Amazon's retail platform effectively turned into a search engine for consumer products.

For traditional companies, strategic alliances can be considered as the dominant form of seeking new competitive advantages related to the digital economy, and takeover deals are the preferred tool for further increasing the competitiveness of digital conglomerates. Amazon, Alphabet, Apple, Microsoft, and Facebook buy large numbers of small firms with innovative technologies and scalable platforms in various industries. For example, to ensure global dominance in promising areas of digital business in the period 2015–2017, they acquired 175 companies. These companies included both unknown firms and major players.

As the use of artificial intelligence and big data increases through more active use of platform ecosystems, competition between digital conglomerates will intensify.

The risks associated with digital conglomerate strategies can lead to a loss of control over completely different lines of business, while overly dispersed investments may not produce the expected effect at all. There may also be problems ensuring cybersecurity. In general, it can be argued that the strategies of digital conglomerates have proven to be more effective in modern conditions than the strategies of traditional conglomerates, which are barely able to adapt to the constantly changing digital economy.

Conclusion

With the dynamic development of digital markets and the digitalization of all public life, a new form of global conglomerate has emerged. It is able to access multiple markets and industries through its use of the core competencies associated with the advantages of this platform ecosystem. The effectiveness of the digital conglomerate strategy is determined by the trailblazer effect, as well as the network nature of business in the digital economy, which leads to a multiplier effect of reaching global customers with decreasing transaction costs while operations are replicated to new business sectors. The ability of current instituitions—firms existing in traditional markets, and industries—to rethink their business models in the face of digital conglomerates is very limited, due to the enormous scale and dynamism of their opponents.

References

Bereznoy, A. (2018). Multinational Business in the Era of Global Digital Revolution. *World Economy and International Relations, 62*(9), 5–17.

Bowen, H. P., & Wiersema, M. F. (2005). Foreign-Based Competition and Corporate Diversification Strategy. *Strategic Management Journal, 26*(12), 1153–1171.

Dawson, A. et al. (2016, April). The Economic Essentials of Digital Strategy. *McKinsey Quarterly*.

Efremov, V., & Vladimirova, I. (2020). Features of the International Activities of Digital Companies. In *Proceedings of the 1st International Conference on Emerging Trends and Challenges in the Management Theory and Practice (ETCMTP 2019), Advances in Economics, Business and Management Research*, Vol. 119, pp. 12–17.

Hausberg, J. P., Liere-Netheler, K., Packmohr, S., et al. (2019). Research Streams on Digital Transformation from a Holistic Business Perspective: A Systematic Literature Review and Citation Network Analysis. *Journal of Business Economics, 89*, 931–963.

Konina, N. (2018). Evolution of the Largest Multinational German Companies. *Sovremennaya Evropa, 2*(81), 49–59.

Lim, Y. (2017). *Tech Wars: Return of the Conglomerate—Throwback or Dawn of a New Series for Competition in the Digital Era?* Available at https://papers.ssrn.com/sol3/papers.cfm?abstract_id=3051560.

Mithas, S., Tafti, A., & Mitchell, W. (2013). How a Firm's Competitive Environment and Digital Strategic Posture Influence Digital Business Strategy. *MIS Quarterly, 37*(2), 511–536.

Ross, J. (2017, September). Don't Confuse Digital With Digitization. *MIT Sloan Review*. Available at https://sloanreview.mit.edu/article/dont-confuse-digital-with-digitization.

Stepnov, I. M., Kovalchuk, J. A., Gorchakova, E. A., & Lukmanova, I. G. (2018). High Technology as a Driver of Changes in Industry (for Example Textile Industry). *Izvestiya Vysshikh Uchebnykh Zavedenii, Seriya Teknologiya Tekstil'noi Promyshlennosti, 3*, 268–272.

Voigt, K.-I., Buliga, O., & Michl, K. (2017). *Business Model Pioneers—How Innovators Successfully Implement New Business Models*. Basel: Springer International Publishing.

Walton, N. (2013, September 5–6). The New Conglomerates and the Ecosystem Advantage. *European Business Research Conference*, Rome, Italy. Available at https://www.academia.edu/16796997/The_New_Conglomerates_and_the_Ecosystem_Advantage.

CHAPTER 12

Digital Transformation Strategies of Oil and Gas Companies: Preparing for the Fourth Industrial Revolution

Anastasia Sheveleva, Sergey Tyaglov, and Peter Khaiter

Introduction

Digital transformation has been the most important factor affecting the competitive ability of international oil and gas companies in the modern era, a time characterized by the high level of instability in both the internal and external business environments. This process

A. Sheveleva (✉)
Moscow State Institute of International Relations (MGIMO University), Moscow, Russia
e-mail: a_sheveleva@rambler.ru

S. Tyaglov
Rostov State University of Economics, Rostov-on-Don, Russia
e-mail: tyaglov-sg@rambler.ru

P. Khaiter
York University, Toronto, ON, Canada
e-mail: pkhaiter@yorku.ca

N. Konina (ed.), *Digital Strategies in a Global Market*,
https://doi.org/10.1007/978-3-030-58267-8_12

implies the integration of digital technologies into various professional spheres, or activities conducted by companies.

Against the current geopolitical, economic, and ecological situation, international oil and gas companies are likely to speed up their response to ongoing changes and enhance their required information uptake to make efficient managerial decisions and to choose the most expedient alternatives, the most accurate plans, and the highest quality control, as well as to optimize business processes and ensure high-performing management.

Achieving these specific goals requires interaction, distribution of data flow, and responsibilities between the company's business units and their staff members to be flawless; it also requires the optimization of their management structure and enhanced planning, record keeping, and control processes. The implementation of such digital technologies as Big Data, IoT, robots (including drones), digital twins (as well as visualization), or distributed ledger (blockchain) is what makes these goals a reality.

In that context, it is pertinent to analyze digital transformation processes in international oil and gas companies, in terms of their management. In modern academic literature there is ample research on digital transformation in the global oil and gas industry in general, as well as in the application of digital technologies by international oil and gas companies in particular.

Many authors highlight the necessity of 'digitalization' in the context of this market's uncertain state (Alekseev et al. 2019; Kapitonov et al. 2019; Bogdanovich and Katysheva 2019; Milovidov 2018; Salygin et al. 2019).

Furthermore, for Russian authors, along with the geopolitical and economic aspects (Simoniya and Torkunov 2015) the preconditions and processes of implementing digital products by international oil and gas companies in their business activities is a particular area of interest; they also aim to identify the advantages and disadvantages of the digitalization of the oil and gas industry (Suloeva and Martynatov 2019; Khodkovskaya and Stoyaltseva 2018). The aforementioned issues have been researched by a number of scientists abroad (Cann and Goydan 2019; Cooper and Crompton 2019). The impacts of digitalization on management processes, as practiced by oil and gas companies, have been studied, albeit to a lesser extent (Balashova and Bolshakova 2018).

However, it should be emphasized that, in these papers, digital transformation is viewed only as one factor in the optimization of the production and business activities of international oil and gas companies; this results in increased efficiency, reduced idle periods, and in totality provides industrial safety. The author suggests that the digitalization of oil and gas company's activity is indispensable for the purposes of enhancing the implementation efficiency of basic managerial functions.

Hence, the aim of this research is to analyze the impact of digital technology on the processes of planning, organization, coordination, management, and control in international oil and gas companies.

Methodology

The author studied the existing scientific literature on this problem, which resulted in them supplementing the currently held views, and suggesting their new vision of this problem; the digital transformation of international oil and gas companies was analyzed with regard to management rather than to production. The applied systematic approach made it possible to regard a number of diverse elements as a whole, whereas formerly they had only been studied separately. Thus, the research looked into digital technologies, oil and gas companies, and management. Careful analysis of the impact of digital technologies on the processes of planning, organization, coordination, management, and control helped to positive results, both qualitative and quantitative, to be identified. Finally, through the generalization and synthesis of the resulting data, some grand conclusions were made.

Results

Key technologies of the Fourth Industrial Revolution in the oil and gas industry are Big Data; the Industrial Internet of Things; robots (including drones); digital twins (including visualization); smart materials (including nano coverage and smart liquids); 3D printing; distributed ledger (blockchain) (Fig. 12.1).

Big Data systems allow oil and gas companies to collect, store, process, and calculate immense data sets (more than 1015 bytes). Also, machine learning and artificial intelligence belong to Big Data system.

Industrial Internet of Things technology, with the help of built-in sensors, enables collecting and exchanging data, as well as supervising production processes and controlling them remotely in automatic mode.

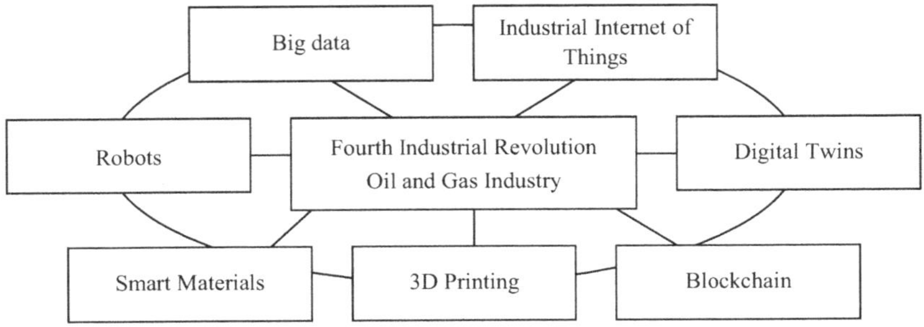

Fig. 12.1 Key digital technologies in the oil and gas industry (*Source* Developed by the authors based on National Oil and Gas Forum. (2018). *Digital Transformation of the Oil and Gas Industry: Popular Myth or Objective Reality?* Available at http://oilandgasforum.ru/data/files/Digest%20site/DAIDJEST%20WEB2.pdf)

Robots (including drones) provide process automation, execute dangerous works, and allow visual studies of inaccessible objects, such as sub-sea wells and equipment for underwater mining. Digital twins (including visualization) are used to model deposit, well, equipment, or infrastructural elements for testing and predicting the consequences of implementing a decision, and for visualizing results in a user-friendly manner. Smart materials (including nano coverage and smart liquids) are materials that preserve or obtain certain qualities in extreme environments during exploration and the mining of oil and gas. 3D printing is used in mining for the creation of models of mining projects and the deposit establishment scheme. Distributed ledger technology (blockchain), in the form of a decentralized app of shared use, provides the possibility of recording all information systems at a high safety level in oil and gas companies.

Digital transformation covers not only the business of international oil and gas companies, but their managerial processes as well. The main functions of management, proposed by practicing French engineer Henri Fayol, are planning, organization, managing, coordination, and control; digital technologies enable these to be optimized.

To plan future activities, oil and gas companies define the goals and tasks of their activities, specify the means and methods to achieve them, and allocate the resources to implement the plans.

To ensure that international oil and gas companies' planning is efficient, the quality of information about the external business environment must be predetermined, and demand should be forecasted in line with the companies' capabilities. In order to speedily receive reliable information and analytical data, companies should actively implement digital solutions. Owing to computerized learning and artificial intelligence, international oil and gas companies accumulate, process, and store their vast amounts of data, then coordinate their strategic and operational plans.

Digital solutions, as designed by big software designers such as SAP, Microsoft, IBM, optimize planning processes and free up time for business development. For example, Annex SAP Business Planning and Consolidation (SAP BPC)—a system designed to enable oil and gas companies to plan, budget, forecast, and ultimately achieve financial consolidation, in compliance with the standards of financial reporting—facilitates the revision of plans and forecasts, and also shortens the process of setting a budget.

The experience of operating this application, obtained by the biggest international oil and gas companies (namely Shell, BP, and ExxonMobil), showed that—due to the prompt request and response—their key business functions has risen in efficiency by 80%.

The introduction of a single integrated software solution for business planning and consolidation has contributed to saving time and error reduction.

Cloud technologies ensure centralized access for top executive management personnel to all available information and records, which improves the accountability of subsidiaries and accuracy of in-house planning.

Analytical built-in tools allow alternative analyses to be conducted, probable scenarios and consequences of activities to be mapped out, adjustments to the adopted strategy (where necessary) to be promptly made, and sustainable management solutions to be found.

Digital twins are a universal tool for company scenario planning.

The IBM Planning Analytics app, being an integrated planning tool based on AI, allows oil and gas companies to automate planning, budgeting, and forecasting, and to introduce more intelligent workflows. Automated model creation, natural language processing, and cognitive assist can be used to elaborate precise plans faster and easier. Real-time plan adjustment, based on obtained analysis results, is also possible. Integrated plan elaboration, based on full data, is possible due to passing fragmentation, data unification, and the synchronization of planning for the whole company. IBM Planning Analytics can shorten planning cycles, increase forecast precision, and elaborate more reasonable business decisions. For companies that have applied continuous planning, the possibility of forecast adjustment taking place every week is 1.5 times higher; these companies are also 4 times faster in adapting to changing market conditions. With continuous planning, it is possible to forecast profit twice as frequently, with $\pm$ 0.5% deviation.

The organization function implies, on the one hand, the building of an appropriate corporate structure which will secure their plans' fruition, and, on the other hand, connections to be made between business units of the given corporate structure.

As for the corporate structure, international oil and gas companies devise specialized centers (so-called digital clusters) to implement digital transformation strategies. A digital cluster is a form of organization of matrix management processes, which perform a search for new ideas and create digital solutions.

As an example, at the end of 2017, PJSC Rosneft Oil Company set up the Digital Transformation Centre and Digital Cluster, which became the key mechanisms of digital program implementation. Their most significant constituent elements are their Analytical Centre, Prototyping Polygon, Partnership Centre, Digital Transformation Centre, and Acceleration Centre.

The Analytical Center specializes in raw data acquisition and processing, analyzes the best practices, and gives overviews of the market with regard to international practices.

The Prototyping Polygon was created for rapid deployment; it partners solution testing, pilot prospects, and the approbation of innovative ideas.

The internal centers of digital pilot projects deal with generating new technological platforms based on the results of research and innovative activities.

The Partnership Centre administers the company partnership development and external structures such as technological companies, funds, universities, which contribute to acquiring new ideas, technological, and human resources.

The Acceleration Centre aims to provide a permanent flow of ideas, enhancing technology approbation and assisting with company copyright protection (Fig. 12.2).

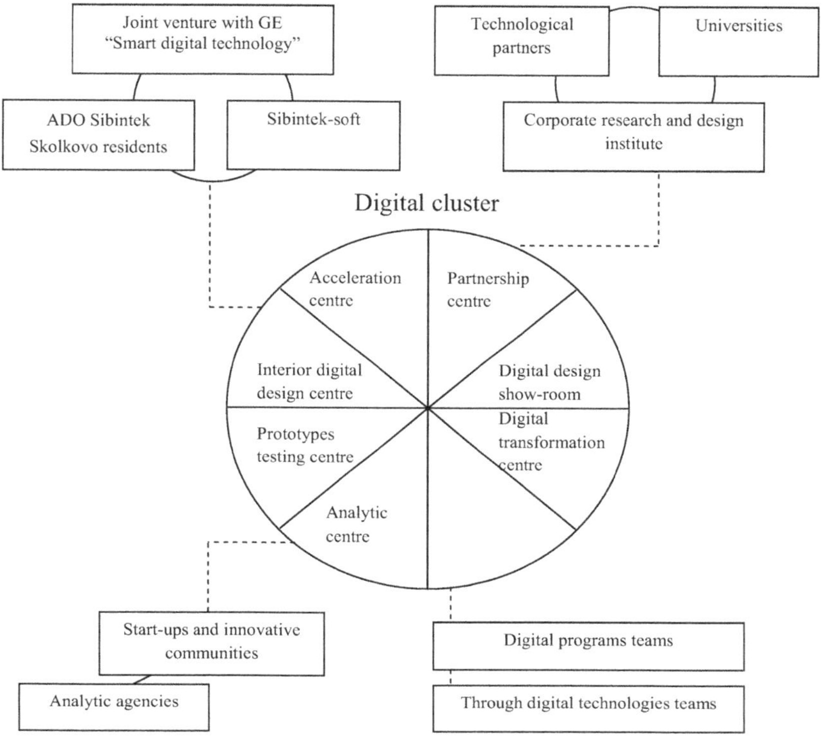

Fig. 12.2 Digital cluster PJSC "Rosneft" (*Source* Developed by the authors based on Petrov, A. S. (2018). *Step into the Digital Field*. Available at http://technefi.ru/images/doc/conf2018/plenarka_25_10/05_Petrov_Rus.pdf [accessed 25 October 2019])

To provide a connection between the individualized business units that exist within the organizational structure of an oil and gas company, there are network activity organization mechanisms; these enable horizontal communication, which lets staff members receive timely access to the information they need to virtually facilitate any solutions of any problem or task should company encounter it.

For advisory, methodological, and expert support for management and employees regarding the introduction of digital decisions and support for digital transformation, oil and gas companies establish centers of competence and special departments as a part of the management apparatus for research, development, and coordination of works related to digital technologies, and for innovative cyber-physical processes.

Also, they establish corporate venture funds, and facilitate their investment and accelerate start-up project activities in the sphere of digital technologies.

Digital technologies of Industry 4.0 create new variants of interaction among company employees, which transform economic relationships among a company and its partners. New efficient methods of cooperation and coordinating relationships among partners are arising, for joint decisions of certain business tasks.

The function of coordination secures the interaction between the company staff members, its business units, its resources, and its technologies, as well as interaction between the company's own activities and the major elements of the environment external to it.

With a view to solving internal interaction problems, oil and gas companies implement those digital technologies that provide some means to computerize document management and which put core business processes into action with more speed. The application of such digital solutions as Big data or IoT ensures a substantial reduction of the company document execution and flow terms.

Various kinds of mobile computer devices favor providing an effective interaction between company staff members and establishing relations with their business partners. Smartphones, tablets, or netbooks, if they support appropriate business applications (including instant messages and video), allow contract partners to cooperate and coordinate, regardless of their whereabouts, so as to solve specified business tasks together.

Digital decision SAP Jam Collaboration facilitates better coordination, as this eliminates barriers among departments, fragments data, and includes tools of social interaction for any business process. This decision allows employees from different departments and regions to be united, and gives easy access to content and experts required for fulfillment of work. Also, it facilitates communication for whichever simple tools for individual publications are applied that facilitate engagement, discussions, and information exchange. Moreover, access to the information is simplified. Unification of business processes with tools and data for joint work is ongoing, which allows employees to obtain necessary information in due time.

The managerial function is aimed at orienting employees of oil and gas companies toward the quality performance of their duties. The manager must arrange it so that the contractor wants, and is able, to fulfill this order in the most efficient manner, and the company has achieved its goals. To do this, the company management needs to know their subordinates well (what connects them with the company, increases employee loyalty), and promptly dismiss those who do not fulfill their duties; meetings should also be held to coordinate the unity of activities.

For taking into account the constant changes in the needs and expectations of staff, decisions are developed to manage the experience of employees, which are able to track, measure, and analyze the quality of interaction with them in real time; from this, surveys can be created of employee engagement, result reports can be issued containing the identified factors to which attention must be paid, and finally actions that quickly increase engagement can be formulated.

For example, digital decision SAP Success Factors have many benefits: they detect and eliminate disadvantages in a system of communication with employees for achieving company goals; create a work atmosphere that facilitates successfully achieving company and employees goals; improve employee experiences through a deeper understanding of key engagement factors.

The SAP Success Factors Performance & Goals decision makes it possible to evaluate and highlight the best specialists, coordinate strategies with the goals of the company, and ensure the continuous improvement of staff productivity. Firstly, this helps to manage employee goals by capturing data on the amount of work and achievements of employees, as well as comments, using a convenient interface on any device, anytime, anywhere. Secondly, there is continuous performance management conducted through regular and productive conversations, to ensure maximum employee productivity. Thirdly, a review and assessment of the effectiveness of employees can be done.

Mobiles and mobile devices also help to fulfill managerial functions. They enable oil and gas companies' management to hold conferences with their staff in order to coordinate areas and efforts which need a united and focused approach, and also keep co-workers informed about their instructions and responsibilities that need to be shared.

Management is tightly connected with employee motivation. In this respect, the relevance of implementing interactive online platforms and production, sales, bonuses, and other visualization systems, tightly connected with an employee fulfilling their duties, is increasing.

Modern information systems allow oil and gas companies to optimize reward programs using advanced modeling and forecasting capabilities based on best practices, efficiently manage rewards and incentives based on real-time analysis using a single unified decision, and motivate employees to maximize work efficiency through timely rewards and recognition of their achievements.

For example, SAP Success Factors Compensation digital decision can be used to develop and implement strategic remuneration programs in accordance with company goals; it is aimed at supporting employee engagement and company performance efficiency.

Control function tasks are to compile, process, and analyze information about business results, compare them with the planned figures, and then take measures to readjust them.

Big Data and Industrial Internet of Things systems enhance record keeping by providing oil and gas company's management, in a timely manner, with precise information about the actual results of their activities, which helps to control the business units performance in compliance with their plan and allows management to identify ineffective and costly units.

The large-scale implementation of information technologies allows those companies that implement them to transition to a new control model, based on the data of information systems and risk management system.

Information systems make it possible to imbed control mechanisms into these processes and to keep track of all operations being conducted. Nowadays, information systems contain all data about the activities of the objects they monitor, thus creating "digital profiles of monitored objects."

The aforementioned approach means that, in the area being controlled and monitored, not only can malfunctions be promptly detected, but also a system for routine observation, monitoring, and analysis can be developed virtually (without approaching the monitored objects). This means that the control can promptly respond to risks when they occur, giving no chance to any actions causing trouble, while also warning about potential problems, or detecting if the relevant areas of monitored objects perform in an unsatisfactory state. The control becomes a built-in element of the

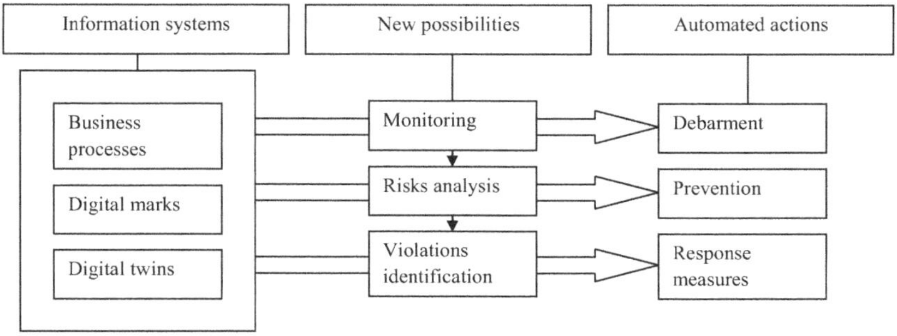

Fig. 12.3 Digitalization of control function (*Source* developed by the authors based on Isaev, E. A. (2019). *Digitalization of Control in the Financial and Budgetary Sphere Approaches*. Finance, No. 5. Available at http://bujet.ru/article/376994.php)

managerial system, whereby every action is checked and accepted in the automatic mode the moment it occurs (Fig. 12.3).

In the integrated digital space, it is possible to provide oil and gas company's management not only with consistent monitoring of the controlled object activity, but also with access to the results of such monitoring, as well as to control measures taken in regard to the controlled objects.

Supervisory authorities can look into the business processes conducted by the information systems that automate financial and economic activities; moreover, they have access to the information systems that automate other aspects of their activities. Therefore, digitalized monitoring will secure consistency, maximum cover, and the transparency of the supervisory activity. Hence, this approach will ease pressure on the monitored object and ensure prompt responses to malfunction probability risks.

Technologies of digital monitoring and consistent dataflow control enhance and ensure more qualitative forecasting of potential changes, which allows oil and gas companies to assess the internal and external state of their environment efficiently, identify key trends and opportunities for their activity, and specify the main tendencies of their development.

A number of the biggest oil and gas companies—Exxon Mobil and Shell in particular—are currently implementing digital monitoring technologies, doing so by using mobile devices. Across all levels, managers use special applications on their mobile devices to get the information they need for control and analysis on a real-time basis. Furthermore, these applications also help to process the information they receive, which optimizes managerial decision-making time.

The app iBase, an analytic app for data control by IBM® i2®, can be used to collect, control, and analyze data obtained by oil and gas companies from different sources of information. It helps to detect and reveal inter-connections, patterns, and trends across the modern world, which are likely characterized by the rapid growth of volumes of complicated structured and unstructured data.

Therefore, it is possible to state that the digital transformation of international oil and gas companies has contributed to significant qualitative improvements of their managerial activity. At the same time, the experts of both ITPS (Information Technology Professional Solutions) and independent information agencies claim that if oil and gas companies start planning thoroughly and implement digital technologies competently, they will achieve the following positive quantitative results:

- the labor intensity planning process will decrease by 20–50%;
- owing to joint planning (helping controls), the budget overrun will decrease by 5–10%;
- the time it takes to maintain management accounting and prepare book-keeping summarizing the company's activities and results will decrease by 50–70%;
- the time needed to realize projects will decrease by 5–15%, albeit at the expense of optimizing, organizing, coordinating, and controlling the planning process (Vasyukov and Tikhomirov 2019).

Obviously, it should be noted that there are risks that expectations may not be met; the impact of digital technologies on the planning, organization, coordination, management, and control processes of international oil and gas companies might fall short, or problems may arise around providing cybersecurity. However, taken as a whole, in the current context, it is evident that effective management is unattainable without digitalization.

Conclusions/Recommendations

Digital transformation is crucially important for business. This is not only for optimizing the manufacturing processes and improving the performance of oil and gas companies; it is also with reference to improving the management system.

The active use of IT in the management of oil and gas companies facilitates the soundness of managerial decisions, due to the rapid collection and processing of information; it also increases the efficiency of company management, and makes decisions at all management levels more consistent.

The adaptation of digital technologies increases the effectiveness of leading oil and gas companies' managerial functions: planning, organization, coordination, management, and control.

Primarily, companies gain qualitative advantages from digitalization. It increases the accuracy of their planning and leadership, brings the relevant techniques to shared standards, optimizes organization structures, and improves coordination, transparency, and control operability.

Moreover, digitalization also provides quantitative improvements for the managerial activity of oil and gas companies: in particular, it decreases the time needed for planning, book-keeping, and control.

Overall, digital technologies facilitate managerial decision-making, enhancing the efficiency of the management of senior executives in oil and gas industries.

Notes. ITPS (Information Technology Professional Solutions) is one of the leading integrated partners for digital transformation of big companies on the basis of modern technologies such as IIoT, Big Data/Smart Data, Predictive Analysis&Optimization, in-house IT-solutions, and platforms of digital production AVIST. For more than 15 years ITPS Group has been implementing large-scale strategic digital transformation projects for fuel and energy complex industry enterprises.

References

Alekseev, A. N., Lobova, S. V., Bogoviz, A. V., & Ragulina, Y. V. (2019). Digitalization of the Russian Energy Sector: State-of-the-Art and Potential for Future Research. *International Journal of Energy Economics and Policy, 9*(5), 274–280. https://doi.org/10.32479/ijeep.7673.

Balashova, A. D., & Bolshakova, O. I. (2018). Change in Business Management in the Context of the Digital Transformation of the Oil and Gas Industry. In *Proceedings of the 23rd International Scientific-Practical Conference "Actual Problems of Management"*. Moscow: GUU (State University of Management), pp. 140–144.

Bogdanovich, K., & Katysheva, E. (2019). Main Directions of the Oil and Gas Industry Innovative Development. In A. V. Babkin (Ed.), *Works of the 10th Research-to-Practice Conference with Foreign Participation 20–22 June 2019 "Digital Transformation of Economy and Industry"* (pp. 265–273). St Petersburg: Publishing House of Polytechnical University.

Cann, G., & Goydan, R. (2019). *Bits, Bytes, and Barrels: The Digital Transformation of Oil and Gas*. USA: MADCann Press.

Cooper, S., & Crompton, J. (2019). *A Digital Journey: The Transformation of the Oil and Gas Industry*. USA: Independently published.

Isaev, E. A. (2019, May 21). *Digitalization of Control in the Financial and Budgetary Sphere Approaches*. Finance, No. 5. Available at http://bujet.ru/article/376994.php.

Kapitonov, I. A., Filosofova, T. G., & Korolev, V. G. (2019). Development of Digital Economy in the Energy Industry-Specific Modernization. *International Journal of Energy Economics and Policy, 9*(4), 273–282. https://doi.org/10.32479/ijeep.8013.

Khodkovskaya, Y. V., & Stoyaltseva, A. A. (2018). Barriers and Effects of the Introduction of Digital Technology in Oil and Gas Business. *Economics and Management: Research and Practice Journal, 6*(144), 27–32.

Milovidov, K. N. (2018). Digitalization Is a New Era in Energy. The Accelerated Development of Information Technologies in the World Economy. In S. V. Zhukov (Ed.), *Global Energy Transformation: Economics and Politics* (pp. 126–137). Moscow: IMEMO RAS.

National Oil and Gas Forum. (2018). *Digital Transformation of the Oil and Gas Industry: Popular Myth or Objective Reality*? Available at http://oilandgasforum.ru/data/files/Digest%20site/DAIDJEST%20WEB2.pdf.

Petrov, A. S. (2018). *Step into the Digital Field*. Available at http://techneft.ru/images/doc/conf2018/plenarka_25_10/05_Petrov_Rus.pdf.

Salygin, V. I., Guliyev, I. A., & Akieva, L. B. (2019). The Impact of Digital Technologies on the Development of Global Energy. *Innovation and Investment, 5*, 41–44.

Simoniya, N., & Torkunov, A. (2015). The European Union's Energy Security and Russia. *Social Sciences (Russian Federation), 46*(2), 78–89.

Suloeva, S. B., & Martynatov, V. S. (2019). The Features of the Digital Transformation of Oil and Gas Enterprises. *Organizer of Production, 27*(2), 27–36. https://doi.org/10.25987/vstu.2019.26.70.003 (in Russian).

Vasyukov, D. E., & Tikhomirov, L. I. (2019). Integrated Digital Transformation of Oilfield Services Company. *Drilling and Oil*. Available at http://itps.com/uploads/files/file_756.pdf.

CHAPTER 13

On Determining the Effectiveness of Digital Marketing in Transnational e-Commerce

Yuri Savinov, Evgeniya Taranovskaya, and Oleg Gavryushin

Introduction

The nature of e-commerce has changed dramatically over recent years. It is no longer limited to domestic commercial activities; instead, is increasingly being used to develop the supply of goods to other countries. This area of entrepreneurial activity is called "transnational e-commerce".

Like any new line of business, conducting these operations requires cost justification: companies must determine the effectiveness of the expenses that arise from marketing and sales organization. The purpose of this chapter is to prove the appropriateness and effectiveness of forming a group of regular customers who make relatively large purchases from one seller, and evaluate the arising marketing costs.

Y. Savinov (✉) · E. Taranovskaya
Russian Foreign Trade Academy, Moscow, Russia

O. Gavryushin
Institute of International Trade and Law, Moscow, Russia

N. Konina (ed.), *Digital Strategies in a Global Market*,
https://doi.org/10.1007/978-3-030-58267-8_13

Methodology

In surveys of specialists, many will answer that they are aware of the need for marketing; indeed, many marketing events are held every day, although not all of these prove effective. Therefore, a new task arises: to determine the effectiveness not of merely one-time activities, but of activities and the costs thus incurred over a relatively long period.

Scientists have made attempts to measure the effectiveness of such costs. It has been determined (Green 2018) that both large and small companies constantly face the same fundamental question, attempting to discover, in addition to sales revenue, how exactly marketing activity can be measured. Marketing's purpose and its importance is universally known, but company to company and event to event, evaluating marketing is done differently by different company's specialists and functionaries. Investments in digital marketing are constantly increasing, while the requirements for efficiency have grown significantly. A typical expectation gap has arisen in the market. Digital marketing is now expected to perform magic: to instantly launch successful projects and generate high profits. Due to the wide range of tools and unique features provided by the internet, it is difficult for advertisers to single out one key indicator to measure performance. The advertiser often has conflicting goals: reaching and engaging potential customers, increasing the number of ad views and responding to them in the form of clicks, developing large advertising banners with minimal costs, and so on. Compromising such conflicting goals leads to campaigns losing focus, and therefore to unsatisfactory results.

Different methodological approaches are used to evaluate the effectiveness of marketing in everyday corporate practice. Analysts quite often proceed from calculating the ratio of short-term profit and investment, but this is not enough to get the full picture, since some costs do not imply immediate returns, and income is only received after some time has passed.

With the development of the internet and the expansion of the possibilities of using digital marketing tools, the importance of evaluating its potential effectiveness has become even higher. It has been noted that the share of digital marketing costs across total marketing costs has begun to increase, but most companies admit that they lack clear methods for assessing the effects of digital marketing (Gaitniece 2018). One company (Freshsparks 2019) proposed 19 methods that can be used to assess the effectiveness of advertising in e-commerce, but this is not the limit. This uncertainty makes it difficult to get a real picture of a company's financial performance.

Therefore, there is an objective need to develop new approaches, taking into account the specific character of trading individual goods in different markets. One proposition is using the AdWords advertising system (now ads.google.com) in electronic commerce (Blair 2019); it has many methods for assessing the effectiveness of advertising. It is necessary to take into account the expenses and income received over a relatively long period. At the same time, it has been proposed that focusing on retaining profitable customers is preferable to the earlier alternative of spending money on acquiring new customers.

Results

Several tools are used to determine the effectiveness of digital marketing in e-commerce; each has its own metrics by which specialists try to calculate this effectiveness. This is essential, since evaluating the effectiveness of each tool makes it possible not only to identify priority areas, but also to weed out frankly weak and ineffective ones.

Here it is necessary to decide what indicators can and should be used to determine effectiveness. Two approaches are most often applied in corporate practice: the first defines "effectiveness" as the amount of incoming traffic, the numbers, and the actions leading to possible purchases that customers demonstrate; the second approach is more specific, and determines the "effectiveness" of marketing through the advertiser's sales growth.

Regarding the first group of approaches, the main goal of search engine promotion is to get more traffic to the intended site from organic search results. However, the amount of traffic alone does not adequately assess effectiveness. For instance:

- Website 1. Attendance—100,000 visitors per week. The number of orders on the website is 1600.
- Website 2. Attendance—100,000 visitors per week. The number of orders is 1200.

The higher traffic to the first site is evidently inefficient; although the traffic of the first website is 66 times higher than that of the second one, the difference between the number of orders is only 400.

Therefore, in order to adequately assess the effectiveness of the site (traffic), the conversion rate is a better metric.

Conversion = (number of orders / number of visitors) * 100%.

In the aforementioned example, the first website has a conversion rate of (1600 / 100,000) * 100% = 1.6%

The conversion rate of the second website is: (1200 / 10,000) * 100% = 12%.

Thus, it is not so much the volume of incoming traffic that matters, but its quality: the higher the traffic conversion to customers or clients, the higher the website's performance.

Other, more reliable methods must be considered for assessing effectiveness. To assess this, we used a contextual advertising performance indicator using the CTR indicator (click-through rate) an indicator of advertising "clickability". This indicator makes it possible to determine how successful a particular advertisement is. It is calculated by: (number of clicks made in response to the proposed advertisement / number of impressions) * 100%. For example, if an ad was shown 1000 times and 200 customers clicked on it, then the CTR would be the following: (200 / 1000) * 100% = 20%. A high CTR indicates that the advertisement is relevant to the target audience, thus is shown to "warm" customers. A low CTR indicates that the advertising campaign or the advertisement itself needs updating.

Another widely used metric is CPC, or "cost per click". This is calculated by dividing the cost of advertising by the number of clicks. It is theoretically possible to determine how much each click on an ad costs. For example: if seven euros were spent on the advertising campaign, and 600 customers clicked on the ad, the average price of 1 click is 0 Euros. The lower the cost per click, the more profitable it is to invest in advertising.

The next appropriate indicator is CPA, or "cost per action"—the cost of any targeted action by the website visitor. This is calculated when an advertising campaign is aimed at ensuring that users perform a certain action: for example, register, fulfil an order, ask for a call, or subscribe to newsletters. For example, a seller company might organize an advertising campaign in order to increase the number of subscribers to brand news, with 2.1e being spent for this purpose, and 500 customers subscribing to the news; therefore, CPA is 2.1 / 100 = 0.2e.

The second group of marketing performance evaluations focuses on determining the company's sales growth depending on marketing and advertising costs. The first indicator is CPS—"cost per sale", or the number of marketing costs per unit of sales. In other words, it is important to determine how much a company spends to make one customer buy something.

Overall, this and all the aforementioned methods are applicable to evaluate individual marketing measures, but not marketing in general. To assess the long-term aspects of marketing costs, a more significant factor is ROI, or "return on investments". This determines whether a company's investment is paying off as a whole, or whether the profit is lower than the cost. The indicator in question can be calculated for any internet marketing tool, or indeed all work in general. For example, in the case of contextual advertising, the calculation will be as follows: (advertising profit–advertising costs) / advertising costs * 100%.

[(28.6 e.–5.7 e.) / 5.7 e] * 100% = 400%—this is an example of a very good ROI.

When using this indicator, it is very important to monitor its dynamics over a long period. If it decreases, then it is advisable to investigate the causes of this phenomenon.

Current economic literature offers many different methods for analyzing the effectiveness of commercial activities through e-commerce channels; many of them, however, are practically useless in most cases. It is advisable to return to the goals of the task and select those indicators that most accurately reflect the seller's activities in moving towards these goals. Key Performance Indicators (KPIs) are numerical indicators of a division's (or enterprise's) performance that help the organization to achieve its goals or optimize its processes. KPIs are the most commonly agreed-upon criteria that help to track the level of work compliance by an employee or an entire department, regarding their assigned strategic tasks. The most basic KPIs include sales and revenue, such as ROI or CPC, but marketing activities can be complex and, often, companies need to break down each action into separate steps to see where the company fails.

Such concepts as "payback period" and "return on invested capital" are very important for each company. This is especially true when a new project is launched at the expense of borrowed funds or a credit line.

In these cases, it is important to answer whether this investment will be profitable, and whether it will give a good return on investment.

The same problem arises when it comes to investing in advertising campaigns and marketing in cross-border e-commerce—how can ROI be calculated when organizing exports?

In the simplest case, it would be possible to calculate how much profit had been gotten from selling goods or services through marketing/advertising, compared with how much had been spent on advertisement. Return on investment in advertising and marketing (ROI) is measured as the ratio of profit to brand advertising expenses.

ROI = [(Revenue—(Cost / Expenses + Cost of ads on the advertiser's website) / (Cost / Expenses + Cost of ads on the advertiser's website)] * 100%. Thus, in order to calculate the ROI, take the amount of income, subtract the total costs, and then divide it by the total costs:

For example, for a month, a company incurred costs of manufacturing goods and organizing sales of 228,028 e, plus 12,114 e for marketing and advertising; sales amounted to 228,040.1 e: ROI = [2,465,857 e–(228,028 e 1,214) / (228,028 1214)] * 100% = 7.56%. Another month's cost (13,000,000 + 85,000) exceeded sales volume [1 714–(185,714 + 1,214) / 185,714 + 1214)] by 17%. It can be seen that, if the organization has expenses that exceed revenues, it makes no sense to calculate ROI using this formula, which is nonsense: advertising is unprofitable, and the ROI is negative.

The bottom line of the analysis is that, in particular cases by particular organizations, using ROI in order to directly assess the impact of advertising investment can seriously distort the true value of marketing; this is because ROI, as an indicator of return on investment, cannot measure the overall effectiveness of marketing in general.

If the goal of digital marketing is to tell potential customers about the company's capabilities, it is difficult to measure ROI at all, without the near-impossible task of figuring out how to reach and interview all potential customers covered by advertising or other marketing promotions and events.

We conclude that although the ROI calculation method for measuring return on investment is applicable, it cannot increase the effectiveness of digital marketing. As an example, a company developed a website for selling souvenir products, and launched an advertising campaign. At the first stage, the costs, of course, were higher than income, the profit was negative, and the cost of attracting customers was higher than the return;

this, however, was in the short term. If this company had kept looking at a negative ROI, then there would have been no point in continuing. However, 2–3 years later, sales turned into profit, and those potential customers became guests/clients and brought the long-awaited profit. Without investing in marketing this would have been impossible! We conclude that most companies that use ROI as an indicator of return on investment in the context of marketing must be misusing it.

Many companies consider digital marketing costs to be investment costs, similar to calculations for one-time (capital) projects. However digital marketing costs cannot be considered and evaluated as a type of investment cost. It was determined that, in this case, costs are expenses, not investments, and this is the main problem (Pauwels et al. 2004).

For example, ROI cannot be taken for water, electricity, transportation costs.; Otherwise, a business would not spend money on it. These things do not bring obvious profit. Without them, though, a business simply would not survive. In financial slang, marketing expenses are profit and loss items, not balance sheets.

Return on investment is, of course, an important indicator for any business owners and managers. ROI, however, helps much less than is commonly believed. In order to understand the real contribution and benefits of marketing activities, it is advisable to use a different approach. It is best to include an indicator of the regular customers in the KPI, and find out how this can be improved. This indicator is CLV (Fig. 13.1).

Sometimes abbreviated instead to CLTV (Customer Life Time Time Value), CLV is the "Customer Lifetime Value", a relatively new and relevant approach to digital marketing. The analysis this indicator provides is invaluable, because it is associated with the profit that the company receives throughout the entire time of client interaction, while also introducing a relative indicator of retention costs of those customers who responded to the company's advertisement into the calculation. These costs are covered by the company's retained earnings: the retention rate (RR), in fact, includes the retained earnings aimed at development.

If RR is 0, the client never returns (the company cannot keep them). If RR is equal to 1, then the client becomes permanent: for example, they will stay at the company's hotel every summer of their life, or will buy the company's products for a long time. In other words, this coefficient refers to a group of loyal customers, from whom the company can receive profit for a practically unlimited time.

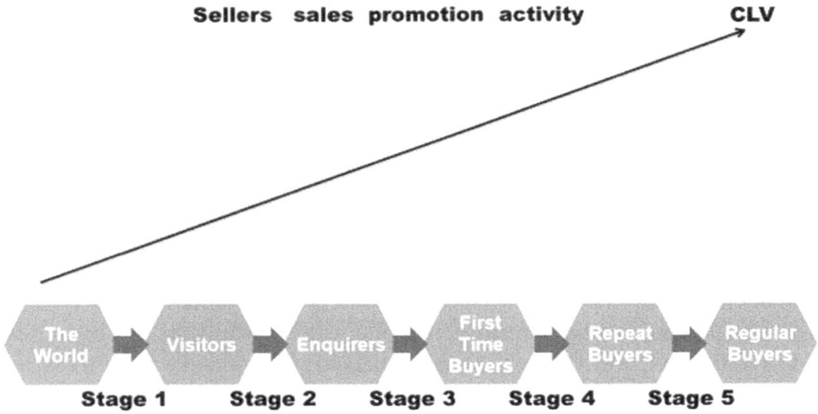

Fig. 13.1 The sequence of actions of the seller to create a group of regular customers (*Source* Created by the authors)

CLV, in the meaning of "customer value", encourages the company's marketing department to shift the focus from making monthly or quarterly profits to a long-term strategy for customer relationships. This indicator is an important criterion for marketing costs, as it represents the upper limit of costs aimed at acquiring new customers. For this reason, CLV, in our opinion, is one of the most important parameters when calculating the profitability of digital marketing (Fig. 13.2).

CLV (Customer Lifetime Value) is calculated as follows:

CLV (e) = Profit (e) * (Retention rate (%) ÷ [1 Discount rate (%)]) * Retention rate (%)).

As an example, PP for the sales department of the company's products equals 0.5 minimum (50%), or 0.8, (80%) maximum, while the discount rate (or discount rate) equals 10%; in these cases, the profit generated by the client in the first case is 71 e, and in the second case is 429 e.

The current profit value in an indefinite period is the profit divided by the discount rate. The above CLV formula gives us the corresponding result:

CLV min = 71 e * (50% / [(100 10): 100] = 325 e.

CLV max = 429 * (80% // [(100 10): 100] = 312 e.

The CLV value, in this case, shows what profit a single client brings to the company as a buyer.

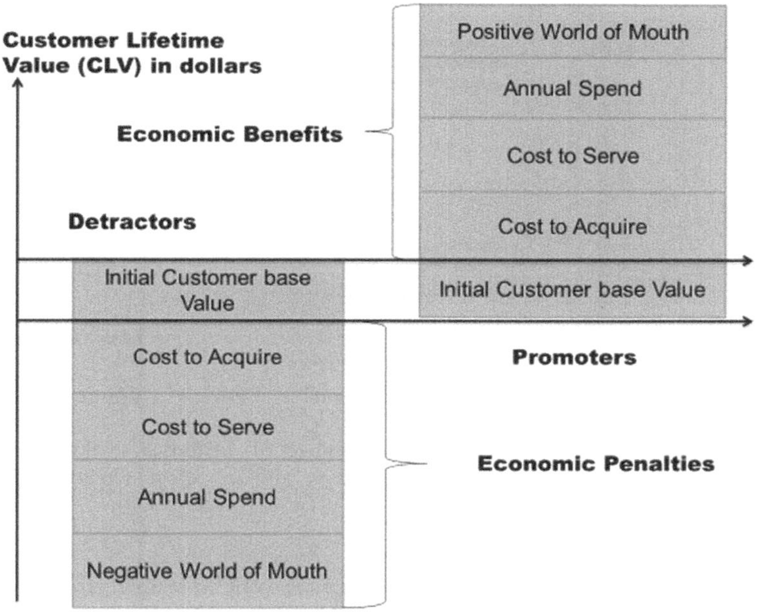

Fig. 13.2 Expenses and income from creating a group of loyal customers (*Source* Created by the authors)

It can also be applied to calculate the effectiveness of advertising/marketing. For example, to attract a client, a company spent 14 e. Then:

Efficiency min = 32 e/ 1000 * 100% = 3.2%.

Efficiency max = 312 e/ 1000 * 100% = 3.1%.

It can now be seen that the cost of marketing/advertising pays off very effectively.

Note that these examples do not take into account several factors, such as the costs of maintaining the marketing department, let alone other costs and aspects of influence. However, knowing the principles and approaches to calculation, any company can introduce correction factors with its specifics.

It is also true that there may be additions and cross-sales: for example, any client of a company visiting a website may make a passing purchase. Therefore, these values may decrease or increase significantly (Fig. 13.3).

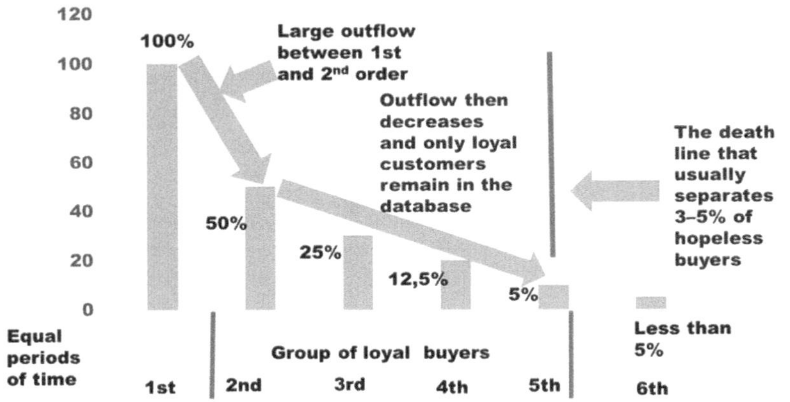

Fig. 13.3 Relative decrease in the percentage of customers making repeat purchases (purchase of the 1st time period = 100%) (*Source* Created by the authors)

The best way to get and retain customers is to build long-term relationships with them. According to research, the ability to sell a new product on the market to existing customers is 60–70%, but this rate for new customers is merely 5–20% (Web Marketing Pros 2020); it is thus advisable to switch focus to assessing customer loyalty behaviour, represented by customer retention over a fairly long time, particularly those making large regular purchases. Additional analysis showed that when advertising on the internet, all customers who responded to the company's advertising messages can be divided into three groups: (A) all respondents, representing the array from which the company's marketing department can work;(B) a reduced number of customers who responded to the ad a second time; and (C) those members who responded to the ad after a long period of time.

In this situation, three courses of action seem appropriate: (1) reducing the time between the first and second response (for the second group of buyers); (2) cutting off the third group of buyers, since these costs are not productive, based on the results of the company's activities for a time (for example, for a year); and (3) increasing activity when working with the second group, from which a group of regular customers can be formed.

Conclusion/Recommendation

Measuring the effectiveness of marketing activities and goals only through ROI indicators has proven to be insufficient. ROI does not measure the way a company builds relationships with consumers, nor how good a marketing strategy or investment in advertising is in the long run.

The aforementioned new approaches to measuring the effectiveness of digital marketing, such as measuring the "customer value" and CLV indicators, paint a more accurate picture of whether to invest in marketing, advertising, and other activities aimed at attracting new customers. Three lines of action seem appropriate in a company's activities: (1) reducing the time between responses; (2) cutting off the third group of customers for a time; and (3) increasing work with the second group, so as to form a group of regular customers.

References

Blair, I. (2019). 18 Essential Metrics to Measure Your Digital Marketing. *Buildfire*. Available at https://buildfire.com/essential-metrics-measure-digital-marketing/2019.

Freshsparks. (2019). *19 Important Metrics for Measuring Digital Marketing Success*. Available at https://freshsparks.com/digital-marketing-success/.

Gaitniece E. (2018). Digital Marketing Performance Evaluation Methods. In *CBU International Conference Proceedings*, Vol. 6.

Green, V. (2018). How to Measure Ecommerce Marketing Performance. *McGaw*. Available at https://mcgaw.io/blog/measure-ecommerce-performance/.

Pauwels, K., Currim, I., Dekimpe, M. G., Ghysels, E., Hanssens, D. M., Mizik, N., et al. (2004). Modeling Marketing Dynamics by Time Series Econometrics. *Marketing Letters, 15*(4), 167–183.

Web Marketing Pros. (2020). *How Customer Loyalty Drives Profitability*. Available at https://www.webmarketingpros.com/how-customer-loyalty-drives-profitability/.

CHAPTER 14

The Fourth Industrial Revolution and Digital Platforms as a Strategic Vector of Global Agribusiness Development

Lilia Revenko and Nikolay Revenko

Introduction

Digital innovations in the agricultural sector have changed manufacturing and distribution processes, thus transforming strategies and the business itself. Furthermore, these innovations affect the competitive and institutional environment and the patterns of monopolization, as well as influencing rural and consumer societies.

The assorted modern technological innovations of systemic importance have been called the Fourth Industrial Revolution. This term and its

L. Revenko (✉)
Moscow State Institute of International Relations (MGIMO University), Moscow, Russia
e-mail: l.revenko@inno.mgimo.ru

N. Revenko
Financial University, Moscow, Russia
e-mail: reni100@yandex.ru

N. Konina (ed.), *Digital Strategies in a Global Market*,
https://doi.org/10.1007/978-3-030-58267-8_14

interpretations were formulated by Klaus Schwab, Founder and Executive Chairman of the World Economic Forum (Schwab 2016). Each previous industrial revolution radically changed the mode of production, the use of resources, and the system of economic and social relationships. The specifics of the Fourth Industrial Revolution lie in the breakthrough nature of end-to-end digital technologies that enable the combining biological, physical, and digital spheres of public life.

The Fourth Industrial Revolution, as a global phenomenon, has affected all sectors of the global economy, including the agricultural sector, where all commercially significant aspects of introducing new scientific and technological achievements into economic life have been updated. In recent years, the dominant trend has been the digitalization of agribusiness, radically changing the production and sales of agricultural produce. The main digitalization elements of the agricultural sector, in line with the Fourth Industrial Revolution, include machine-to-machine communication (M2M), the Internet of Things (IOT), artificial intelligence (AI), Big Data, and cloud computing. Almost all of these belong to so-called end-to-end technologies, used in all sectors of the economy. "Smart" or "intelligent" agribusiness also refers to new areas of development, which actively involves a range of technological and technical solutions based on automation and robotics, and helps companies to come to production decisions without (or with minimal) human involvement. This has given rise to new competitive conditions in agriculture, called the digital divide.

The digital platform is often considered the key element of digitalization not just in the agricultural sector, but globally. This article refers to the definition provided by Moazed and Johnson: "A platform is a business model that creates value by facilitating exchanges between two or more interdependent groups, usually consumers and producers" (Moazed and Johnson 2019).

In terms of its characteristics, it is methodologically important to specify how "digital platforms" are defined in agribusiness, so as to classify the object of study. There are multiple approaches to this topic; it is therefore essential to distinguish between the interdisciplinary differences when classifying platforms. As early as in the late twentieth century, information technology sciences classified platforms according to their functions, application, and tools. Defining and measuring the digital economy, as Bukht and Heeks discovered, cannot be done by a universal measure; the classifications of platforms are numerous and varied, and all tend to downplay the actual output of the digital economy in the agricultural sector (Bukht and Heeks 2017).

Analysing the categories of digital platforms, Koskinen, Bonina, and Eaton specify the scope of relevance. They emphasize that the layered architecture and modularity are the characteristics prioritized in research into these platforms. Within the framework of the economic theory, the supply and demand feature of these platforms, as well as their differences from other types of market models, is extensively discussed. When studying information systems, considerable emphasis is placed on their social and technical aspects, such as their impact on organizational structures and international standards (Koskinen et al. 2018).

For the agricultural sector, the need to classify platforms arose later. As of yet, in this field, there is still no unified system of classification. When classifying platforms, the target type is considered. According to Ognivtsev, the Russian agribusiness platform can be broken down into 9 industry-based subplatforms (Ognivtsev 2018). In early definitions, taking into account the target approach, we distinguished between market, production, information, and academic platforms in the agricultural sector (Revenko and Revenko 2019).

The aim of the given research is to reveal the tendencies common for the market, and suggest the operating and information platforms to be developed in the agricultural business sector.

Methods

To research digital agribusiness platform performance, a complex approach whose core principle is its interdisciplinarity (with end-to-end digital characteristics and their utilization) is used. The analysis was carried out using statistics, trends, system-analysis, and matching methods.

Considerable emphasis was placed on the current approaches looking into data, information, and analytics, as received from international companies and agricultural businesses. These have been developed by Russian and international scientists studying platform economy and the digitalization of the agricultural sector, and are theoretically grounded in generalizing and summarizing information about the object of study. Performing these proprietary research methods involves using the author's own classification and definitions.

Results and Discussion

The platform model turned out to be very attractive to agribusiness, due to the automation capacity it offers when dealing with mundane tasks inherent to the agricultural industry. Moreover, digital innovations have contributed to competitive advantages, engaging a more diverse number of participants who pursue global value chain opportunities into production, distribution, and consumption processes in the agricultural market. Figure 14.1 shows what the value chain looks like in the agricultural sector.

The process of developing platforms is based on a wide range of digital innovations and is linked to end-to-end digital solutions. Analysing these ledger technologies, Tripoli and Schmithuber emphasize emerging opportunities for the agri-food industry which enhance its transparency and traceability, lower uncertainty, and make agricultural supply chains more efficient (Tripoli and Schmithuber 2018).

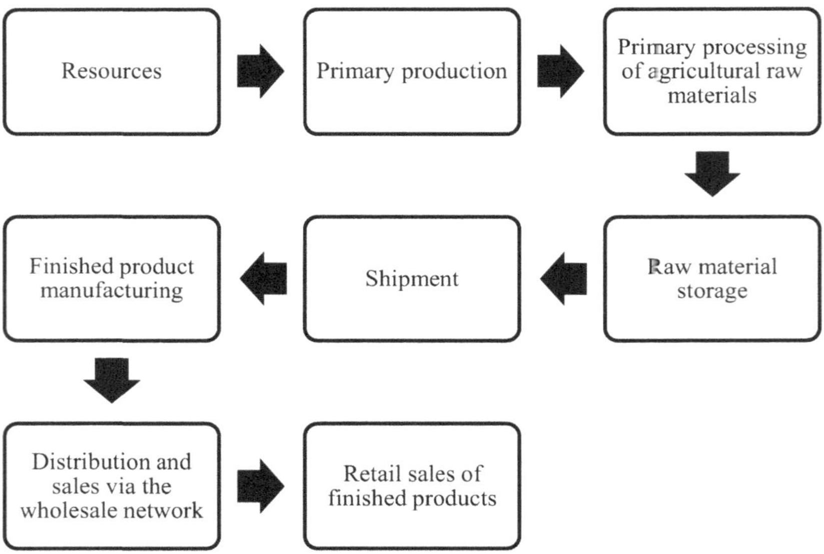

Fig. 14.1 Value chain in the agricultural sector (*Source* Created by the authors)

As commodity and food-processing industries are characterized by loose coupling, developing business platforms in the agriculture sector is considered highly significant.

The level of technology adoption is directly related to the level of maturity across all other business processes, as well as readiness to assume both the advantages and the risks that come from this. However, only industry leaders are able to develop platforms to find solutions to optimization and distribution. The ultimate ambition is to make the digital network accessible to all market players such as commodity traders, producers, sellers, and buyers. The ideal digital platform must facilitate inclusive participation of agriculture giants (integrated both vertically and horizontally), small and middle-sized producers, and their consumers. Such a "one-size fits-all" platform model is hard to achieve, however, as there are gaps—economically, socially, and in knowledge—between market participants, which therefore renders a competitive environment's accessibility uneven. Nevertheless, platform economy contributes to cost and investment reduction. Small and middle-sized companies gain more access to information and management resources, increasing sales and distribution opportunities. Barriers hindering platform development in the agricultural sector are characterized by the overall economic situation from country to country, or region to region, in their particular agriculture market. According to Kiselev, '... the very need to develop digital technology should be based on objective prerequisites and conditions. The industry and economy must be ready to embrace its development and application. The level of human potential, financial capabilities of producers, the degree of development and the state of agricultural production should be highlighted among these conditions' (Kiselev 2018).

There are several types of digital platforms depending on their purpose (Fig. 14.2).

Production and market platforms are fastly growing in the global agriculture sector. One former platform is an Internet of Things platform (IoT-platform), connecting together the production cycle and value chain process.

In agriculture, IoT platforms transmit data between devices installed in places (greenhouses, farms, fields, and other such locations) and data storage centers where information is analysed; this helps companies make better decisions, and monitor and manage production processes without human-to-human intervention. IoT platforms that provide fertilization,

Platform type	Purpose of platform creation
Information platform	• improving the sustainability of the agricultural sector by alining it with the business environment • SDG 2 implementation: achieving food security • environment transparency • monitoring of land resources, alongside weather and climate conditions
Education platform	• improving the overall educational background of rural populations, in particular in developing countries • training young farmers in agricultural skills • transformation of best practices in agriculture and agribusiness • identification of effective methods of agribusiness in inclusive systems
Manufacturing platform	• improving the overall efficiency of economic activity • innovative transformations of the operating process • introducing end-to-end digital technologies in the production of agricultural raw materials and finished goods
Market platform	• transforming business processes • modernizing global operations • optimizing commodity flow chains • transitioning to platform supply models

Fig. 14.2 The main types of digital platforms in the agricultural sector, depending on their purpose (*Source* Created by the authors)

irrigation, pest control, harvesting, and other agrotechnical activities are currently the most widely used in horticulture. In livestock farming, they provide full control over animal health and location, determine the time of feeding, maintenance and milking, and provide care. IoT platforms are widely used in the global agriculture sector to optimize the entire logistical process coordinating shipment, distribution, and storage. Deploying IoT technologies is economically effective, reducing production costs.

The building and launching stages are not as cost-consuming as other hi-tech systems, which makes them economically attractive. The study conducted by Accenture estimates the IoT deployment costs as lower than those of conventional mobile networks (Accenture 2019).

IoT platforms empower resource integration, and spur labor productivity and the optimization of managerial solutions. However, there are also drawbacks, such as employment declining among both qualified and low-skilled workers.

Early market platforms were built as open information platforms, mainly for a price survey and to indicate the situation in supply and demand. Market monitoring was carried out at both global and regional levels. Later functions of agriculture market platforms broadened their scope. Using the analysis of the market changes and artificial intelligence, they started to offer recommendations on facilitating access to banking and insurance products, promoting goods on the market and increasing market transparency.

As in other economic sectors, developing platforms in agriculture businesses (besides optimization and sales) involves a number of objectives, such as an exchange of values between consumers and producers. However, their fulfilment significantly depends on political, macroeconomic, social, and geographical factors. One of the keys to successful digitalization is technology infrastructure, such as a broadband network interface, which allows platforms to reach their full potential. Another barrier to effective performance is a lack of digital skills among workers engaged in agriculture.

The cooperation of companies who are otherwise competing to set up digital platforms is a new trend in the global agriculture market. As noted earlier, transnational agriculture corporations may have subsidiaries in different countries, but they have developed operating activities to coordinate these (Konina et al. 2018). At present, platforms have a great impact on developing business process synchronization.

Thus, in 2018, six global transnational agriculture leaders—Glencore Agriculture Limited, Archer Daniels Midland Company (ADM), Bunge Limited, Cargill Incorporated, COFCO International Ltd, and Louis Dreyfus Company (LDC)—announced the upcoming launch of a new platform with open access for other industry participants (Cargill 2019).

This group of companies intends to modernize global agricultural commodity trade operations. Their digital platform has the potential to transform the industry, making contract execution processes more accurate and transparent. It has been declared that companies of all sizes will benefit from the advances along the post-trade value chain.

Initially, the platform is supposed to automate grain and oilseed post-trade execution processes to move agricultural and food products all over the world. Collaborating on essential issues, such as a business model, adoption strategy, functionalities and capabilities, and choices of security and privacy technology, the group ensures that all the requirements of the entire industry are met.

The group of six companies jointly states that customers, partners, and other industry participants recognize the platform's technological advances. Interestingly, third parties were encouraged to partner with the initiative at the early stages. It was also announced that a pilot will cover shipments of soybeans from Brazil to China. The launch of the new platform is projected for the second half of 2020, subject to regulatory approval.

Global practice proves that introducing digital platforms in agriculture business empowers innovation and technological advances. Contracts made on platforms enable online payments for agricultural goods without delay, reducing costs and minimizing risks for both sellers and buyers. Consequently, the more efficient the supply chain process is, the more sustainable the financial growth.

Monetization is a widely used process in the information and data sector. However, due to unequal levels of digital and technological penetration and skills, access to analytical data is unevenly distributed among agriculture entities, hindering market solutions.

Studying the impact of digital technologies on the global agricultural system, Es and Woodard point out that technological innovations spur movement into developed countries' agricultural and food processing industries, thus increasingly influencing developing countries' economies. Nevertheless, localized resources, low coupling, knowledge and research gaps in rural areas, and unevenly distributed government support are challenges to tackle. All these efforts are necessary and economically justified to support the food security program (Es and Woodard 2017).

The multilateral regulatory policies imposed on digital platforms also must be considered. Many experts, including Bureau, Guimbard, and Jean, emphasize the specificities of the agricultural sector, and note serious contradictions between actors of the international trading system (Bureau et al. 2019). The need to regulate the activity of digital platforms makes these contradictions more acute.

The need to regulate economic activity during the Fourth Industrial Revolution has emerged in all sectors of the economy. Digitalization entailed the development of new rules for regulating the production of agricultural goods and trade in them. To achieve competitive advantages, the goal of accelerating the commercialization of accumulated scientific and technological potential was included by a number of countries to the priorities of their agricultural policy. Hopes for equalizing competitive conditions in agricultural markets are pinned on building a new regulatory environment within the multilateral trading system, although it is fair to assume that the regulatory problems in the agricultural sector, in the context of digital transformation, will grow. This statement is based on an increase in the degree of extraterritoriality of the production and exchange of agricultural goods, when a number of production functions and market decision bases are at a distance from the main land and water resources. The focus of the international community on intensifying the development of a new agricultural policy in the digital area is obvious.

Sustainably providing the population with food and agricultural raw materials is the main reason for international organizations and government agencies to support technological and managerial initiatives. They are aimed at introducing digital technologies, including digital platforms in all links of the production chain and in all countries and regions of the world, taking into account their economic development levels.

In this context, the problem of a certain lag in shaping agricultural policy, from the dynamic implementation of platforms and principles based on them in economic activity, is very acute.

In view of sectoral regional specifics affecting the agricultural sector and common features inherent to the global agricultural system, government support and assistance from international organizations has been called for to aid the development of certain types of platforms, in order to bridge the divide on the competitive digital market. The first important step is to provide producers with all the reliable market information and data required for supply chain engineering.

The driving forces framing digital strategies and concepts in the agriculture sector are twofold: UN specialized agencies, and other international organizations involved in solving market problems. For example, the Food and Agriculture Organization of the United Nations has been contributing to designing national strategies in order to support agricultural development, based on digital technologies and the use of various tools for digitalization by modern agribusiness. There has been a tendency to create digital information platforms by international organizations. These platforms play different roles in the agricultural sector (Table 14.1).

Taking the importance of managing natural resources in agriculture sustainably into account, the FAO launched the System for Earth Observations Data Access, Processing and Analysis for Land Monitoring (SEPAL), a set of free and open-source software tools to help countries

Table 14.1 The role of digital information platforms in the global agricultural sector

Role of digital information platform	*Platform feature*
Innovation role	• Establishing a digital ecosystem • Exchange of best practices • Technological diffusion • Bridging the digital divide
Economic role	• Optimizing the cost structure • Promoting saving resources
Social role	• Exchange of cultural and production traditions • Achieving food security and improving nutrition through better access to food (SDG 2) • Reducing social inequality • Addressing gender-based discrimination
Trade-political role	• Shaping the regulatory environment in the context of digitalization • Searching for digital platform regulatory tools • Global information exchange on regulatory measures for digital interoperability • Identifying risks of insufficient or improper regulation
Market role	• Communication between market actors • Information on the production, distribution, and consumption of agricultural raw materials and food • Price information in various regions of the world
Ecological role	• State of land resources monitoring • Weather and natural disaster monitoring • Data acquisition and exchange on the vital activity of insects and pests • Phytosanitory information exchange

Source Created by the authors

improve their climate change mitigation plans and land-use policies. The FAO estimates that nearly 80% of developing countries are not able to independently collect and analyze information on their land resources.

These tools and reports are used by government agencies, research organizations, and companies to monitor, detect, and assess changes such as state of ground during a plague of locusts or droughts. In 2018, the platform registered 225 organizations in 85 countries among its active users (FAO 2018b).

At the beginning of 2019, the FAO, joined by NASA, developed Collect Earth Online (CEO), a custom built, open-source, satellite image-viewing, and interpretation system integrated in SEPAL. This promotes consistency in monitoring any global land use or landscape changes. The full functionality of the platform makes it easier for agriculture and forestry companies to conduct surveys (FAO 2018a). Through it, any location on Earth can be inspected, providing reference data for landscape assessments.

Another function of information platforms is pest control. This is especially relevant in the fight against desert locusts in Africa and other regions of the world. Data from the global information platform, developed by the FAO in cooperation with the National Aeronautics and Space Administration (NASA) and the European Space Agency (ESA), is available to both national regulatory authorities and farmers through a specially designed application (FAO 2020).

The FAO's global knowledge platform is related to those types of platforms that help users receive information and analytics to empower sustainable supply chains in the food industry (FAO 2019). The platform allows representatives from government agencies and agribusiness companies, project managers, and researchers to communicate and exchange value chain data (FAO 2017).

However, there are other information platforms or information portals, such as Agricultural Market Information System (AMIS), set up by a number of international organizations.

Currently, the information platforms support small and medium-sized agriculture businesses most considerably, reducing the digital divide in the sector.

Conclusion

Digital technologies determine the overall vector of agricultural business strategies in the era of the Fourth Industrial Revolution. The modern paradigm of agriculture and agribusiness development is based on the principle of interconnectedness between the production and the sale processes of agricultural raw materials and finished products. This creates not only new advantages, but also new risks for business and society.

The influence of digital platforms, both on agribusinesses and on the global agriculture goods trade, is quite ambiguous. On the one hand, platform models enable agribusinesses to accelerate and optimize their activities, thus saving their resources. Increasing market transparency encourages small and medium-sized companies to offer their produce to the market, changing the distribution pattern. On the other hand, the digital divide between companies working at different high-tech levels means competition is increasing. This situation leads to negative social and economic consequences, such as a layoff of up to 15%.

The problem of digital divide in the agricultural sector can be reduced by implementing efficient corrective measures. This would regulate the agricultural commodities market against the backdrop of ever-developing platform-based business models. However, this process is far from complete. One positive trend is joining the efforts of civil society, market regulators, and business representatives to develop new rules for agribusiness operations in the digital environment. With proper regulation, such platforms will provide agribusiness entities at the stage of the Fourth Industrial Revolution with greater income while maintaining social balance.

References

Accenture. (2019). *Accenture Technology Vision 2019*. Available at https://www.accenture.com/_acnmedia/PDF-94/Accenture-TechVision-2019-Tech-Trends-Report.pdf#zoom=50.

Bukht, R., & Heeks, R. (2017). Defining, Conceptualising and Measuring the Digital Economy. Paper No. 68, *Center for Development Informatics, Global Development Institute, University of Manchester, Manchester*. Available at http://hummedia.manchester.ac.uk/institutes/gdi/publications/workingpapers/di/di_wp68.pdf.

Bureau, J.-C., Guimbard, H., & Jean, S. (2019). Agricultural Trade Liberalisation in the 21st Century: Has It Done the Business? *Journal of Agricultural Economics, 70*(1), 3–25.

Cargill. (2019). *Glencore Agriculture Limited Joins ADM, Bunge, Cargill, COFCO International and LDC in Industry-Wide Initiative to Modernize Global Agriculture Commodity Trade Operations*. Available at https://www.cargill.com/2019/glencore-agriculture-limited-joins-industry-wide-initiative.

Es, van H., & Woodard, J. (2017). Innovation in Agriculture and Food Systems in the Digital Age. *Global Innovation Index 2017, World Intellectual Property Organization, Cornel SC Johnson College of Business and INSEAD*, Geneva, 97–104.

FAO. (2017). *Building Agricultural Market Information Systems: A Literature Review*. Available at http://www.fao.org/3/a-i7151e.pdf.

FAO. (2018a). *FAO and NASA Launch Next-Generation Geospatial Tool*. Available at http://www.fao.org/news/story/en/item/1173756/icode/.

FAO. (2018b). *Open FORIS and SEPAL (System for Earth Observation Data Access, Processing and Analysis for Land Monitoring)*. Available at http://www.fao.org/3/CA1085EN/ca1085en.pdf.

FAO. (2019). *Sustainable Food Value Chain Knowledge Platform*. Available at http://www.fao.org/sustainable-food-value-chains/home/en/. Accessed 15 December 2019.

FAO. (2020). *In East Africa, a Race to Outsmart Locusts with Drones and Data. In Conversation with Keith Cressman—FAO Senior Locust Forecasting Officer*. Available at http://www.fao.org/fao-stories/article/en/c/1270472/.

Kiselev, S. V. (2018). *Prospects, Risks and Challenges of Digital Technologies Development in the Rural Sector of Russian Economy*. In Lomonosov Readings 2018, Economic Sciences Section, Digital Economy: Human Being, Technology, Institutes: Collection of Essays, Economic Department, Lomonosov Moscow State University, Moscow, pp. 241–247. Available at https://www.econ.msu.ru/sys/raw.php?o=50907&p=attachment (in Russian).

Konina, N. Y. et al. (2018). *Current Issues of Management, Marketing and Entrepreneurship*. Moscow: MGIMO-University (in Russian).

Koskinen, K., Bonina, C., & Eaton, B. (2018). *Digital Platforms in the Global South: Foundations and Research Agenda*. Paper No. 8, Center for Development Informatics, Global Development Institute, University of Manchester, Manchester. Available at https://diodeweb.files.wordpress.com/2018/10/digital-platforms-diode-paper.pdf.

Moazed, A., & Johnson, N. (2019). *Platform, Practical Application of a Revolutionary Business Model*. Moscow: Alpina Publisher (in Russian).

Ognivtsev, A. B. (2018). The Conception of the Digital Platform in the Agricultural Complex. *International Agriculture Journal, 2*(362), 16–22 (in Russian).

Revenko, L. S., & Revenko, N. S. (2019). Digital Information Planforms as Driver for Increasing Agricultural Markets Transparency. *Russian Foreign Economic Journal, 7*, 21–33 (in Russian).

Schwab, K. (2016). *The Fourth Industrial Revolution*. Geneva: World Economic Forum.

Tripoli, M., & Schmidhuber, J. (2018). *Emerging Opportunities for the Application of Blockchain in the Agri-Food Industry*. Rome and Geneva: FAO and ICTSD.

CHAPTER 15

Retail Business Models in the Era of the Fourth Industrial Revolution

Ekaterina Bostoganashvili

Introduction

The recent trend for digitalization is paving the way for a transformation of traditional business models, spurring competitive advantages and effective business performance. The process is accelerated by several key factors, such as newly developed end-to-end digital innovations, or changes in customers' behaviour and competitors' activities.

The phenomenon of digitalization was first mentioned by Don Tapscott, a Canadian scholar, in 1995. In his book 'The Digital Economy' he defined it as founded on information and computer technologies (Telekhov 2016). At the same time, the term 'data economy' was coined by Negroponte, who identified the digital economy as a new technological trend based on digital technologies (Negroponte 1995). According to Peres, the digital economy is the fifth technological paradigm, and

E. Bostoganashvili (✉)
Moscow State Institute of International Relations (MGIMO University), Moscow, Russia
e-mail: eka_94@live.ru

N. Konina (ed.), *Digital Strategies in a Global Market*,
https://doi.org/10.1007/978-3-030-58267-8_15

is capable of restarting competition (Peres 2011). In 2015, the Organization for Economic Cooperation and Development (OECD) explicitly defined the digital economy as the amalgamation of several non-specific technologies for general use in the sphere of information and communication (Osterwalder et al. 2005). Nevertheless, it is worth stating that one universally acknowledged definition of the digital economy is yet to be established.

At the end of the twentieth century, various types of information and communication technologies, alongside robotics, into many processes were actively being implemented; however, automation had predominantly local character, whereby each company or unit within a company used its own control system that was incompatible with other systems. Further development of the internet, information and communication technologies, cloud technologies, and digital platforms has provided the emergence of global industrial networks and open information systems. Such networks and systems transform all sectors of business and the modern economy, and transfer industrial automation to a new, fourth stage of industrialization. The key components of Industry 4.0 should include the elements of the Internet of Things, artificial intelligence, machine learning, Big Data technologies, additive manufacturing, cybersecurity, integration system, augmented reality, and so on. Many of the above elements have long been used in practice; their integration into a coherent system made it possible to develop the concept of Industry 4.0, as well as generate additional income through the use of end-to-end digital technologies, the implementation of innovative business models, and the formation of network interaction with other market entities.

A prerequisite for maintaining the competitiveness of modern retail companies is the use of advanced digital technologies. The technologies of artificial intelligence, the Internet of Things, and Big Data are called the drivers of the Fourth Industrial Revolution. Such technologies open up wide opportunities for optimizing business processes, improving the quality of customer service, and cutting costs (Stonehouse and Konina 2020). For example, analysis of Big Data in retail opens the way for price adjustments, geolocation data analytics (to determine the most attractive locations for outlets), optimization of supply chains based on analysis of traffic congestion, a better understanding of needs structure, and so on. In turn, artificial intelligence technologies analyze CCTV and collect all the necessary information for predictive analytics. Based on the analysis of the movement of customers, decisions are made on the organization of the trading space. Such technologies can predict the flow of customers, calculate the need for staff, and, accordingly, create a flexible schedule. Of course, all modern technologies, which are called the drivers of the Fourth Industrial Revolution, are at different stages of their development, but despite this, it is now obvious that they have great potential for improving the efficiency of managing retail companies, strengthening automation processes, conducting high-quality data analytics, and being employed in many other ways.

The main principles of Industry 4.0 lie in interoperability, virtualization, decentralization (cyberphysical systems should be able to make their own decisions), functioning in real time (data collection should take place in real time), service orientation, and also modularity. Functional interoperability implies that cyber-physical systems and people should be able to communicate through the Internet of Things technologies. Virtualization involves virtual copies (digital twins).

Analysing the theoretical and methodological background behind the digital economy, several main scopes of its study can be seen. Firstly, most scholars describe the impact digital technologies have on different aspects of people's lives; at present, end-to-end innovations is one particular focus of analysis. Secondly, they study how traditional institutions apply particular aspects of digital transformation. Thirdly, researchers pay attention to the technical features of digital economy, such as its infrastructure, digital platforms, and others.

The transformation process consists of several inter-related stages. The journey towards digitalization requires three key steps: working with clients, developing operation processes, and building up a company's business models (Garifullin and Zyabrikov 2018). Working with clients involves profound knowledge of their needs and experience, revenue growth from loyal customers, and identifying customer touchpoints. Operation processes include production automation, encouraging staff creativity, and improving performance management based on big data. Transforming business models means implementing digital innovations with pinpoint accuracy, and introducing revolutionary business models and digital globalization (Garifullin and Zyabrikov 2019). Companies grounded in traditional sectors tend to adopt digital solutions to suboptimize their business processes rather than to transform them fundamentally. The business landscape has been significantly changed by the implementation of such novel models (digital platforms) (Stepnov and Kovalchuk 2018); these have transformed several areas, including, for example, the retail sector. The term 'digital globalization' means that companies embrace structured information and digital technologies to enjoy global synergy, whilst at the same time being able to adjust to local criteria. The process of combining localization and globalization is called 'glocalization'. Through these stages, digital transformation is shown to be a well-conceived strategy that is based on integration of technological innovations.

B2C sectors have always been at the forefront of implementing end-to-end digital technologies; taking this into account, the author looks into the problem of business model transformation as provoked by the Fourth Industrial Revolution (particularly within retail companies), and conducts a comparative analysis of business models.

Chesbrough defines a company's business model as its plan for making a profit and creating value (Chesbrough 2006). Mustafa and Werthner identify it as a conceptual description of the goods and services the company buys and sells (Mustafa and Werthner 2011). According to Osterwalder et al. a business model is a tool comprising of a set of assumptions, hypotheses, and interactions; upon these, the company's intention for making its money is logically founded (Osterwalder et al. 2005). The author interprets the term 'business model' as a way of organizing a particular business, reflecting the logic behind the business' activity and how it creates customer value.

Methodology

The present research was conducted using general scientific methods and took a comprehensive approach to solving problems. The given work is founded on papers by both Russian and international scholars who studied different aspects of the Fourth Industrial Revolution and its impact on business activities.

Results

At present, there are more and more companies transforming their ineffective business models and embracing sophisticated ones in order to meet higher customer demand. Whilst there are indisputably different approaches to the classification and comparison of business models, the author suggests emphasizing two significant groups in particular: traditional and platform business models.

Platform models create value via digital innovations; this makes real time cooperation more effective, and provides trust and equal access to information for all participants of this platform or ecosystem. Also, unfair competition, and the abuse of market power, is prevented through this model.

Traditional business models, however, create value through linear processes or value chains; a company's profit increases by decreasing input value and reducing production costs, as well as by increasing output value.

Economic ecosystems are similar to natural ecosystems. A natural ecosystem is the habitat and environment in which living organisms interact together, where each component is responsible for a particular function. Similarly, an economic ecosystem consists of its participants (for example, companies and individuals) and the resources these participants contribute to it (for example, software applications, ideas, information, etc.) As a rule, companies working with business platforms build up not physical products, but non-physical (e.g. digital) products; these include platforms which enable other participants of this ecosystem to interact with each other, or tools which can regulate such interactions and distribute resources within an ecosystem. The value of any ecosystem depends on its size; thus, the more participants join in, the more valuable it is for each participant, and the more attractive it is for new participants. This phenomenon is called the 'network effect'. Today it plays an important part in ecosystem business models (Gawer and Cusumano 2014). Ecosystems reflect the direction of economic development and undermine the position of companies adhering to traditional business models.

There is a large number of diverse business ecosystems, yet despite their variety they all have a set of characteristics that distinguish them from other business models. The first is modularity. Unlike hierarchical supply chain models, in business ecosystems, parts of a proposal are developed by participants independently of each other. Customers are free to formulate combinations of components. The second feature is adaptation. Each ecosystem member contributes and adapts to the concept of their ecosystem. The third characteristic is their dependency. Ecosystem business models take the form of a large network of business relationships, within which all participants are dependent on each other. The fourth aspect is their coordination. Ecosystem business models do not imply standard control methods; instead, there is a mechanism for coordinating all business processes through upholding standards and following certain rules. Ecosystem business models have several important benefits: they provide access to a wide range of possibilities, are flexible and stable.

Table 15.1 Comparative analysis of traditional and platform models

Criteria	*Traditional business model*	*Platform business model*
The methods of interaction	Low speed of interaction based on one or more links in the value chain	High-speed platform-based interaction
Additional restrictions	Country and territorial restrictions	No additional restrictions
The level of costs	High level of costs; Low cost of entering the business;	Low level of costs; High cost of entering the business

Source Created by the author

Traditional business models use a number of intermediaries (sometimes merely one) between the customer and the company providing services in order to create value. Business platforms eliminate intermediaries, reducing time and money expenditure. Platform models offer direct interaction between market participants in real time, as well as minimal transaction costs and a low barrier to entry (see Table 15.1).

Traditional business models have limits and barriers which hinder effective cooperation between market participants, such as territorial restrictions between countries. Before e-commerce platforms, delivering goods from one country to another was impossible at minimum cost.

Comparative Analysis of Platform Models

Two main types of platforms (ecosystems) can be distinguished: innovation platforms and transaction platforms (Evans and Schmalensee 2016). Table 15.2 presents the examples of such platforms.

According to another classification, there are three types of business platforms: internal platforms (based on digital twin technology), integration platforms, and multi-sided platforms. Digital twin platforms are particularly popular with companies engaged in the production sector, as the development and the introduction of complex physical products to the market requires working within the extended ecosystem their partners use. Integration platforms are a market type; as a rule, companies in a similar sphere unite two users, facilitate their communication on the platform, and adjust supply to the demand of this particular market, and if a solution can be found which makes both parties content (for example,

Table 15.2 Transaction and innovation ecosystems

	Transaction ecosystem	*Innovation ecosystem*
Benefits	The provision of the transactions between the different organizations; The possibility for the exchange of information, goods, or services;	A large number of developers are working on the creation of unique products and applications for the ecosystem, which allows third-party companies to add additional products and services to the main product;
Examples	Amazon Marketplace, Uber, Airbnb, eBay, Alibaba, etc.	Google Android, Apple iPhone, Amazon Web Services, etc.

Source Created by the author

online shops help to reduce costs through supply chain network optimization), the platform is considered a success. Multi-sided platforms involve at least four groups of participants: although other participants can be a factor, the four key groups are a platform owner, independent app developers, marketing partners, and consumers. Unlike integration platforms, multi-sided platforms hire independent app developers, who become responsible for creating and maintaining surplus goods and services and who greatly contribute to their success. Multi-sided platforms benefit from mass cooperation based on transparency, international activity, and information exchange. Importantly, in this context, API tools are what makes it easy for independent developers to access platforms. Consequently, the most remarkable feature of multi-sided platforms is their transparency and their permeability; for example, Amazon evolved from an integration platform into a multi-sided platform after it gave free data access to third parties and invited its rivals to use the platform. Whilst integration platforms benefit from the network effect, multi-sided models thrive on the activity of independent participants who create value—their resources, knowledge, or time. Such digital platforms play a crucial role in the sharing economy or peer economy, being the most integral part. Consequently, collaborative innovations, generated by big-data technologies, contribute to development of multi-sided platforms.

Accordingly, in the given paper, the author carries out a detailed comparative analysis of integration platforms and multi-sided platforms according to a number of criteria, such as their purpose, particular characteristics, participants, level of transparency, and the owner's activity.

Integration platforms provide the capabilities to simplify communication between different participants and to enable access to the market; multi-sided platforms are built up to develop business ecosystems with different partners. As for specific features, activities within integration platforms are based on providing service solutions (for example e-commerce platforms); multi-sided platforms provide network access for independent participants working according to established rules and standards. Integration platforms operate as a closed central system; multi-sided platforms offer differentiated levels of transparency for different actors. Integration platforms are used by suppliers and clients (who in some cases can become partners); the actors who perform on multi-sided platforms are independent third-party developers, marketing partners, clients, or partners providing services. Owners of integration platforms act as aggregators, arranging the interaction amongst the participants; owners of multi-sided platforms are responsible for designing its architecture, levels of transparency, collaborative mechanisms, management, and the rules and standards for accessibility and development.

It is important, regarding business platform models, to consider the multiple user groups these models cater to. Platform owners have to build up relationships with consumers and other concerned parties; however, the author assumes that platform owners are more interested in fostering relationships with partners and third-party developers, as they provide maintenance services for the platform. As a rule, network partners generate profit, which is why value propositions are offered to both customers and partners. A crucial, challenging task for any platform-based company is to decide on how to monetize their work, and to develop a motivational system to encourage new participants to join in. Analysing a company's activity allows the most common approaches to monetization to be identified, including: commission (for example, Uber), transaction fee (for example, Visa), subscription, advertising (Alibaba, Google), franchising, affiliate programme or revenue sharing programme (Amazon), and others.

Platform holders enjoy the monopolization of their chosen ecosystem, letting other products and services have access to their database's user interface. Furthermore, they dictate the platform's terms and define its regulations, yet, as a rule, the ecosystem's value increases without much effort from its holder. In this context, it should be noted that—compared to traditional strategies—platform businesses are highly regarded by investors; for example, in the S&P 500 Index, they are estimated to earn nine times as much annually as the average, compared to traditional companies who earn approximately four times as much as the average annually. Platform companies are growing faster than traditional ones, and their market capitalization is significantly higher than that of traditional companies (see Table 15.3). Besides business platform holders, manufactures and clients also benefit from them. Ecosystems facilitate easy access to products and services produced by independent developers, making them visible and available.

The author emphasizes several common mistakes when building up business platform models: choosing the wrong pricing strategy, failing to instil consumer confidence, underestimating competitors, and being unable to determine market viability. Eventually, many platforms tend to develop due to the network effect, which means designing appropriate pricing strategies and choosing subsidized sides. For example, Amazon and Aliaba have resorted to aggressive subsidizing strategies which spurred their rapid profit growth. Trust is also one of the keys to success. For example, eBay failed to establish trust in China, but in contrast, the Taobao platform succeeded in providing the necessary mechanisms.

Obviously, not all retailers use business platforms such as e-commerce platforms, but there is no doubt that, for companies working in the retail market sector, integrated digital infrastructure and pinpointed solutions have considerable advantages reducing customer response time. Online trading is enjoying a fast growth compared to offline trading methods, as it is usually preferable. In addition, it should be noted that platform

Table 15.3 Top retail companies in the world by market capitalization (as on 01.03.2020)

№	*Company*	*Country*	*Market capitalization (US$B)*
1	Amazon	US	929.6
2	Alibaba	China	600.5
3	Walmart	US	330.7
4	Home Depot	US	238.3
5	Comcast	US	216.7

Source Developed by the author on the base of PwC. (2020). Global Top 100 Companies by Market Capitalization—Mode of Access. https://www.pwc.com/gx/en/audit-services/publications/assets/global-top-100-companies-2020.pdf business models, combined with a high customer focus, provoke the transition from the sale of goods to the provision of services. For example, in the current conditions, an increasing number of consumers prefer not to purchase goods into property, but to pay for the provision of a service to which they gain access through various kinds of digital platforms. This trend has great potential and allows for more sustainable and transparent models for the exchange of goods and services.

Traditional retailers tend to fully embrace omnichannel strategies, which provide an integrated approach and enable customers to choose the most suitable way of making a purchase. As a rule, the term omnichannel is used to describe technologies for synchronizing various sales channels, as well as optimizing interaction with customers. From a technological point of view, an important condition for the development of omnichannel sales is the availability of specialized software. The growing interest in omnichannel business models is evidenced by the steady increase in revenue for software companies. An analysis of the American B2C markets shows that the effect of implementing an omnichannel business model is 2–4 times higher than the combined effect of multichannel sales (Gasparyan 2015). With an efficiently built omnichannel business model, the consumer should not feel the difference in sales channels. The omnichannel approach implies that the buyer has the right to choose across every stage of their journey purchasing goods. Omnichannel involves providing seamless integrated trading, which requires several important steps: calculating long-term investments in the development of technological infrastructure that supports omnichannel sales, defining organizational, technological, and process rules for synchronization between channels, and forming an approach to pricing in various sales channels. Building such a business model requires a clear understanding of how omnichannel management will affect inventory management, logistics, product policy, marketing, etc. In addition, it should be noted that, in a truly omnichannel model, the consumer should not see the price differences in various channels, although the magnitude and the structure of costs in the online and offline segments are different.

Moreover, there are other business models that aim to make the most of the advantages of the Fourth Industrial Revolution; one such example is those business models based on the type of customer focus. Within the framework of such business models, the activities of companies are focused on processes directly related to customer service. In turn, business models—reinforced by data—create new sources of revenue through access to valuable consumer information. To a greater extent, such companies rely on analytics and data retrieval software. Of course, these transformations suggest that companies will invest heavily in data security and cybersecurity systems to prevent direct hacking of their systems, as well as unintentional failures of the digital infrastructure.

New business models also increase the need to rethink corporate culture and professional skills due to new qualification requirements. Companies must learn to work on the basis of the so-called 'talentism' concept, which focuses on highly qualified personnel. This is one of the highest priority factors for the development of competitiveness in the era of the Fourth Industrial Revolution. Over time, an increasing number of retail companies will move away from hierarchical structures to network-type models defined by network collaboration and interaction. The development of many companies in the industry reflects such changes, based on the rapid growth of their introduction of the latest technologies in combination with the Internet of Things. All this gradually gives companies the opportunity to combine the physical and digital spheres.

In addition, it should be added that the Fourth Industrial Revolution creates both enormous advantages and problems. The platform effect leads to the concentration and dominance of several powerful platforms.

Conclusion

Digital information is the core resource of the digital economy. Digital innovation and data facilitate economic growth. The digital economy can be characterized by growing knowledge of, and innovation with, implemented digital strategies, depending on company's organizational knowledge.

To successfully implement digital technologies and transform business models, a consistently articulated executive vision and strong leadership are necessary, and well-conceived strategies for changing the internal culture, as well as the coordination and prioritization of transformation initiatives, are also required.

As noted earlier, the platform, which was made possible due to the emergence of network effects during the transition to digital space, is one of the highest priority models for the industry. Even during the Third Industrial Revolution, digital platforms emerged, but a distinctive feature of the Fourth Industrial Revolution was the emergence of so-called global platforms, which are very closely connected with the physical world.

With growing demands, there are more and more companies moving towards the virtual sector and business platform models. Platform strategies help to combine the economy of scale effect and offer a customized approach for every consumer. Thus, companies provide speedy services due to costs being reduced and intermediary chains being eliminated. Ecosystem business models utilize external resources which require minimal expenses (ideas, information, clients, etc.), but their deployment is rather cost-intensive and requires considerable changes in management strategies.

Traditional retailers often aim to integrate digital platforms in their business models, or to use them partnering with other companies (i.e. Walmart). In the given context, the significant challenge is to leverage ecosystems contributing to traditional business models. Furthermore, digital technologies and virtual companies transform conventional business models and spur omnichannel growth, providing seamless and on-going communication with consumers.

References

Chesbrough, H. (2006). *Open Innovation: The New Imperative for Creating and Profiting from Technology*. Boston, MA: Harvard Business Press.

Evans, D. S., & Schmalensee, R. (2016). *Matchmakers: The New Economics of Multisided Platforms*. Boston, MA: Harvard Business Review Press.

Garifullin, B. M., & Zyabrikov, V. V. (2018). Tsifrovaya transformatsiya biznesa: modeli i algoritmy [Digital Transformation of Business: Models and Algorithms]. *Kreativnaya ekonomika, 12*(9), 1345–1358. https://doi.org/10.18334/ce.12.9.39332.

Garifullin, B. M., & Zyabrikov, V. V. (2019). Vidy biznes-modeley kompaniy v tsifrovoy ekonomike [Types of Business Models of Companies in the Digital Economy]. *Kreativnaya ekonomika, 13*(1), 83–92. https://doi.org/10.18334/ce.13.1.39720.

Gasparyan, V. (2015). Omnikanal'nyj ritejl v Rossii: mify i real'nost' [Omni-Channel Retail in Russia: Myths and Reality]. Retail&loyalty, *7*, 80–86.

Gawer, A., & Cusumano, M. (2014). Industry Platforms and Ecosystem Innovation. *Journal of Product Innovation Management, 31*(3), 417–433.

Mustafa, R., & Werthner, H. (2011). Business Models and Business Strategy—Phenomenon of Explicitnes. *International Journal of Global Business & Competitiveness, 6*(1), 15–30.

Negroponte, N. (1995). *Being Digital*. New York: Knopf.

Osterwalder, A., Pigneur, Y., & Tucci, C. L. (2005). Clarifying Business Models: Origins, Present and Future of the Concept. *Communications of the Association for Information Systems, 15*(1),1–25.

Peres K. (2011). *Tekhnologicheskie revolyutsii i finansovyy kapital: dinamika puzyrey i periodov protsvetaniya* [*Technological Revolutions and Financial Capital: Dynamics of Bubbles and Periods of Prosperity*]. Moscow: Delo (in Russian).

PwC. (2020). Global Top 100 Companies by Market Capitalization—Mode of access. https://www.pwc.com/gx/en/audit-services/publications/assets/global-top-100-companies-2020.pdf.

Stepnov, I. M., & Kovalchuk, J. A. (2018). Platform Capitalism as the Source of Digital Rentier's Superprofit. *MGIMO Review of International Relations, 4*(61), 107–124 (In Russ.). https://doi.org/10.24833/2071-8160-2018-4-61-107-124.

Stonehouse, G. H., & Konina, N. Y. (2020). Management Challenges in the Age of Digital Disruption. Conference Paper. *Conference: Proceedings of the 1st International Conference on Emerging Trends and Challenges in the Management Theory and Practice (ETCMTP 2019)*. https://doi.org/10.2991/aebmr.k.200201.001.

Telekhov, I. I. (2016). *Analiz innovatsionno-investitsionnyh proektov so vstroennymi realnymi optsionami* [*Analysis of r&d Innovation Projects with Embedded Real Options*]. Bulletin of St. Petersburg University. Series 5, No. 3, pp. 155–175 (in Russian). https://doi.org/10.21638/11701/spbu05.2016.309.

CHAPTER 16

Digital Tools in Empirical Marketing Strategies of Global Hotel Companies

Raisa Nozdreva and Anna Churakova

Introduction

Fundamental technological transformations, which are currently taking place in all areas of activity, indicate the beginning of a qualitatively new stage of industrial development. According to Schwab, the founder of the World Economic Forum, humanity is at the beginning of the Fourth Industrial Revolution, which "began at the turn of this century and builds on the digital revolution. It is characterised by a much more ubiquitous and mobile internet, by smaller and more powerful sensors that have become cheaper, and by artificial intelligence and machine learning" (Schwab 2016). Schwab furthermore emphasises the historical importance of the ongoing processes.

R. Nozdreva · A. Churakova (✉)
Moscow State Institute of International Relations (MGIMO University), Moscow, Russia
e-mail: a.a.churakova@yandex.ru

R. Nozdreva
e-mail: rbnauka2020@rambler.ru

N. Konina (ed.), *Digital Strategies in a Global Market*, https://doi.org/10.1007/978-3-030-58267-8_16

Schwab also considers that the fundamental difference of the Fourth Industrial Revolution is in "the fusion of technologies and their interaction across the physical, digital and biological domains". Interdisciplinary research creates opportunities for breakthroughs in a wide range of technologies which can instigate a sharp increase in production efficiency and labour productivity. The processes of profound transformation are interdependent; they affect the economic, social, cultural, and humanitarian spheres of life and society in general.

Rapid integration of technologies in all spheres of public life, as well as the rising dynamism of the global economy and changing consumer behaviour, increase global competition. Existing business models are put under considerable pressure as traditional companies try to compete with tech-driven start-ups (Stonehouse and Konina 2020). These challenges accelerate the development of marketing; new concepts are being formulated based on the use of digital technologies. The famous American marketing theorist Kotler introduces the concept of "Marketing 4.0", which characterises the marketing activities of companies in the digital environment (Kotler et al. 2017).

The principal characteristic of the new marketing phase is the dominant influence of the consumer. Digital technologies enable consumers to publicly express their opinion about the quality of products and services and the quality of experience provided by the company. Consumers can leave comments on companies' public pages and on review sites, whose reputation depends on the veracity of left comments. Moreover, digital technologies allow customers to express a general need for new products and services. The client becomes the primary driving force of business development in the modern digital economy. "Prosumer", as the combination of "Producer" and "Consumer" (Toffler 2008). According to the scientist, this term highlights the active role of consumers in product creation. Establishing long-term relationships with consumers becomes an indispensable condition for the company's economic success.

With respect to studying customer experience management and its influence on companies' competitive strength, a considerable theoretical base has recently been developed by the works of such authors as Grewal, Puccinelli, Jaakkola, and Nozdreva. Empirical marketing is based on modern ideas regarding consumer decision-making, and particularly the irrational nature of this process. The new theoretical approach suggests customer behaviour is based not on economic expediency (minimised costs and maximised benefits), but on the influence of various mental and social factors (Nozdreva 2018).

Whereas prior research in this area was focused on customer satisfaction, the formation of positive customer experiences currently attracts more attention. Contemporary researchers believe that this approach exerts the greatest influence on the establishment of successful relations between the company and the customer. Customer experience comprises of every contact held between the customer and the company, whether before, during, or after the consumption of a product or service. This includes the aggregate of physical, intellectual, and emotional contacts experienced by an individual when communicating with a given brand (Kandampully et al. 2015).

Customer experience management is especially important for the hospitality industry (Kandampully and Solnet 2015), because this industry involves extensive customer-company relations. According to Gartner, 89% of its players aim to offer a better experience to their customers (Gartner 2014). It is noted that customer experience influences their loyalty, and a company's market performance. Currently, customer experience management is recognised as one of the most promising approaches towards achieving success in service industries (Homburg et al. 2015).

Until recently, many dominating brands based their reputation on meeting consumer expectations, delivering products and services stably. Developing any new products or services had to meet the needs of a certain group of customers. However, as digital products actively evolve, consumer standards undergo transformation (Churakova 2019). The emergence of digital companies in the field of services, such as Airbnb and HotelTonight, significantly influences the shaping of customer expectations and values and, as a consequence, the modes of decision-making. Demands regarding communication with hotel companies are changing accordingly. Digital companies transform the standards for customer interaction by creating a simpler and more intuitively understandable interaction, which is also characterised by a high degree of personalisation and adaptability. Any customer who has experienced comfortable interactions with high-tech companies expects a similar level of communication from other hospitality businesses too. Excellent service is no longer a guarantee of brand loyalty (Lin et al. 2019). Customers expect a personalised experience, and value it so highly that it has become the basis for loyalty and a critical advantage in effective brand promotion (Sabre Hospitality Solutions 2018).

The process of customer-company interaction is evolving in both physical and virtual spaces, through interactive communication: websites, social media, mobile applications, etc. (Ponsignon et al. 2015). Contemporary researchers stress that it is important for the company to establish a continuous long-term connection with its customer, particularly via online activities. Many authors, including Litvin, Zhou, Park, Hailey, Chaffey, and Smith, study the potential of using certain digital marketing tools in order to support interaction with customers. It is emphasised that success hinges on convenient, intuitively understandable and integrated interaction between the brand and its customer, and furthermore on the capability of offering each guest a unique personalised product at any and every point of contact with the brand, be that in a virtual or a physical space. In this regard, the need remains to measure the quality and efficiency of cross-channel interaction (Hossain 2017).

Despite the evident importance and necessity to perform tasks relating to shaping positive customer experiences, most initiatives along this line fail, and very few companies has achieved an in-depth understanding of the customer experience management process (Forrester Research 2014). The decisive factors of empirical marketing efficiency are a comprehensive approach and cross-channel interaction. While technologies are being invested in and developed in order to increase the scope and efficiency of particular elements, without a focus on personalisation and guest experience, such investments do not, as a rule, produce any perceivable outcome, since they are based on multi-channel rather than cross-channel interaction. This results in fragmented communication, without a clearly formulated idea as to what the customer will perceive at each point of contact and to what extent it will influence his or her relationship with the brand. This lack of personal connection with the customer results in a failure to understand the degree to which various technology tools influence the customer's behaviour. Studies regarding this issue do not give any specific idea as to the methods for practical use of empirical marketing strategies by global hotel companies.

That being said, the hospitality market is one of the fastest-growing and highly competitive international markets, and therefore major hotel chains worldwide continue to enhance their efforts to develop and implement various such tools.

This article seeks to systematise the practical approaches of some of the largest international hotel chains towards managing customer experience with the use of digital tools. The purpose of the study is to analyse the experiences international hotel companies have had using Internet-based tools in order to implement their empirical marketing strategies.

Methodology

This paper reviews the experience of practically implementing empirical marketing methods with the use of digital tools by six international hotel chains: Wyndham Hotels & Resorts, Marriott Hotels and Resorts, Radisson Hotel Group, AccorHotels, InterContinental Hotels Group, and Hilton Hotels and Resorts. *The share of chain hotels in the global market is currently about 13% (2018) and is predicted to grow to* 21% *by 2027.* The chain hotels' business is anticipated to increase from $74 bn in 2018 to $178.6 bn by 2027 (Transparency Market Research 2019).

For the purposes of this analysis, the largest international chains were selected, since it is those companies that possess the technology, the physical potential, and the human potential to implement empirical marketing strategies, and have sufficient reasons to invest in the creation of an integral online infrastructure in order to gain a competitive edge in the growing market. Using a system analysis, the author has reviewed the practical activities of the hotel chains in the following areas: the operation of a website, presence on social media, and the functioning of an Internet application. The author has examined whether these areas are integrated and whether it is possible to put together an integral online infrastructure as the basis for forming a unified customer digital path.

In order to conduct this study, the author has used data from the hotel chains' official websites, the Google Play and AppStore application stores, and the companies' official accounts on the following social media: Facebook, Twitter, YouTube, Instagram, and Pinterest. The functionalities of the mobile applications under review have been determined from the descriptions of their respective developers and the author's testing. The study has identified 49 factors that shape digital customer experience. Based on the aspects they are aimed at, all of the factors have been grouped into six major categories:

1. The operational stability of an interaction channel
2. The functionality of an interaction channel
3. The convenience of an interaction channel
4. The ability to personalise the approach and the ability to select the communication language

5. Integration among the interaction channels and the ability to switch into another channel without the loss of any data
6. The updating of information and the generation of digital elements

Furthermore, the author has analysed whether the digital channels being used by the hotel chains conform to the criteria for the shaping of a positive digital customer experience.

Results

Each of the global hotel chains has developed its own unique infrastructure, intended to support its interaction with customers by using numerous digital channels belonging to three key areas: a website, social media, and mobile applications (Fig. 16.1). In addition to the above areas, email campaigns could also be a criterion, but it would be difficult to

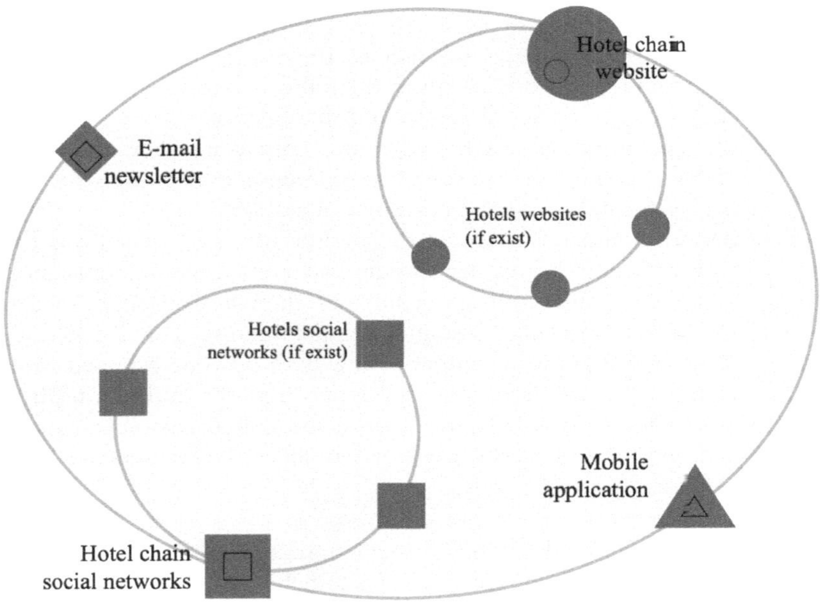

Fig. 16.1 Hotel chain Digital communication channel (*Source* Created by the authors)

study this area since this tool is not used on a continuous basis and statistical data are unavailable. This analysis includes only a welcome email at the time of registering for (where this is a possibility) one of the hotel chain's loyalty programmes.

It is determined that all of the hotel chains have respective company-wide websites, enabling a customer to search for their required accommodation alternatives and which affects online booking and payment. All hotel chain websites operate in a sufficiently stable manner; when the study was carried out, all of them were active and did not have any difficulties with respect to accessing and registering for loyalty programmes, authenticating a personal account, or booking. The functionality of the websites is generally expressed by a certain set of functions. Notionally, one could divide them into the following groups:

- searching for and selecting an accommodation
- registering for a loyalty programme
- the possibility of "sharing" information on any selected accommodation (in social media, messengers or by email)
- booking
- payment for booking
- the availability of a customer support service
- getting bonuses under a loyalty programme
- the possibility of posting a review upon completion of stay

Seeking to provide their customers with wider digital experience, some hotel chains have expanded the functionality of their websites by adding an "enlightening" function to their website contents. They create subsections, or even external resources, and fill them with information on travel destinations: recommendations from local residents on "secret" places in a city, the best restaurants and routes, unusual leisure ideas, etc. Marriott Hotels and Resorts has introduced the "enlightening" function directly into the booking process by supplementing its web pages and its external resource "moments.marriotttbonvoy.com" with a large amount of information on unusual travel destinations. Acquainting customers with unique travel experiences in addition to the accommodation itself is an innovative approach. This hotel chain invested in an American tour and event management firm, PlacePass, which provides Marriott Hotels and Resorts guests with access to an online travel trips' platform. When making a direct booking via the Marriott Hotels and Resorts website or mobile app, the search engine offers more than 100,000 events in 800 cities around the world: concerts, gastronomic tours, historical excursions, active recreation, and VIP tours. The management of Hilton Hotels and Resorts represents its hotels on the corporate website in a more traditional manner, but also offers a separate resource called "experiences.hiltonhonors.com" in order to "enlighten" customers. AccorHotels issues its online magazine *the magazine*, which also expands its customers' positive digital experiences. Some websites, in particular that of Marriott Hotels and Resorts, also feature unconventional systems for filtering their accommodation offerings in terms of hobbies or leisure types.

An interaction channel's convenience is determined by the aesthetic quality of its resource design, the freedom of action enjoyed by a visitor, the ease of use of the system (the number of steps required to register for the loyalty programme or to select, book and pay for an accommodation), the intuitive manner of interaction, and other such factors. The smallest number of simple steps for the purpose of registration or booking is on the website of Marriott Hotels and Resorts, which supports the option of quick registration and quick access via Facebook. Registration on the Wyndham Hotels & Resorts website is divided into several simple stages, supplemented by process visualisation. Some hotel chains adhere to traditional methods by asking their guests to complete longer questionnaires during registration, such as Hilton Hotels and Resorts or InterContinental Hotels Group. Furthermore, personal profiles at hotel chains offer various degrees of convenience, with the highest visualisation characterising personal profiles at Marriott Hotels and Resorts and AccorHotels. It may be interesting to analyse the influence visualisation and design has, within personal accounts, on the digital experience of customers in more detail.

The personalisation of customer experience starts with selecting the language of communication and the payment currency, which is mostly carried out via the personal account. The websites of all international hotel operators are localised for various regions, but it should be noted that the number of languages differs. The greatest number of languages is offered by AccorHotels; its website supports 29 local versions, which is patently convenient for a larger number of customers. Marriott Hotels and Resorts supports only 11 languages, although this chain boasts a significant presence in most major regional markets. It should also be noted that the local versions of its website contain much less information, and this lowers the quality of digital experience for non-English-speaking customers. This tendency has been noted for other hotel chains as well; InterContinental Hotels Group offers wide localisation and 18 languages on its website, but the destination must be typed in Latin letters, so booking may prove more difficult for some prospective guests.

All international hotel chains have a customer's personal account on their websites; this personalises interaction and can be used to implement their loyalty programme. The personal profile is the most important personalisation tool, as the guest can use it to make and monitor bookings, accumulate bonus points, order additional services, and maintain communication with the hotel chain. The hotel is able to record the customer's details as well as information on his or her preferences, which can be used in the future for formulating personalised offerings and helping to establish long-term relations with guests. Hotel chains websites offer an opportunity to switch to other communication channels: to follow brand accounts on social media, to subscribe to an email newsletter or to download the mobile application (Table 16.1). The more extensive the "digital footprint" left by the client is (more devices connected, more channels used, more pages visited, more comments left), the more information the hotel chain managers can receive about the

Table 16.1 Website channel switch options

Hotel chain name	*Link to social media websites*	*Link to mobile application*	*Link to email newsletter*	*Support*	*Phone number*
Marriott Hotels and Resorts	+	–	–	+	+
Radisson Hotel Group	+	+	+	+	+
Accor Hotels	+	+	+	+	+
Intercontinental Hotel group	+	+	–	+	+
Hilton Hotels & Resorts	+	–	–	+	+
Wyndham Hotels & Resorts	+	–	–	+	+

Source Created by the authors

client. Data collected from customer interactions can help deeply analyse the customer's behaviour and preferences.

The highest degree of personalisation is offered by Marriott Hotels and Resorts, whose customers are able to choose a particular room and to book extra services. Customer preferences are saved in the personal account and will be taken into account in any further interaction with the hotel chain. The use of the personal profile allows integration with a mobile application, thus synchronising data and providing access to the personal details and booking history of customers both in the personal account on the corporate website and on the guests' mobile devices via the application.

An analysis of the hotel chains' presence on social media has demonstrated that all of the selected hotel chains have opened their brand accounts on the key social media websites: Facebook, Instagram, and Twitter. These hotel chains diversify their content with unusual stories by guests and interviews with popular persons; they also cover new travel destinations, supplementing their photo and video content with stories by local residents, thus providing a positive digital experience for their subscribers. Subscribers are particularly interested in user-generated content. International hotel chains motivate their guests to share pictures from their visit and tag the chain. They offer discounts for some services and small presents for subscription, post or comment. Blogger reviews are also beneficial for hotel chains. Management of many hotels arranges luxury press tours for bloggers and influencers, to get high-quality content. The latest trend is to include the most beautiful sights of the country instead of just the hotel in the press tours, to let influencers create positive experiences they can transfer to their audience. Via the Facebook accounts of Marriott Hotels and Resorts, InterContinental Hotels Group and Radisson Hotel Group, it is possible to make a direct booking, and the accounts of Hilton Hotels and Resorts and AccorHotels offer localised versions for other regions with regular information updates. Other international hotel networks, despite their wide presence in regional markets, do not maintain any separate accounts or versions for those who reside in non-English-speaking regions. In these cases, interaction with foreign tourists in social media is implemented through the individual accounts of accommodation facilities. It has been noted that all international hotel networks have accounts on the Chinese social media Weibo and Wechat. Some of them (for instance, AccorHotels) have also focused on YouTube and Pinterest.

Digital technologies create an opportunity to involve customers in the process of constant interaction. The client becomes an active participant in service creation that is personalised by its nature. The mobile app is one of many possible ways to communicate with the hotel and personalise the client experience. Guest requests may include all kinds of information regarding amenities, comfort, entertainment, food, and other nuances of their stay at the hotel. Data about the guest's wishes are saved in the CRM, and the guest will be able to receive the same personalised offer when making subsequent trips or can change the preferences if necessary. The speed of response to consumer requests and the technical stability of applications are of great importance. The client assumes that the answer to the request will be received quickly, and a delay or lack of response negatively affects the client's satisfaction. All international hotel chains have their own mobile applications with different sets of features. Users mention some stability problems with respect to the Radisson Hotel Group, InterContinental Hotels Group, and Hilton Hotels and Resorts applications, which prevent guests from using all the applications' functions and hinder pleasant experiences interacting with them. As part of our analysis, 10 of the application's key functions that are used by guests in their relations with the relevant brands have been examined. All applications allow the customer to book and pay for accommodation, and review his or her information and booking history. Many applications are intended to save the customer's time, featuring in-built functions for credit card scanning and access to the Apple Wallet. The applications of Marriott Hotels and Resorts and Hilton Hotels and Resorts also offer their guests a mobile chat, a mobile key, mobile check-in and check-out, the ability to order additional services, and the selection of a specific hotel room. AccorHotels' application offers 17 language versions (the maximum number of languages), whereas the application of Hilton Hotels and Resorts supports only English—a fact to which users often refer. All applications support a hotel loyalty system, offering various bonuses for the installation of the application and for any booking made directly from the application. The applications acquaint tourists with the infrastructure of each hotel, as well as relevant places of interest and leisure options at the selected location during the guest's stay, thus generating an additional digital experience. Some applications include a personalised selection of offerings based on the guest's preferences and his or her prior experience with the relevant hotel chain.

The practice of using the Internet of Things by the most innovative hotel chains represents a great interest. For instance, in hotels of Hilton Hotels located in the US, clients use the Hilton Honors mobile app to control the lighting and air conditioning and to choose the subject of media content. They receive access to this type of personalization, even before check-in. Marriott Hotels and Resorts' management are also developing "smart" rooms. International hotel chains build their own digital solutions and apply those of Samsung, Legrand, Amazon, and other companies. Implemented technologies support interaction between many systems, devices, and applications for guest services.

As regards virtual integration, contemporary hotel brands invest in platforms which ensure dynamic and personalised interaction at every stage of the guest's travel, through various channels and devices on the basis of unified guest profiles. Information in the applications of all international chains is synchronised with data from the personal account on a website. In this manner, the guest receives all information on his or her booking history and personal status in the loyalty programme on any mobile device, as may be convenient for him or her (Fig. 16.2). Many developers have released application versions for iPad as well. AccorHotels' application is supported on iPad and Apple TV, and the application of Marriott Hotels and Resorts can use iPad and Apple Watch, so that interaction with customers becomes even more versatile. Integration is

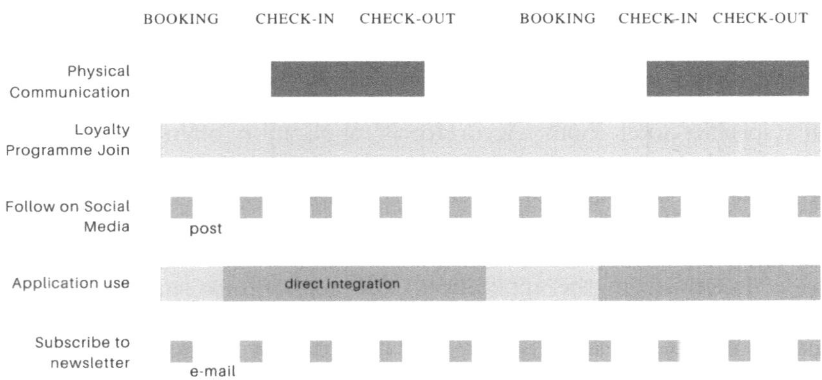

Fig. 16.2 Physical and virtual communication process (*Source* Created by the authors)

also used for a customer support system; for instance, customer support at Hilton Hotels and Resorts can be initiated via a CRM system, in which each request is assigned a reference number, and then uses the channels preferable to the customer. However, the future of cross-channel integration lies in the implementation of complete interrelation among all digital channels without destroying any established links. For example, one could carry out a booking process on a given device while switching to various other devices while still retaining the progress of the purchase.

Conclusions/Recommendations

Ongoing fundamental technological changes allow hotel chains to apply marketing strategies focusing on bilateral communication with the consumer instead of unilateral. Hotel chain management creates meaningful, continuous relationships with the client to get the most accurate picture of their guest—their needs, purchasing behaviour, way of thinking, lifestyle, habits, and hobbies. The interpretation of received information is particularly important, remaining the most challenging stage of customer understanding. Hotel chains use data to create a personalised service and better understand their market. Modern customers particularly value an individualised approach, which has become the most critical element of increasing trust and loyalty. In general, interaction with the client leads to the strengthening of competitive positions and higher sales.

The intention to convey a positive experience on an individual basis has become a catalyst for innovative changes in all internal and external processes of hotel company operations. In building an infrastructure for interaction with customers, emphasis is shifting towards adaptability, the implementation of innovations, and the ongoing testing of state-of-the-art technologies.

Among the hotel chains reviewed, digital "innovators" have been identified, namely AccorHotels and Marriott Hotels and Resorts. These hotel chains test innovations along several lines, generate a lot of information valuable for travellers, and are focused on the provision of a personalised digital experience. The digital infrastructure of the other hotel companies contains less information and is less personalised. Generally, it can be stated that most international hotel chains have achieved a certain degree of integration among their interaction channels, and the experience that customers receive from their communication with digital platforms is at a rather high level. However, the personalisation of the digital experience is still difficult to achieve—a fact which may be due to the insufficiency of human, physical, and technological resources. An efficient marketing strategy requires a complex system of well-balanced, coordinated, consistent marketing activities, including digital marketing and traditional marketing. Undoubtedly, the comprehensive implementation of high-technology digital transformations requires considerable physical resources as well as the appropriate highly qualified personnel training. International hotel chains must quickly adapt to constantly evolving digital technologies. The implementation of technological solutions should not lag behind the level of technologies used by consumers. In most cases, only large international hotel chains are able to meet such requirements. They have the potential to put together a complex information infrastructure in order to generate a personalised customer experience.

As concerns its practical application, this study can help various hotel chains and independent hotels evaluate their progress in developing channels for their interaction with customers along three lines—via a website, via social media, and via a mobile application—and identify the degree of integration and cross-channel communication. They can analyse their operations with respect to the factors identified from user reviews.

In the future, researchers could develop a valid model in order to determine satisfaction in each single interaction and to assess the overall experience of interaction with the entire infrastructure. The technology-related features of a CRM system and loyalty programme functioning could be investigated in more detail as well.

References

Churakova, A. A. (2019). Experience Marketing as a Modern Strategy for the Promotion of Hotel Chains. *Marketing and Market Research* (3) (July), 186–198.

Forrester Research. (2014). *Customer Experience Maturity Defined*.

Gartner. (2014). *Importance of Customer Experience is on the Rise: Marketing is on the Hook*. https://www.gartner.com/en/documents/2853519.

Homburg, C., Jozić, D., & Kuehnl, C. (2015). Customer Experience Management: Toward Implementing an Evolving Marketing Concept. *Journal of the Academy of Marketing Science, 13*(3), 13–25.

Hossain. T. et al. (2017). *The Impact of Integration Quality on Customer Equity in Data Driven Omnichannel Services Marketing*. Procedia Computer Science, January, 784–790.

Kandampully, J., & Solnet, D. (2015). *Service Management: Principles for Hospitality and Tourism*. Iowa: Kendall Hunt Publishing.

Kandampully, J., Zhang, T., & Bilgihan, A. (2015). Customer Loyalty: A Review and Future Directions with a Special Focus on the Hospitality Industry. *International Journal of Contemporary Hospitality Management, 27*(3), 379–414.

Kotler, P., Kartajaya, H., & Setiawan, I. (2017). *Marketing 4.0: Moving from Traditional to Digital*. Hoboken, New Jersey: John Wiley & Sons, Inc.

Lin, P., Fan, X., Zhang, H., & Lau, C. (2019). Spend Less and Experience More: Understanding Tourists' Social Contact in the Airbnb Context. *International Journal of Hospitality Management., 83*(October), 65–73.

Nozdreva, R. B. (2018). The Development of a Marketing Concept on the Basis of Empirical Economics. *Marketing in Russia and Abroad, 4,* 3–10.

Ponsignon, F., Klaus, P., & Maull, R. S. (2015). Experience Co-Creation in Financial Services: An Empirical Exploration. *Journal of Service Management, 26*(2), 295–320.

Sabre Hospitality Solutions. (2018) *Digital Transformation of Guest Experience*. http://www.skalroma.org/wp-content/uploads/2018/03/Digital_Transformation_of_the_Guest_Experience.pdf.

Schwab, K. (2016). *The Fourth Industrial Revolution*. Moscow: Eksmo.

Stonehouse G. H., & Konina N. Y. (2020). Management Challenges in the Age of Digital Disruption. Conference Paper. *Conference: Proceedings of the 1st International Conference on Emerging Trends and Challenges in the Management Theory and Practice (ETCMTP 2019)*. https://doi.org/10.2991/aebmr.k.200201.001.

Toffler, E. (2008). *Metamorphosis of Power: Knowledge, Wealth and Power at the Threshold of the 21st Century*. Moscow: Publishing House AST.

Transparency Market Research. (2019). *Hotel Market*. https://www.transparencymarketresearch.com/Hotels-market.html. Accessed 25 october 2019. https://www.forrester.com/report/Customer Experience MaturityDefined/3/E3RES59376.

CHAPTER 17

Digital Transformation of Marketing Strategy of Western Firms in Chinese Cosmetic Market

Elena Ponomareva and Elena Nozdrenko

Introduction

The global cosmetic market is developing steadily as part of the global economy. In the era in which multinational companies are dominant, perfume, and cosmetic firms have accordingly expanded their markets as a part of diversification. Taking the rapid development of China's market into account, and acknowledging its increasing role in the global economy, many Western companies have set out a goal to expand their presence in the thriving Asian market and, in particular, in the fast-growing cosmetic market in China.

Due to the increase in consumers' purchasing power and the holistic growth of the middle class, Chinese consumers more often prefer premium cosmetic products. This fact makes the Chinese market very attractive to foreign companies in this field.

E. Ponomareva (✉)
Moscow State Institute of International Relations (MGIMO University), Moscow, Russia

E. Nozdrenko
Siberian Federal University, Krasnoyarsk, Russia

N. Konina (ed.), *Digital Strategies in a Global Market*,
https://doi.org/10.1007/978-3-030-58267-8_17

The volume of the Chinese cosmetic market is growing steadily, and the presence of foreign players within it is expanding. International experts make forecasts that, in the next five to ten years, China will occupy a leading position in the global perfume and cosmetic market. At the same time, it is obvious that effective promotion of imported products in the Chinese market will be possible only with a well-developed marketing strategy, including modern features—due to the digital features of the economy—to sell goods, and ways to influence consumer preferences using digital technologies.

The digital transformation of business in the perfume and cosmetic field is the most important driver of success. Currently, in the business of Chinese perfume and cosmetics, digital transformation takes place across all areas—production, equipment and software, fundamental changes in strategic approach, marketing and sales policy, and communications.

Methodology

The theoretical basis of the research is the modern system of economic, cultural, and sociological knowledge that underpins the basic requirements for the scientific theories, essence, structure, and methods for applying various analytical tools in the field of marketing. Research methods obtain the fundamental principles of marketing theory. During the research, the scientific works of domestic and foreign scientists on various aspects of strategic marketing, economic analysis, consumer culture, and digital strategies were used. To lay the empirical base of the study, the researchers used the data officially published on cosmetic industry web sites and portals, including expert evaluation and statistics.

Results

Modern marketing strategies are focused on ensuring a high level of global competitiveness. According to researchers, "if a business does not have a unique advantage over competitors, it does not need to exist" (Kotler 2015).

Therefore, ensuring the concept of "uniqueness" in marketing is the most important factor in a business' competitiveness. According to Nirmalya Kumar (Kumar 2008), the key factor for a company creating its own unique marketing strategy lies in exploring and determining its target market and those requirements, putting forward a profitable value proposition and building its own sales network for offering this value. In the era of digital economy, we believe that the digital transformation of business is the key driver of successful operations and global expansion.

Taking the rapid development of the Chinese economy into account and understanding its global impact, Western companies are focused on expanding their presence in Asian markets. Moreover, due to national consumer behavior, the Chinese population's increasing purchasing power, and the growth of the middle class in general, Chinese consumers more often prefer premium cosmetic products and especially demand foreign skincare products, which accounts for 70% of the entire cosmetic market. These trends make the Chinese market very attractive for foreign companies, especially the premium segment which is of a particular interest for Western companies (Investments.miraeasset 2019).

The positive dynamics of the Chinese market are due to the complete development of the consumer society in China. Today, it is best to say that the cosmetic market is a capital-intensive sector of the Chinese economy, subject to the competent implementation of digital strategies. Companies manufacturing products for the mass market are predominantly national. For national producers, the majority of their sales are achieved in cities of the second and third categories, where the middle class is the dominant social group within the population. The low popularity of national cosmetic manufacturers among Chinese consumers is due to their distrust. Most potential consumers believe that national cosmetic companies have less experience in branding and marketing, as well as insubstantial financial resources for research and development.

Despite the fact that the perfume and cosmetic market in China is developing according to global trends, it is characterized by national characteristics, which are primarily associated with the characteristics of consumers. The development of the cosmetics industry in China is inextricably linked to an increase in the well-being of the population. Along with an increase in revenue, consumer demands and expectations for cosmetic products are growing.

Firstly, the female audience has begun to pay more attention to the properties and effects of the product, as well as the brand's popularity, whereas previously price was the key factor in choosing cosmetic products. According to *Morgan Stanley's* AlphaWise study, 84% of survey respondents are willing to purchase higher or similarly priced products next year (Morganstanly 2016).

Secondly, due to rising incomes, the population has the opportunity to travel, which has a direct impact on consumer awareness of brands and shopping abroad. The proportion of people traveling as part of tourist groups is growing steadily, and recently amounted to almost 12% of the total population, or 164.9 million people (Morganstanley 2016).

Thirdly, the share of online purchases is rapidly growing among Chinese cosmetic consumers. According to an AlphaWise study in 2018, 26% of all domestic purchases were made online. According to the results of that survey, more than half of the respondents highlighted the following reasons they were in favor of online shopping: the ability to compare prices from different representatives; lower prices than retailers; the ability to read consumer reviews; some products are only available for purchase online.

In cases when a perfume and cosmetic company enters the Chinese market, marketing specialists have to develop the optimal sales chain that ensures the most efficient and uninterrupted sale of products. Experts identify three main ways of marketing in the Chinese market, sometimes combining several of them at once: export, outsourcing, and offshore production.

All of these three features can be found in the marketing activity of those Western companies that are successfully expanding in Chinese cosmetics.

The application of the above methods in the context of digitalization is associated with the development of artificial intelligence technologies. We clarify the following exceptional features of artificial intelligence: the ability to control and reduce incoming large amounts of information in real time; the ability to make decisions and conduct complex tasks despite a lack of time; the ability to coordinate decisions with other parts of the process or object; the ability to maintain and disseminate the knowledge gained as a result of many years of work by experts (Naumov and Chistyakov 2017).

Accordingly, the use of digital strategies in modern marketing provides obvious competitive advantages when using *export, outsourcing, or offshore production*. Digitalization ensures the effectiveness of marketing strategies, creating favorable conditions for an effective marketing policy and cost reduction (Table 17.1).

Depending on the category to which the company's products belong, it is advisable to use one of the distribution channels (Table 17.2).

Table 17.1 Main marketing methods by criteria

Criteria	*Export*	*Outsourcing*	*Offshore production*
Brand image	High	Low	Middle
Quality control	High	Low	Middle
Intellectual Property Protection	High	Low	Middle
Copy risk	Low	High	Middle
Access to local market information	Low	Middle	High
Delivery time	Long	Short	Short
Production costs	Low	High	Middle
Delivery costs	High	Low	Middle
Flexibility to changes in demand	Low	High	High
Tariffs	High	Low	Low

Source Developed by the authors based on Fang, C., Gao, F., Liu, D., Tang, Ch. S, Wang, W., & Wu, T. (2008). *Supply Chain Analysis: Supply Chain Configurations of Foreign Cosmetics Companies Operating in China*. Boston: Springer

Table 17.2 Distribution channels by categories

Distribution channels	*Premium*	*Mass-Premium*	*Mass-Market*
Premium Shopping Centers	X	X	
Professional cosmetics stores	X	X	
Supermarkets		X	X
Pharmacies		X	X
Direct marketing			X

Source Developed by the authors based on Fang, C., Gao, F., Liu, D., Tang, Ch. S, Wang, W., & Wu, T. (2008). *Supply Chain Analysis: Supply Chain Configurations of Foreign Cosmetics Companies Operating in China*. Boston: Springer; Created by the authors

Estée Lauder, for example, is one of the successful global brands operating in the Chinese market, and is further developing as part of a global marketing strategy for geographic market expansion. The features it uses for its sales organization are worth consideration. It has located its facilities in a number of European countries, such as France, Great Britain, Belgium, and Germany, as well as in the USA and Canada, through investment in infrastructure construction. At the same time, *Estée Lauder* refused to place production facilities in China, preferring to use a segmentation strategy. The company directly exports products to China, which favorably affects the preservation of the brand image, allows the quality of goods to be controlled and the protection of its intellectual property, which also reduces the risk of selling counterfeit products. However, there are a number of drawbacks to direct exports: high transportation costs and customs formalities, and long transportation times (Wu et al. 2008).

Estée Lauder has successfully used integrated marketing communications to penetrate the Chinese market. The organization of integrated marketing systems allows the company not only to use a set of means of communication with the consumer for multichannel, comprehensive impact, but also to maintain its corporate identity. Brand recognition is of great importance in the promotion policy of each company operating in the premium arena. *Estée Lauder*'s corporate identity has been successfully achieved in three ways: *corporate branding*, *branding in the sales area*, and *branding of flagship stores*. The corporate identity of the company manifests itself in both the ATL—and BTL—communications of *Estée Lauder*.

Among the ATL tools, outdoor visual advertising is most often seen in the form of advertising posters and signs, which are placed in shopping centers, on busy streets, and at points of sale. The company also uses digital technology, and carries out image advertising on electronic billboards in the center of large cities. Other popular advertising channels are print media, including glossy magazines on electronic devices and the Internet. The company's digital advertising is most successful due to the prevalence of Internet use in the country.

Estée Lauder's online direct marketing is carried out by sending e-mails. Thus, the company keeps in touch with regular customers, notifying them of new products, upcoming discounts, and personal offers.

An analysis of *Estée Lauder*'s communication policy revealed the prevailing use of online platforms to promote the brand. A study of *Bain&Company* in 2017 emphasizes the increasing share of digital marketing costs among the complete marketing expenses of *Estée Lauder*. In its promotion strategy through social networks, *Estée Lauder* uses a number of popular Internet sites, among which are *Sina Weibo* and

WeChat; premium segment companies allocate from 30 to 60% of the digital marketing budget for promotion through the *WeChat* platform.

Sina Weibo is an analogue of American Twitter, but has a number of features for writing informational posts not limited by the number of characters, as well as for writing comments in the public domain. *Estée Lauder* uses the *Weibo* platform primarily to disseminate information about its products, as well as to receive feedback from consumers. Each of the brands produced under the *Estée Lauder* brand has its own page; the total number of subscribers amounts to more than 20 million people. It should be noted that all information posts on *Weibo* are accompanied by photographs of models of Asian appearance, which indicates the uniqueness and difference of the company's strategy for the Chinese market from its global promotion strategy.

One of the successful strategies for promoting *Estée Lauder* is to use influence marketing, due to the predominance of millennials among the brand's target audience. In 2017, 40% of *Estée Lauder* purchases were made by customers between the ages of 18 and 30 (Forbes 2017).

Thus, the company combined two key factors affecting the target audience: influence marketing, and digital media. Representatives of *Bain&Company* call influence marketing the most effective tool for influencing the millennial generation: according to the survey, 64% of respondents are guided by recommendations from "opinion leaders" when making a purchase in the premium market. Moreover, almost 60% of respondents say that they receive information about premium products through electronic devices (Bain 2020).

Estée Lauder also used influence marketing on another popular social site, *WeChat*, which is used by about a billion people daily (Statista 2020). In 2016, *Estée Lauder* conducted an interactive EyeQ campaign with Chinese model Liu Wen. The idea of this campaign was that users online can see the contents of the model's handbag, where—besides *Estée Lauder* products—there was her handwritten diary, pages of which can be scrolled through to reveal this celebrity's favorite *Estée Lauder* products. Also, users could pass a test showing their knowledge of the company's products, and then receive prizes. This campaign was recognized as one of the most successful projects to attract a young audience. Moreover, *Estée Lauder* has become one of the most frequently mentioned brands, with the most frequently mentioned campaigns, by opinion leaders on the *WeChat* platform.

Another example of a successful *Estée Lauder* campaign is the recent collaboration of the MAC brand and the *Honor of Kings* series of mobile games, which was developed by the Chinese video giant *Tencent*. In February 2019, the companies jointly released a line of lipsticks in five shades, which could be purchased on the official *MAC* website and on the *Tmall* platform. The idea for this co-branding came to *Estée Lauder* management after they studied chat in a game where the *MAC* brand was mentioned many times—the reason for this was the need to choose the appearance of your character in the game. The key audience for the mobile game is between 18–24 years old, which partially coincides with the age of the target audience of *Estée Lauder*.

Moreover, in 2017, the female audience of the mobile game outweighed the male one. In total, the number of players is more than 200 million people per month. The success of this campaign is confirmed by the number of users who pre-ordered lipstick on these online platforms—after the announcement of the new item, 14 thousand copies were bought within one day (Jingdaily 2019).

Estée Lauder's sales policy in the Chinese market is in line with current consumer trends and national features. In China, the company uses a multi-channel combined marketing system, which combines both direct and indirect sales methods, due to rapidly changing market conditions, as well as its desire to expand its market presence (Fig. 17.1).

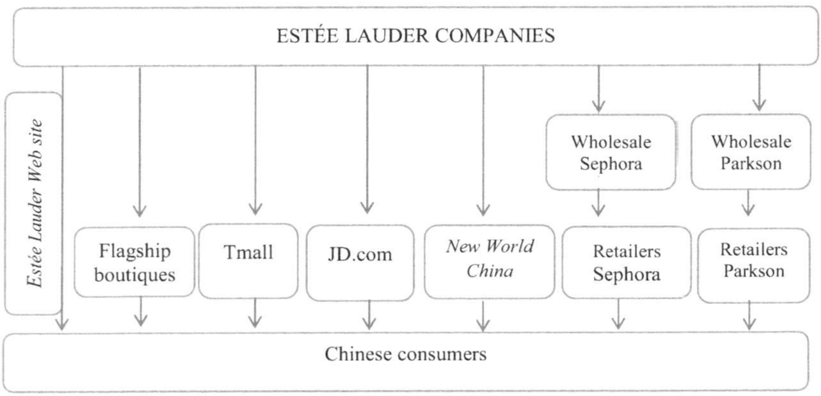

Fig. 17.1 Estée Lauder's multichannel combined marketing system (*Source* Created by the authors)

A study of factual materials and accessible analytical resources demonstrates that the main sales method of *Estée Lauder* is indirect: that is, the sale of products through intermediaries, including perfume stores, cosmetic stores, and shopping galleries. After 26 years of maintaining a presence in the Chinese market, *Estée Lauder* has opened a corner brand of the same name in perfume and cosmetic stores in more than 50 cities. For other brands that are part of the *Estée Lauder* companies, their most common flagship stores are in large shopping centers and on busy streets.

The direct marketing method is represented mainly by online trading, the rapid development and popularity of which is due to the national characteristics of the Chinese population. Over the past few years, online trade in China has been increasing rapidly. In 2017, the number of consumers making online purchases reached more than 530 million people (Statista 2020).

Online brands have begun to compete with offline brands in traditional markets. Online stores are in competition with traditional retail sales, combining the quality of the services of a physical store with the information, flexibility and capabilities of a digital office.

Against the backdrop of increased consumer activity in the social space, brands have also stepped up sales on social networks. According to analysts' forecasts, in the near future, brands will be able to offer their products directly on the pages of social networks, thus ensuring true global reach and multiple new venues for branding in social media (Ponomareva 2017).

China is becoming a global leader in the fashion market, consumers are changing behaviors, and the emergence of "challenger brands" breaks the familiar landscape of the industry (Sostav 2019).

Firstly, such figures are associated with an increasing number of trading platforms on the Internet: mobile applications, ease of access to platforms, and a convenient way for instant payment through a virtual wallet. According to experts, in 2019 the total volume of goods turnover in the Chinese online market will be $4.87 trillion. Moreover, during Single Day (November 11, the Black Friday analogue held in China), the cost of online purchases amounted to $25 billion, which is 40% higher than the total US sales on Black Friday and Cyber Monday (Sostav 2019).

According to research, the largest group of Internet users who shop online is the age group of 18–24, part of *Estée Lauder*'s target generation of millennials. A 50% increase in online sales was recorded in 2017 (Elcompanies 2017).

In addition to selling goods on their official website, *Estée Lauder* sells its products on popular market places: *JD.com* and *Tmall*. These are the two largest sites, together accounting for 85% of online commerce in the B2C sector in China at the end of 2018 (Chinainternetwatch 2019).

Tmall, part of the *Alibaba Group*, is the largest trading platform on the Internet, with a market share of 61.5% and an active audience of more than 500 million users every month. *Estee Lauder* launched the sale of its products on the *Tmall* site in May 2014, and the first day brought incredible results: almost 8 thousand transactions were completed for a total of 2.7 million yuan. Thus, one day of online sales at *Tmall* brought *Estée Lauder* more profit than a month of sales in an offline store (Chinainternetwatch 2014).

Estée Lauder uses a number of sales strategies that differ according to the following criteria: sales intensity, distribution of efforts, and responsibilities among participants in the distribution system. As for the marketing strategy for sales intensity, the company adheres to selective sales of its products, due to the characteristics of the product and its market niche. *Estée Lauder* products belong to the premium segment, which makes intensive mass marketing impossible, as this would negatively affect how consumers perceive the brand and entail the loss of the target audience.

At the same time, it is impractical to apply an exclusive sales strategy; the product would become difficult to access and the company would consequently significantly limit its sales opportunities, entailing a loss of market share. Thus, applying the strategy of selective sales, *Estée Lauder* carefully selects resellers and pays considerable attention to building supply chains. To sell products from brands such as *MAC Cosmetics*, *Jo Malone,* and *Bobbi Brown*, *Estée Lauder* is opening flagship boutiques in major malls.

At the same time, other brands owned by the company are being sold through retailers in perfume and cosmetics stores. The main intermediaries of the company in China are the American network of perfume and cosmetics stores *Sephora,* the Malaysian shopping gallery *Parkson*, and *New World China*—a network of shopping centers in mainland of China.

Taking into account the significant efforts *Estée Lauder* are taking to develop and implement a special marketing strategy that will attract Chinese consumers, we can conclude that the company uses the PULL marketing strategy, since measures to promote products in the Chinese market are aimed at the end consumer. This is reflected in the features of *Estée Lauder*'s promotion policy, which is based on digitalization.

Conclusions/Recommendations

China has become an active participant in the global economy, which is a factor in attracting Western investors. One of the fast-growing sectors of the Chinese economy is the perfume and cosmetic industry, which is dominated by large foreign companies. *Estée Lauder* has been one of the global leaders in cosmetics and perfumery for decades. It should be noted that *Estée Lauder* specializes in premium quality products that meet the demands of consumers in China. The American company entered the US market in 1993, and since then *Estée Lauder* has firmly established itself in the luxury cosmetics market. According to the Gartner L2 Digital IQ Index (Gartner L2 Digital IQ Index is a rating calculated by Gartner L2, reflecting the degree of the company's digitalization) *Estée Lauder* ranks first among more than one hundred perfume and cosmetic brands in China.

Estée Lauder's marketing strategy for penetrating the Chinese market has been developed by especially taking into account the characteristics of these consumers, their business traditions, and current trends in the marketing world, which makes it unique. *Estée Lauder*'s wide portfolio of brands allows to employ several global marketing strategies when entering the Chinese market: segmentation strategy, expanding market boundaries, an active expansion strategy, and differentiated marketing strategies for goods.

In the process of studying the available analytical resources, it was revealed that *Estée Lauder* uses a combined sales system, combining direct sales and an indirect sales method through intermediaries. Direct sales of products are carried out through the company's official website and through the placement of flagship brand stores. Indirect marketing is actively carried out both through distributors and through electronic trading platforms that act as intermediaries in the sales chain. At the same time, the prevailing sales method is the indirect one, which is explained by the widespread use of the market place in China. In this way, *Estée Lauder* has achieved a wide market reach by combining traditional trading methods and e-commerce opportunities.

It should be noted that *Estée Lauder*'s promotion policy is mainly aimed at the millennial generation, the predominant percentage of the company's target audience. Thus, the company uses those communication policy tools that are most effective with this group of consumers, which explains the use of digitalization in promotion.

Thus, the Chinese cosmetic market is developing successfully using the concept of "digitalization" as the only opportunity to meet the rapidly changing conditions of the digital economy. Digital strategies in the cosmetics market in China are a key driver of marketing, as they provide the flexibility to respond to ongoing changes and market needs.

References

Bain. (2020). *China Luxury Market Study*. Available at: http://www.bain.com.cn/pdfs/201801180441238002.pdf. Accessed 20 January 2020.

Fang, C., Gao, F., Liu, D., Tang, Ch S, Wang, W., & Wu, T (2008). *Supply Chain Analysis: Supply Chain Configurations of Foreign Cosmetics Companies Operating in China*. Boston: Springer.

Forbes. (2017). *Social Media Helping Estee Lauder Grow Its Presence In China*. Available at: https://www.forbes.com/sites/greatspeculations/2017/06/05/social-media-helping-estee-lauder-grow-its-presence-in-china/#267ed12b1507. Accessed 05 June 2017.

Jingdaily. (2019). *Beauty Battle: Lipstick Sales Soar With Tencent Mobile Game Tie-In*. Available at: https://jingdaily.com/lipstick-tencent-game/. Accessed 07 February 2019.

Kotler, P. (2015). *Marketing Insights from A to Z: 80 Concepts Every Manager Needs to Know* (7th ed., Transl. from English). Moscow: Alpina Publisher.

Kumar, N. (2008). *Marketing As Strategy: Understanding the CEO's Agenda for Driving Growth and Innovation* (Transl. from English). Moscow: Pretext.

Morganstanly. (2016). *Beauty in the Eye of the Chinese Consumer*. Available at: https://www.morganstanley.com/ideas/china-beauty-market-consumer-boom. Accessed 04 November 2016.

Naumov, M., & Chistyakov A. (2017). Application of Artificial Intelligence Systems in Various Fields of Activity. *Journal of Postulate, 5*.

Ponomareva, E. (2017). *Brand Management*. Moscow: Urait.

Statista. (2020). *Number of Active WeChat Messenger Accounts 2011–2018*. Available at: https://www.statista.com/statistics/255778/number-of-active-wechat-messenger-accounts/. Accessed 20 January 2020.

Wu, T., Wang, W., Tang, C. S., Liu, D., Gao, F., & Fang, C. (2008). How Do Foreign Cosmetics Companies Align Their Supply Chains and Distribution Channels in China? *International Journal of Logistics Research and Applications, 11*(3), 201–228. https://doi.org/10.1080/13675560701635500.

"Asians Drive The Premium Skin Care Market", Available at: http://investments.miraeasset.us/files/5413/9640/9810/emi-q22013-story03.pdf.

"Eight Western Brands Running Innovative Campaigns on China's WeChat", available at: https://econsultancy.com/eight-western-brands-running-innovative-campaigns-on-china-s-wechat/.

"The Estée Lauder Companies Delivers Strong Fiscal Year 2017 Results", available at: https://www.elcompanies.com/en/news-and-media/newsroom/press-releases/ 2017/ 08-18-2017-114420311.

"Estee Lauder First Day Tmall Sales Data Leaked", available at: https://www.chinainternetwatch.com/7538/estee-lauder-tmall-sales/.

"Fashion Market in 2019: View of The Business of Fashion and McKinsey & Company", available at: https://www.sostav.ru/publication/rynok-mody-v-2019-godu-vzglyad-bof-i-mckinsey-and-company-36771.html.

"New Faces: Estée Lauder Grows Younger in China", available at: http://www.pci-mag.com/features/featurenew-faces-6753510.

"Tmall and JD had a Combined Market Share of Over 85% in China's B2C E-Commerce Market in Q4 2018", available at: https://www.chinainternetwatch.com/28169/b2c-ecommerce-q4-2018/.

CHAPTER 18

Management by Values in Digital Transformation Strategies of Russian Companies and the Fourth Industrial Revolution

Alexander Gaponenko, Anastasia Erokhina, and Maria Pokrovskaya

Introduction

Digital transformation has spread across all areas of economics, with relevant modifications—both at strategic and operational levels—being introduced, and with regard to companies positioning. At the same time, digital transformation means material changes in company management. Weill and Woerner, widely recognized experts in digital transformation, have plenty of reason to state in their book that digital transformation is not about technology—it's about change. The main difficulty consists in managing these changes; the main factor for success is efficiency in managing these changes (Weill and Woerner 2018).

A. Gaponenko (✉) · A. Erokhina · M. Pokrovskaya
Institute of Business Studies, The Russian Presidential Academy of National Economy and Public Administration, Moscow, Russia

N. Konina (ed.), *Digital Strategies in a Global Market*,
https://doi.org/10.1007/978-3-030-58267-8_18

In a business' digital transformation, transformation of management is fundamental. Within the system "machine – human," new skillsets are formed: the skillset for machines includes automation tasks, with speed ensured by software; the skillset for people encompasses creativity, emotions, context & complex problem solving, and values. Simultaneously alongside digital transformation, new and emerging leadership skills are being strengthened. Among these are collaboration, openness, curiosity, empathy, and emotional maturity. Digital transformation makes many traditionally managed companies alter their management and introduce innovative management technologies. Management by values—one such innovation—implies that employees hold shared values that serve as a basis for making everyday decisions.

Today, digital transformation is in even greater demand. In the new digital world, goods and technologies can be readily replicated, buyers have increasingly more pricing power, and competition is less and less reliant on price. Under these circumstances, a company should rely not only on product-related and technological innovations, but also on innovations in management.

The essence of the subject considered herein is the following: nowadays, when many businesses are undergoing digital transformation, it is clear that management by values is advisable, and its formation and development is possible. Still, many entities hold back from implementing this, and instead keep practicing conventional—and inefficient—management methods. The study contemplates the forms and methods of management by values, as adopted in leading companies, and detects the main ways they can be used by organizations in Russia.

Literature Review

The concept of management by values emerged as one possible source for improving management practices several dozen years ago. In management-related literature, various authors presented their approach to management by values. Ginsburg and Miller ultimately defined this management type as "…plans, decisions, actions and rewards regulated by the value focus" (Ginsburg and Miller 1992: 23). Continuously following this scheme is of great significance for value-driven management (Pohlman et al. 2000).

Hamel raises a question: what is important in management today? For him, the answer is values, innovations and passion (Hamel 2012). Note that Hamel deems values to be not an auxiliary tool, but one fundamental aspect in modern management.

The concept of a company's values is also outlined by Rampersad in his works, suggesting the use of certain tools to align the company's goals with the employees' goals; defining the company's mission, its vision, and its strategic goals—as well as organizing the team work, managing the changes and analyzing the organization culture—are of crucial importance (Rampersad 2004). The impact of management by values on investments' cost-effectiveness is furthermore shown by Dolan, Garcia and Richley (Dolan et al. 2006).

Other authors have referred to such key values as deeply established principles, which define all the company's activities and serve as its cultural cornerstones (Collins and Porras 1994). According to another approach, in management literature, to using values as a management tool, value initiatives have nothing to do with building consensus, but are about imposing a set of fundamental, strategically sound beliefs on a broad group of people (Lencioni 2002).

The research performed by Kaptein and Schwartz is focused on the Business Code as a tool for implementing values, and draws a distinction between measuring the actual and the potential effectiveness of business codes for a company (Kaptein and Schwartz 2008). Among potential methods for introducing a sustainable value-driven management system, Lavoi highlights visual means, including printing, of communicating values, assessing candidates, and rewarding workers for exhibiting behavior that is in line with the company's character (Lavoie 2017). Marek highlights the importance of HR policy for establishing and augmenting values (Marek 2018). Having compared different regions, Florea and Florea note that levels of awareness, and stages of implementation, of the Value-Driven Management concept are not uniform place to place (Florea and Florea 2013: 65).

Another branch in studying management by values consists of analyzing personal and organizational value congruence (Gulbovaite 2017) (Hoffman et al. 2011). As has been noted, the experiences of many organizations that practice value-driven management shows the difficulty—and near impossibility—of finding and recruiting staff who hold personal values a priori in line with corporate values.

There has been considerable interest in the study of corporate values in modern literature, particularly in the context of digital business transformation. On one hand, research show that single values can foster and improve a company's innovations (Hartl and Hess 2017). On the other hand, digital tools can be used to integrate and maintain culture and values, facilitating their spread and embedding them in the organization, and optimizing business processes (Schumann and Tittmann 2015). Interestingly, however, corporate culture and organizational features are reflected in the combining of information technology, practices and values, and studying the way such digital tools are implemented (Hinings et al. 2018).

Among scientific literature, there is a considerable number of studies dedicated to the values impacting work efficiency—not only the contents of these values, but also how they can match personal values. However, there is a deficiency of works reviewing techniques and special technologies for forming and strengthening shared values in today's companies. Moreover, there are virtually no papers assessing existing practices to form and strengthen corporate values, almost no papers dedicated to values influencing the digital transformation of business, and also almost no papers analyzing digital methods of enhancing common values in an organization.

The purpose of this research is to detect and estimate the value-driven management practices that have been adopted in Russian entities, and then to define how having and developing this management pattern impacts an entity's competition ability, as well as what potential digital transformation could do for its business.

In 2019, the authors performed a sociological survey among employees and managers of Russian commercial companies, and from its results, the respondents' attitude to value-driven management, and their assessment of whether these management methods are used efficiently, could be determined. The survey set out to tackle the following issues: defining the extent to which management by values has been implemented in modern Russia, defining the efficiency rate of value-driven management technology, and developing recommendations for introducing management by values.

Methodology

Through a questionnaire with 215 respondents, data was obtained, which provided the primary empirical evidence for the research. Statistical data, taken as secondary empirical evidence, were used to compile a profile of the companies in question, and to classify them for analytical purposes.

Additionally, 20 cases, featuring leading entities that practice value-driven management (for example, as part of digital business transformation), were expanded upon; through these cases, the most frequent practices adopted by these companies for forming and strengthening their values could be detected.

Employees of Russian and international entities, as well as representative offices in Russia, acted as empirical subjects of the survey. All the respondents are 22–50 years old, are graduates of leading Russian universities with a Magister or an MBA degree, and currently work as specialists, middle management, executives, or business owners. The respondents provided comprehensive answers to the questionnaire items, which allowed us to define the management methods currently used in their respective organizations. As a method of forming the sampling population, stratified sampling with typical subject selection was taken.

The method of obtaining primary empirical evidence was a questionnaire. The grouping, the minimum and maximum weight values, and the correlation analyses were used as methods of processing and consolidating primary empirical evidence.

In addition, we performed a comparative case study of companies that successfully use management by values. A pool of companies whose value-driven management had already been described in detail in scientific literature was selected; the approaches and management technologies, which had and commonly been adopted in their practices, were defined.

At present, researchers agree that management by values is efficient; however, scientific literature still lacks data on what technologies are capable of, to ensure successful management by values. This research, thus, and its conclusion—on successful value-driven management technologies and the relevant recommendations—is something of a scientific novelty.

Results

Despite the obvious advantages of value-driven management, the research discovered that many companies still do not practice it. A considerable percentage of respondents—27%—commented that values are not stated in their organization.

In certain companies, corporate values are declared, yet no further work is conducted regarding these: among those respondents who stated that values had been adopted in their companies, 11% were unable to recall their values themselves. This demonstrates the lack of further work to maintain values in these companies, and as such employees are not just unable to use their corporate values in their work, but are even unable to name them. Values proclaimed by an organization are not always at the forefront of their employees' minds—16% of the survey participants could not state that the values declared by their companies are fully in line with those of the employees.

The respondents' opinions, and the cases considered, suggested certain areas of improvement. For example, during the introduction of value-driven management into these companies, it is particularly important to focus on technologies aimed at clarifying each organizational value—methods for this include discussion, fixing values, and storytelling. There are value-aimed technologies that make employees think over their values and assess to what extent their work corresponds to these corporate values—mandatory reports showing what company values have been implemented, or discussing values as part of every work meeting, are potential techniques. Other techniques, which take a visual bent to try and maintain values, could include displaying corporate values on the website, on documents, on the office walls, or by e-mail. As the research shows, most companies—having at least the prerequisites for management by values—are practicing technologies belonging to the second group; 88% noted that their corporate values can be found on the website, on documents, on the office walls, showing values are already being visualized. 44% of the respondents indicated that they receive regular e-mail distribution describing the main values of their companies. However, as successful entities have shown from their experiences, these technologies are efficient only if combined with other techniques to change an employees' perception. Technologies with the highest efficiency are only used in a few companies. In particular, according to the poll, values are discussed during work meetings in only 16% of the questioned companies, while a periodic report on values implementation is standard practice for only 12% of companies.

In most cases, according to the respondents, values act as a criterion when hiring a person (64%). It is virtually impossible, however, to select and hire persons already holding a set of values fully in line with the organizational ones above all other candidates, as more comprehensive interviews with these respondents revealed. Consequently, in reality, only one or two values (e.g. team work or client-oriented approach) are focused upon during the hiring procedure.

The survey proved a hypothesis which suggests that the more a company works on its values, the more successful it is. One reason for such a correlation could be that competitive ability is directly dependent on how strongly value-driven management has been developed.

As part of the survey, cases with Russian and foreign companies were analyzed to define what value-driven management technologies they use (Table 18.1). Table 18.1 provides data on the experience of twenty Russian and international companies in management by values, as represented in scientific literature. Despite the fact that the table contains data on well-known companies, in certain cases there was no significant difference between companies which are successful or well-known and those that are not; this corresponds with the data from the MBA graduates poll that suggested such a hypothesis.

As the extent of business and business processes digitalization is constantly increasing, it is important to define precisely and exactly where the interface points are between digital technologies and value-driven management. At present, a considerable number of value-driven management techniques (specified in Table 18.1) can be fully implemented or drastically improved by using digital technologies. Very frequently, text or other visual value representation (corporate design/brand, infographic) is provided through distribution of emails, which, due to the massive digitalization of business communication processes, ensures a fairly wide range of recipients and a high viewing frequency, which helps not only

Table 18.1 Value-driven management technologies in Russian Companies

Value-driven management technologies	*% used in companies*
Clearly defined missions, visions and values	100
Printed or other visual representation of values (corporate design/brand)	50
Systematic guidance based on selected values integrated in working procedures	40
Assessment of employees considering the use of values in work	70
Assessment of candidates considering the use o values in work	25
Coaching and mentoring on values	40
Corporate values induction program for new employees	30
Encouraging value implementation and usage through gamification	20

Source created by the authors

company employees but also company clients to memorize and understand the company's values. All the companies that were analyzed had defined and adopted their mission, their vision and their values.

In the world's fastest growing companies, one of the main growth drivers is ensuring their personal understanding exactly the purpose and values (Malnight et al. 2019). Traditional corporate HR practices are still practiced to introduce and maintain values. Thus, 70% of the studied bodies use an employee's ability to practice company values as one criterion for evaluating his/her work; one quarter of the companies assess candidates based on their accordance to the values adopted in the company; 30% have developed induction programs that acquaint newcomers with their corporate values; Furthermore, 40% use coaching and mentoring for communicating and strengthening their values.

For 50% of the companies questioned one popular value-driven management technique was visual communication, whereby values were visually combined with corporate branding. For example, internal e-mail distribution, posters on office walls, and other visual means will regularly include articles and videos on the values of the company.

Apart from that, 40% of the companies use established systematic value guidance; after selecting values, these are integrated into working procedures. For example, dedicated guidelines have been developed, which then help an employee to define which behavior model he/she should follow in a certain situation, in compliance with the corporate values.

Lastly, another method widely used by these organizations to promote values within the company is gamification: using gaming approaches for processes that are usually not game-like. This tool is aimed at improving the participants' involvement in solving tasks where gaming elements are introduced.

Assessing if candidates and employees use values is also partially performed with up-to-date technologies. Personal interviews are still widespread, but electronic testing, offline video questionnaires (without any direct involvement from HR personnel) and other such methods are increasingly being engaged with; this effectively optimizes man-hours spent, as well as the quality and the speed of the relevant data processing. Employees can receive feedback on their work, inter alia via, dedicated information graphics generated by the software, based on feedback from their managers and other team members, which would show their strong points and weak points, such as using the value usage parameter and compliance with the adopted corporate culture. Information graphics such as these normally contain guidelines on the expected technical abilities and the personal characteristics of the employee.

For new employees, an induction program on values is often offered as an online PC course. Also, many software products can monitor activities of the company and each employee and produce statistics; within the software, this can include, or can be supplemented by, gamification components, to show levels or scores that would indicate the progress of applying the organizational values and other goals, as established.

The Navicon case can serve as an example of how digital tools have been used to introduce and maintain values. At Navicon, a virtual currency was invented, which helped the employees themselves encourage each other to implement corporate values. The virtual currency could be earned by helping colleagues and fulfilling ideas, so each person tries to accumulate as much as possible for each value. Each employee was assessed on a 360-degree basis against the corporate values, and their feedback was implemented as a virtual currency. This example demonstrates how, by virtue of a virtual corporate currency, an environment is formed where employees can more fully comprehend the key values of their company, and which implements these values across all levels of employment. Corporate management notes the consequences: team members become more attentive to each other's work, everyone gets more involved in helping each other, and employees show their gratitude. As colleagues can gain virtual currency for being helpful and for implementing ideas, each of them strives to accumulate gratitude tokens related to all the values.

Navicon employees can spend this currency in their corporate shop to buy a pizza or a cinema ticket, to rent a Ferrari for one day, or to have a cup of coffee served by the manager in person. This electronic currency has materially assisted the team in absorbing the corporate values. The trick that made it work was organizing efficient feedback and publically appreciating team efforts; this is shown both among employees and on the management level too.

One particularly prominent example of a Russian-based company that has successfully implemented management by values is the largest Russian bank, Sberbank. This company has clearly established and well-explained values and guidelines, which serve as an important reference point in decision-making processes and for conflict resolutions. The three core values of Sberbank are: "I am a leader"; "We are a team"; "All for the customer." The official site not only names values but gives guiding points for them. For example, for the "All for the customer" value, it is said that "all our activities are built around clients and are in their interests," "we aim to surprise and delight clients with the quality of our services and attitude," and "we exceed client expectations" (Sberbank official website[1]). Moreover, the company provides a detailed explanation on how values should impact and enhance the experience of its various stakeholders: clients, employees, shareholders and investors and society. Such an approach allows Sberbank to have more precise value-driven vision and adhere to internally set standards and rules.

The Russian retail chain VkusVill is also considered a successful case of choosing, planning, and integrating values into the company's functioning. VkusVill identified and promoted six core values: honesty, trust, responsibility, mutual aid, decency, and social significance. The values are implemented on all levels within the company. On the basis of these values, core principles were developed, among which are such statements as "we are used to solving problems together, rejoicing in success and experiencing defeat" and "we help each other and understand that our company values a worthy joint result" (VkusVill official website[2]). As the responses of VkusVill employees show, trust and value competence are one of the key success factors of the company.

Another company which has successfully formed its corporate culture and values is the printing company Neoprint. Taking into consideration the specifics of the company's business operations, the company has chosen to communicate its values through informative corporate publications, giving the employees a chance to impact the way they are done, showcase skills, and naturally integrate values into their common operations and systems.

There are many examples of companies which have their own set of values. Still, it is not commonly known what the effective methods are to make these values be shared by personnel. One of the hypotheses is based on the following key methods: discussion, storytelling, coaching, and assessment of employees, considering the use of values in work. In addition, there are supplementary methods: value guideline, gamification, and assessment of candidates, through considering the use values

[1] Sberbank official website: https://www.sberbank.com/about/mission.

[2] VkusVill official website: https://vkusvill.ru/mission/.

in work, printed or other visual representation of values, missions, and visions including special materials for new employees (Fig. 18.1).

Management by values is one efficient means by which a vibrant enterprise management system can be formed; this system then becomes a competitive advantage. This is of particular importance today, when digitalization entails transparency and the free flow of information; as a result, new goods or new technologies no longer represent a stable competitive advantage. As one of the features for boosting competition, the new reality promotes corporate culture aimed at corporate values. This statement is justified by the experiences of successful enterprises around the world, where a powerful corporate culture is taken as a given, resting in its turn on values shared by any and all employees.

In some cases, management transformation, and introducing value-driven management, is carried out as part of digital transformation and is influenced by a robust ecosystem. Alibaba, the international Chinese colossus, is one such example. A small manufacturer of bags (INM Bag Manufacture) incorporated the Alibaba ecosystem, but in order to create

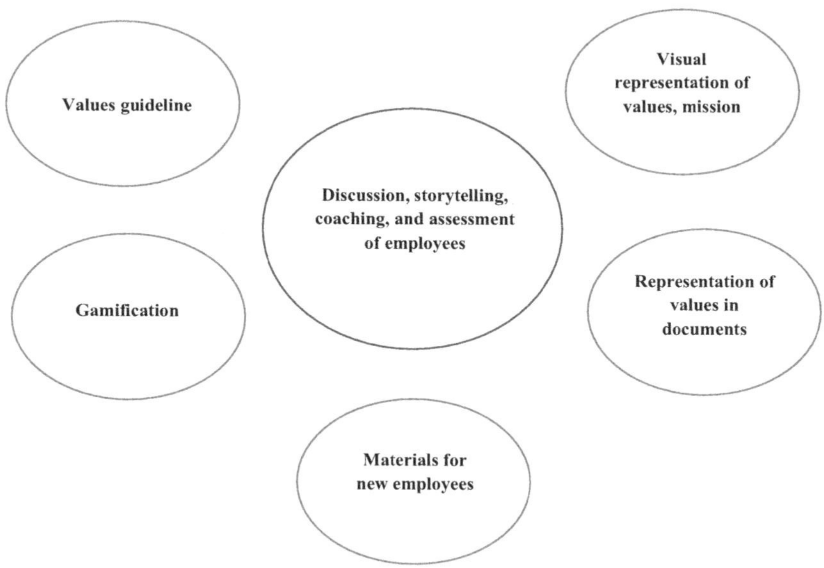

Fig. 18.1 Core and supporting methods of management by values

a positive development and growth environment for themselves, introduced the following principles: "to be a bag manufacturer that has happy and healthy employees; to create a smart bag-producing plant; to make clients happy."

Business basics often need to be changed due to digitization. Thus, in China, a lot of minor retail stores in rural areas have totally changed their business functions in partnership with Alibaba. This major digital entity, having a database on the sales dynamics and the structure of thousands of similar stores, and using Big Data to estimates needs from similar stores, regularly forms a pool of goods that certain stores will need in the short term. The precise required goods are brought to such stores by a truck at the very time when stock needs to be replenished. As a result, the store owner needs just to organize customer service and issue receipts while receiving payments. Many functions, such as forming orders and planning purchases, are gone. One can now focus on improving service and customer needs. This is where value-driven management can help.

Conclusion

The research shows that management by values makes digital transformation more efficient, and plays a key role in such transformations.

Similar value-driven management technologies are used in a number of companies. Proclaiming a company's mission, its vision, and its philosophy, along with its values, is a popular practice, and almost all the companies questioned were committed to doing so. Visual campaigning practices have become widely spread, with values being prominent across many printed materials, on the website, in the brand book, or in the office's interior design. Besides, forming value-driven management regulations—a kind of a corporate "white book"—is also a widely popular practice. Such regulations are used both in everyday work and as a part of orientation for new employees. Among management technologies, using values criteria while hiring and assessing employees can also be popularly seen. The gamification of value building, and strengthening such procedures within a company, has clearly become a trend over the last years. The gaming format is a quick and efficient way to transform an employee's conscience, filling it with corporate values and implications.

Analyzing the best practices shows that promoting and strengthening shared values among employees is most efficient as part of collective discussions, where the entire team is involved in comprehending value benchmarks. Shared values are formed and enhanced during such discussions.

Digital technologies can be used in value-driven management without any limits. To start with, digital tools help to streamline crowdsourcing while searching for and identifying the paramount corporate values. Digital solutions serve to assess each team member's input in implementing corporate ideas, and to ensure that such assessments are up-to-date. Even candidate selection and induction programs for newcomers can use electronic means.

For management in leading companies, both in Russia and abroad, every participant of any business process participant is expected to act independently. Therefore employees get involved—voluntarily, consciously and actively—in their own transformation. In these circumstances for such a transformation, creating and developing direction vectors is of particular importance. Consequently, values that are shared by the team and help in decision-making, such as forming plans and carrying out day-to-day business activities, become increasingly valuable. These values form an entity's ethical framework, which helps to ensure that activities across the team are all aligned.

References

Collins, J., & Porras, J. (1994). *Built to Last: Successful Habits of Visionary Companies*. New York: HarperBusiness.

Dolan, S., Garcia, S., & Richley, B. (2006). *Managing by Values: A Corporate Guide to Living, Being Alive, and Making a Living in the 21st Century*. Basingstoke: Palgrave.

Florea, R., & Florea, R. (2013). Value Driven Management Implementation—A Comparative Study in EU SMEs. *Alytus College Academic Papers*. 1/2013.

Ginsburg, L., & Miller, N. (1992). Value-Driven Management. *Business Horizon, 35*(3).

Gulbovaitė, E. (2017). Strengthening the Congruence of Personal and Organizational Values. In J. Vveinhardt (Ed.), *Congruence of Personal and Organizational Values* (pp. 43–52). Zagreb InTech.

Hamel, G. (2012). *What Matters Now: How to Win in a World of Relentless Change*. San Francisco: Wiley.

Hartl, E., & Hess, T. (2017). *The Role of Cultural Values for Digital Transformation: Insights from a Delphi Study*. 23rd Americas Conference on Information Systems (AMCIS 2017), Boston, USA.

Hinings, B., Gegenhuber, T., & Greenwood, R. (2018). Digital Innovation and Transformation: An Institutional Perspective. *Information and Organization, 28*(1), 52–61.

Hoffman, B., Bynum, B., Piccolo, R., & Sutton, A. (2011). Person-Organization Value Congruence: How Transformational Leaders Influence Work Group Effectiveness. *Academy of Management Journal, 54,* 779–796.

Kaptein, M., & Schwartz, M. S. (2008). The Effectiveness of Business Codes: A Critical Examination of Existing Studies and the Development of an Integrated Research Model. *Journal of Business Ethics, 77*(2), 111–127.

Lavoie, A. (2017). 4 Ways to Bring Your Organizational Values to Life. *Entrepreneur*. https://www.entrepreneur.com/article/247288.

Lencioni, P. (2002). Make Your Values Mean Something. *Harvard Business Review, 80*(7), 113–117.

Malnight, T., Buche, I., & Dhanaraj, C. (2019). Put Purpose at the Core of Your Strategy. *Harvard Business Review, 97*(5) (September/October), 70–78.

Marek, A. (2018). Adjusting the Employee Management Process to Key Organizational Values. *The Central European Review of Economics and Management, 2*(4), 111–126.

Pohlman, R. A., Gardiner, G., & Heffes, E. (2000). *Value Driven Management: How to Create and Maximize Value over Time for Organizational Success*. New York: AMACOM.

Rampersad, H. (2004). *Total Performance Scorecard: Redefining Management to Achieve Performance with Integrity*. Oxford: Routledge.

Schumann, C. A., & Tittmann, C. (2015). Digital Transformation in the Context of Knowledge Management. *European Conference on Knowledge Management, 1,* 671–676.

Weill, P., & Woerner, S. (2018). *What's Your Digital Business Model?: Six Questions to Help You Build the Next-Generation Enterprise*. Boston, MA: Harvard University Press.

CHAPTER 19

Conclusion: The Fourth Industrial Revolution—Further Research Agenda

Natalia Konina

The monograph "Digital Strategies in a Global Market: Navigating the Fourth Industrial Revolution" examined various aspects of digital strategies associated with the Fourth Industrial Revolution.

Wrapping up this book, I would like not so much to summarize the main ideas of the authors already discussed, but instead to look ahead and talk about those issues that have not been disclosed.

Today, at the very beginning of the Fourth Industrial Revolution, many of its trends are hard to pinpoint as of yet; more generally, we can talk about the fog that covers these problems. At the same time, the modern world is diverse, and it is very difficult to predict the main directions of development that society and the economy end up taking at the beginning of radical technological transformations.

Studies on digital strategies and the Fourth Industrial Revolution typically focus on technologies such as Big Data, Cloud Computing, or Artificial Intelligence (Big Data, Clouds, AI), but very little is given to the

N. Konina (✉)
Moscow State Institute of International Relations (MGIMO University), Moscow, Russia

N. Konina (ed.), *Digital Strategies in a Global Market*,
https://doi.org/10.1007/978-3-030-58267-8_19

impact of technologies such as AR/VR, 3D, robots, nanotechnology, and biotechnology. Moreover, with ever-accelerating scientific and technological development, the manifestation of dominant technologies requires a certain amount of time; it is still difficult to say which trends will develop and to what extent they will affect strategies and operations.

The changes associated with digital technologies are begin with small steps, yet advance very quickly to giant steps; for example, twenty years ago there was no such device as a smartphone, yet now smartphones are the very heart of digital communication. At the same time, it is important to note that the key for the consumer quickly stopped being the smartphones themselves as devices, but their applications and the information they store, create, and process. However, economic phenomena and processes are characterized by variability and cyclicality; they are largely related to people's behaviour, judgments, and expectations. When complex processes take place in human society, scientific understanding and research will always lag behind real life.

Although the new technologies of the Fourth Industrial Revolution are the subject of wide public and scientific discussion, a comprehensive view and understanding of the holistic picture of changes in strategies is yet to be drawn; the functioning of markets and companies under the influence of radical technological changes remains relevant.

Several issues related to digital strategies and the prospects of the Fourth Industrial Revolution have not been adequately covered in this book, and can be studied in subsequent works. We need research of an interdisciplinary nature with the widest possible and conceptual views, working at the intersection of management, marketing, international business, macroeconomics, and sociology.

Industry 4.0. involves the introduction, to various degrees, across the activities of all companies and industries, of new digital and biotechnologies, materials, and renewable energy. Many different companies are actively trying to digitally transform their business, massively automate processes and production, and introduce artificial intelligence, 3D printing, and robotics. The speed of change and technological advances is impressive, rapidly changing the prevailing markets and business models of many companies. The volume of global traffic based on the Internet Protocol (IP)—which provides an approximate idea of the scale of data flows—has grown from approximately 100 gigabytes (GB) per day in 1992 to more than 45,000 GB per second in 2017 and will exceed

150,700 GB per second in 2022. About 90% of all the information accumulated in the world was created over the past two years. It takes three minutes for the latest quantum computer to complete a calculation that would take 10,000 years for a modern supercomputer. There will be 21 billion devices connected to the Internet of Things (IoT) by 2020. In 2023, there will be more than 3 billion gamers in the world. The IoT medical segment will grow by 19% annually over the next few years, and by 2025 its global volume will reach %322.2 billion. The use of Artificial Intelligence (AI) will lead to an increase in global GDP by 14%, which will amount to more than $15.7 trillion. By 2030, Artificial Intelligence (AI) will be used in more than 40% of digital transformation projects and 100% of Internet of Things projects. Forbes data shows that since the turn of the century, AI startups have been launched 14 times more often, and investment in AI startups has increased sixfold. AI will automate at least 16% of jobs in the US.

The concept of "the future that has already come", was introduced Peter Drucker as the new millennium was on the horizon (Drucker 1964). Now the future of the Fourth Industrial Revolution has already come. Changes in technology, in society, in culture, in consumers, and in the structure of the economy are the signs of this bubbling revolution. At the same time, this future is only partially reflected in business as of now.

The technologies of the Fourth Industrial Revolution will affect various sectors and economies to various degrees. It will likely take from 15–20 years for these technologies, mostly currently in the initial stage of development, to reach their full potential. At the same time, the impact of digital technologies on business is usually manifested with a cumulative effect.

Even 10 years ago, it seemed to automotive companies that the technologies of the Fourth Industrial Revolution would change car design, optimize planning and supplies, and gin up the use of automated systems and robots. However, the development of this technology has taken a slightly different path; today, there is a completely different approach to mobility: autonomous vehicles are becoming the most important concern, and the whole model of the mobile service consumption is changing. Moreover, this is happening on a global scale. The combination of environmental issues and digitalization has led to a sharp demand for electric cars, which, combined with a change in the approach to mobility among younger generations of consumers, has led to radical changes in the entire automotive industry.

An important issue for possible future research is a new understanding of the role of the state. How can—and should—the state respond optimally to the challenges of the Fourth Industrial Revolution? It is likely that, in general, the role of the state will not decrease, but what new forms and types of regulatory activity of states can there be? Recommendations for regulating such issues as moving, storing, and using data when using the internet, cybersecurity, preserving intellectual property rights, and some issues related to artificial intelligence and robots must be dealt with, with such policies underlain by thorough scientific understanding.

Studying and understanding the new types of firms and new business models generated by the digital revolution and the sets of issues thereof is of considerable scientific and practical interest.

New leaders—digital multinational corporations—have already appeared, but importantly, these are not companies dealing with hardware. Most of them, except for Apple, are new firms, not older than 15–20 years. Over the past 10 years, a group of major leading companies has emerged. New companies are actively shaping global digital trends; traditional transnational corporations (TNCs) are still using business models that have not yet changed so much. However, such MNEs are beginning to experience the threat of breakthrough technologies generated by the onset of the digital era. The study of the negative digital experience many large companies have had in the digital era, and their unsuccessful and expensive attempts at digital transformation, can provide a very interesting and important topic for further research.

Digital multinationals are actively invading new areas of business. Business in wholesale and retail trade, hotel business, and leisure are rapidly changing. Soon, radical changes will occur in the field of mobility. Companies dealing with information and communication technologies have come to the forefront of the global economy, overtaking previous leaders in terms of sales growth, rate and weight of profits, market capitalization, and size of mergers and acquisitions. Particular successes here are oil and car companies.

Digital TNCs are defined here as companies operating on a global scale in the field of digital technologies as goods and services, where most of the turnover is associated with digital activities. These are companies working in both the real economy and the service sector, most of whose income is related to the Internet, information and communication technologies, and digital technologies.

This approach to digital TNCs is broader than the concept introduced in the UNCTAD report (World Investment Report 2019), here implying that TNCs include companies engaged in hardware+software, particularly such companies as Apple Inc., Alphabet Inc., IBM, Facebook Inc., Twitter, HP Inc., Dell Technologies, Intel, Amazon.com, Microsoft, Oracle, Netflix, Adobe Inc., Salesforce.com, Uber, Zoom; Chinese Alibaba, Tencent Holdings, Baidu, JD.com, Lenovo Group, Huawei, Xiaomi; Tata Consultancy Services, Infosys, Wipro, Capgemini, SAP, Siemens; Softbank, Sony, Hitachi, Panasonic; and Hong Hai (Foxconn), Quanta Computer, TSMC, Samsung Electronics, LG Electronics.

The radical and dynamic changes in the global economic landscape generated by the Fourth Industrial Revolution set the questions for further research dealing with major international companies. How will TNCs operate in the context of the Fourth Industrial Revolution? Will the largest TNCs of developed countries remain the most important force in the global economy? How will the balance of power between transnational corporations change? In the meantime, we are facing an unprecedented depreciation of companies' tangible assets, for example, those of General Motors, Ford, General Electric, Yahoo, Hewlett Packard, Motorola, Lucent, etc. This can be explained through the prisms of increased competition and the radical transition to another production base, but so far everything that has been created around the world is created using already established technologies that transformed the technologies of the Fourth Industrial Revolution at the very beginning.

The development of technologies of the Fourth Industrial Revolution leads to a significant change in not just the way they are consumed (including the consumers themselves and their expectations), but also the companies' business models. We need to investigate whether the international fragmentation of the manufacturing system and its geographical dispersion have reached their limits. How will the relationship and balance of power between parent and subsidiary companies develop in the Fourth Industrial Revolution? What will the life cycle of modern large companies be? According to Fortune magazine, only 12.2% of companies from the Fortune 500 list in 1955 were still there in 2014, 59 years later; the rest either went bankrupt or were taken over. At the end of the twentieth century, the average life cycle of a successful company was 60–75 years; today, the company's life cycle has decreased, as has the life cycle of goods.

It is traditionally noted that with the change of technological modes and the transition from one industrial revolution to another, redistribution and overflow of wealth occurs. How quickly will this happen to the largest modern transnational corporations? We are witnessing how the market capitalization of high-tech companies has significantly increased over the past twenty years since the Dotcom crash of March 10, 2000, when investors reevaluated the effectiveness of so-called post-industrial technologies which failed to meet the expectations attributed to them. The global business landscape is changing under the influence of changing investor sentiment. Industry 4.0 is changing investment approaches and investment priorities. Before 2007, oil and gas and retail companies, along with banks headed the list of the largest companies by market capitalization, yet in 2019, the 5 biggest high-tech companies and 2 largest online marketplaces were among the most expensive global firms by capitalization. The market capitalization of the most successful digital companies has reached unprecedented proportions. For example, in June 2020, Apple's market value was $1.516 trillion, while Amazon's was $1.334 trillion, Microsoft's $1.48 trillion, Alphabet's $976.6 billion, and Facebook's $680.33 billion. How stable are the competitive positions of these companies? Will they maintain market dominance and leadership in the coming years? To which firms, how, and when will the wealth created by the largest companies of the industrial era flow?

Digital companies using the online platform model are of particular interest. Online platforms, thanks to their breakthrough technological innovations, have made new products and services available, often for free. The breakthrough nature of the changes caused by the use of online platforms is due to the ability of firms to scale the effect, which has led to a change in the structure of industries and the way competition between firms occurs. Online platforms provide a digital infrastructure for various services and have exerted unprecedented market influence: in particular for marketplaces (Amazon), application stores (Apple), social networks and instant messengers (Facebook, Instagram, Twitter, WhatsApp), and search engines (Google). Global online platforms are estimated to have added $2.7 trillion to global GDP by 2025, created 72 million new jobs, and improved production results for 540 million people (World Investment Report 2017). Seven of the eight largest companies in the world in terms of market capitalization use platform business models (Digital Economy Report 2019). Thanks to digital platform solutions, the market for online outsourcing services is growing significantly and employees can work anywhere in the world with internet access, primarily in areas such as software and technology development, multimedia projects, sales and marketing services, office work and data entry, translation, and various other professional services.

One of the most frequently discussed aspects of the Fourth Industrial Revolution of Industry 4.0 is the potential impact of technology on labour. From a staff perspective, will a large number of temporary non-staff employees be a hallmark for certain jobs? Further research awaits quite specific questions of how work itself will change. Perhaps, for example, everyone will work remotely: how if so, can the corporate organizational culture be recreated, the work of temporary teams controlled and organized, or the safety and security of the most important company data ensured—especially when the boundaries of companies are becoming more vague and unsteady? Will it be possible to ensure the loyalty of temporary specialists that everyone finds on the platforms, and how? Are support services going to completely disappear? How will the companies diversify? On a less existential note, it is likely that soon there will be no desks allocated for a particular employee in their office. A change is taking place in the content and nature of labour: in the next 15–20 years, half of the routine tasks will be completed by artificial intelligence or robots; this can happen now, even at the current level of technology development.

Training employees to work in the new digital environment is a critical business requirement. Most companies do not have a clear idea of what kind of employee qualifications are needed, nor how to achieve this. In surveys, only 10% of firms reported that they generally understood what skills would be required in the future, and only 20% thought they were ready. At the same time, three-quarters of firms believe that, for their company, the formation of a corporate culture of lifelong learning and staff development is the most important activity in the framework of the transition to Industry 4.0.

How the technologies of the Fourth Industrial Revolution influenced—and still influence—management is another important and interesting question. Modern technologies of the Fourth Industrial Revolution determine the network nature of modern firms with increasing de-verticalization and the modular nature of goods, services, and processes. Fast and mobile networks with a large number of participants interacting in real-time using digital technologies will replace inflexible linear value chains. Many tasks can be performed by employees remotely in corporate networks. There will be no offices with open space for hundreds of people. Paper contracts and personal meetings for forty people are likely a thing of the past. Emerging trends indicate that the corporate structure itself will become different: there will be no need for several management levels, especially those in the middle. The coronavirus pandemic has highlighted once again that many issues of organizing work, especially in large firms, are out of date. Nevertheless, more than 40% of firms noted that when using remote access employees seem significantly less effective, which puts forward new challenges for management. Perhaps the moment predicted by Peter Drucker has come when companies of the future become "flotillas of independent mobile firms" (Drucker 1992). Will firms be virtual structures with blurred, fuzzily limited boundaries? What is the essence of the new type of firms in the digital age?

Researchers are interested in studying the patterns of how this entire network of companies can and will work. As Kelly notes, the main objective of a company is to maximize the value of the company network (Kelly 1998). Today, the global value chains managed by the largest TNCs increasingly include R&D based on open innovation; by their nature, modern Special Communications Main Centres are flexible; modular international networks are dispersed between different locations. Who should be the driving force behind the development of such networks? How are these forces able to provide an innovative culture within networks? What is the relationship with the institutional environment, in particular with regional authorities, with clusters, or with universities?

An important research topic is the impact of digitalization on competitiveness and competition in the global market. It is necessary to analyze the difficulties faced by large companies (including global ones) in conducting digital marketing and management transformation. Digital technologies create a peculiar effect: they lower transaction costs and entry barriers while increasing competition, which leads to lower profit margins. At the same time, due to the scale, competition becomes more severe, many firms leave the market (being unable to reduce their costs to an acceptable level), and in some cases leading firms become even more dominant. At the same time, a firm's competitiveness is increasingly determined by non-material aspects associated with the skilful use of critical digital technologies. This produces a situation when the winner takes it all, or almost all. The competitiveness of firms in the new digital environment is becoming less and less stable but instead is very mobile, increasingly depending on the properties associated with the organizational culture of the company: on its openness to innovations, on its selection of talented employees, and on the competence and adequacy of senior management decisions. At the same time, the innovative ability of firms, the skilful use of knowledge, and innovative openness are of critical importance for competitiveness.

Along with the changing nature of competition and the competitiveness of firms, the influence of digital technologies on geo-economic competition is separately raised. The new state of the productive forces has already led to a shift in the focus of the geo-economic struggle (Konina 2018). The heated conflict between the US and China over the Chinese Huawei technology corporation is a clear example of this. For the first time, sanctions against Huawei were imposed in May 2019, but then the Chinese company's temporary license to operate in the United States was extended five times. The sanctions imposed by the US administration against Huawei are aimed at ensuring technological leadership in 5G networks, which are the basis of the Internet of Things and a large number of other technologies associated with the Fourth Industrial Revolution. The new sanctions of the US Department of Commerce are not aimed at undermining Huawei's business by depriving the company of key sales markets and of the opportunity to purchase semiconductor products created by American companies. As part of the geo-economic confrontation, to avoid a catastrophic deterioration in positions on some key technologies of Industry 4.0, the US authorities are ready to impose even more restrictions on the access of Chinese competitive companies to the most important technologies. The stakes in the geo-economic confrontation associated with technologies of the Fourth Industrial Revolution are very high, and in response, China is ready to recognize some US companies as "unreliable organizations"; leading American computer companies have seen restrictions imposed or economic investigations initiated against them, such as Qualcomm, Cisco, and Apple; the purchase has also been suspended of Boeing aircraft.

Undoubtedly, it important to understand how the Fourth Industrial Revolution will influence traditional transnational corporations from the industrial point of view. In some industries, new technologies have not yet become widespread, but they may be widely used in the future. In many respects, the application of technology will be determined by the characteristics of the goods, raw materials, and available technologies, the need to ensure the uniqueness of the goods offered, and the speed of updating in response to changing consumer desires. Digital strategies differ across companies in different industries, yet all industries are characterized by the increasing importance of services in their work. Research is focused on such issues as how information and new digital technologies are changing industry boundaries (for example, those between manufacturing and non-manufacturing industries), deconstructing traditional industries, and encouraging the emergence of new sectors and/or cross-industry convergence.

Digital breakthrough technologies require operating companies from almost all industries to respond dynamically and quickly to new challenges, as everything is amplified and aggravated by the network nature of interactions, establishing the "winner takes it all" environment. Such breakthrough technologies include virtual and augmented reality and big data.

Smartphones and autonomous vehicles are examples of a combinatorial technological explosion that changes consumer behaviour and the work of many firms. Smartphones and autonomous vehicles are not separate innovations, but both are cardinal complex phenomena that have led to profound changes in business models, consumer behaviour, and the economy of supply and demand.

The heart of the modern economy is connected with smartphones. It took about 15–20 years for smartphones to dominate the market. In a few years, according to forecasts, even more smart gadgets will replace smartphones. By 2021, there will be augmented reality devices that will be no different from ordinary everyday glasses. Many top IT companies, including Facebook, Microsoft, and Apple, along with numerous startups, are actively working on augmented and virtual reality projects. In 2014, Facebook bought Oculus VR startup for $2 billion. Microsoft has recently released the second generation of HoloLens Augmented Reality Glasses. Apple, according to recent news, is going to release its VR/AR gadget in 2022. Such gadgets may become the new leading platform after smartphones in the future. The VR and AR market is expected to reach $1.5 trillion in 2030 and will grow rapidly. Equally, markets will change under the influence of new mobility.

The unmanned aerial vehicle market, including helicopters, may grow from $615 billion to $2.9 trillion by 2040. The autonomous vehicle market will grow to 30.4 million cars a year by 2035, the main stage of growth beginning in 2025. Annual sales of drones will increase up to $364.8 billion by 2035. As early as 2021, level 3 autonomous driving will become a reality. Autopilot technologies will reduce travel time by 250 million hours per year.

Amazon is an example that shows that a lot of data is great. After a certain scale, available customer behaviour and data therein can be used to customize personal offers, which gives higher sales rates, larger scale, greater network reach, and new opportunities to minimize costs and increase sales.

Virtualization and digitalization of the top manufacturing activities of TNCs, especially in mechanical engineering, significantly enhance their involvement in the trade of digital services and products that continue or complement the core business. Businesses such as Caterpillar, among several others, have experiences testifying to this. According to surveys, by 2030, at least one of the largest car makers will receive more income from selling data and services online than from selling cars and spare parts.

Accordingly, this will increase competition in the global service market as previously non-core suppliers will enter it, but at the same time will create additional demand for information, computer, management, technological, and other services from such suppliers.

Answers must be found to the question of how digital strategies in the global market differ from those in national markets. How, for example, are companies affected by digitalization programs implemented at the level of country or regional groupings? Most researchers are inclined to the idea that the question of the impact of digital strategies on the prospects of emerging markets remains a complex and controversial one.

Special attention should be paid to issues related to robotics. Automation and robotization of the economy will become a key development trend in the coming decades. In 2018, the Nobel Prize laureate in Economics Christopher Pissarides noted that robotization and automation will become the main threats to the twenty-first century economy; according to him, the development of digital technologies has already spawned a kind of monopolist that is widening the property gap (Pissarides 2018). McKinsey notes that as a result of technological changes, up to 375 million jobs may disappear from the global labour market, while 30% of functions for 60% of existing professions can be automated soon (McKinsey 2017). In Germany and the USA, automation potential is 24% and 23% of man-hours, while in China it is 16%. $16 billion makes up the current volume of the world industrial robotics' market. 74% of sales of industrial robotics come from five countries—China, Japan, South Korea, the USA, and Germany. $6.5 billion can make up the robot surgeon market by 2023. The robotization of economies will differ in developed and developing countries; in developing countries, this could provoke a narrowing of their domestic demand and accelerate the brain drain to developed countries due to the inability to find jobs for educated youth and those who have lost their jobs.

Many things will likely be determined by the market size and the specific socio-economic conditions of the future, because the technologies of the Fourth Industrial Revolution also create new opportunities for access to competencies, technological solutions, and effective business models.

It is also important to further study digital strategies themselves. We need to analyze why the percentage of failures is so high. The preliminary review shows the significant responsibility of TNC senior management, in particular the board of directors and management boards. As a rule, these are representatives of previous businesses who are not sufficiently aware of digitalization, do not have adequate digital skills, and are not fully aware of the threats and opportunities associated with new technologies and the industrial revolution. All company in any sphere should be constantly checking whether its strategy is sustainable and which areas have the greatest threats for undermining the company's significance for consumers.

It is interesting to study the role of mergers and acquisitions in digital strategies, as well as the set of conditions that ensure the effectiveness of mergers. The inorganic growth of companies, through mergers and acquisitions, remains important in the era of transition to the Fourth Industrial Revolution, primarily due to its speed. It can take a long time—or even be impossible to develop—the necessary digital competencies and skills within a company. Mergers and acquisitions in the digital sphere have shown their effectiveness in developing business models for finding new sources of growth and increasing profitability. It is important to note that creating in-house capabilities or giving access to the market can be long, difficult, and time-consuming. The necessary mergers and acquisitions require a concerted effort, usually over several years. Leading companies are one-and-a-half times more likely to take bold steps in launching brand new digital offerings than everyone else. Similarly, they spend three times as much of their income on mergers and acquisitions as ordinary companies in their industries. At the same time, leading digital transformation companies account for at least two-thirds of their acquisitions in digital business or creating digital opportunities, while the remaining companies have less than 50%.

Noteworthy are changes in global value chains organized and led by large international firms. Manufacturing globalization has contributed to forming complex, network-centric, global and regional value chains. The manufacturing system of all countries is increasingly dependent on imported intermediate goods and semi-finished products. Thus, in the United States alone, the volume of national industrial production in 2019 amounted to $2.856 trillion, while imports of intermediate goods and semi-finished products amounted to $1.045 trillion. According to the researchers of the World Economic Forum, open innovation, distributed manufacturing (based on 3D-printing technologies and reinforced by new software solutions), and horizontal communications between companies will seriously change the manufacturing process (WEF 2018).

Reducing the cost of extracting, storing, and processing large amounts of information, and combining this change with easily accessible, low-cost, large computing capabilities and other new digital technologies, is a process that has accelerated changes in the production base. Industrial companies have about 4–6 years to rebuild their entire manufacturing process based on the digital solutions of the Fourth Industrial Revolution.

As one possible promising form for organizing industrial manufacturing, multi-site operations involve placing factories as close to the consumer as possible and actively involving local factors in creating value, by participating in the development of design and other product parameters based on the digital double of the brand owner. Such a manufacturing model may look like a decentralized network of 3D printers and robotic machines connected with manufacturing companies through the cloud. The Internet of Things—together with the exchange of data among firms that own digital product data—can allow firms and households to decentrally release products adapted to local conditions. 63% of companies producing consumer goods believe that by 2030, production of localized goods directly by households will become the main development vector.

Sustainable development issues, instead of increasing the shareholder value, is a matter company executives are increasingly shifting their attention to (Renjen 2020). Issues related to climate change and environmental safety are increasingly attracting managers' attention. Increasing pressure from internal and external stakeholders—employees, investors, and consumers—has lead to a rethinking of the social role business play. Almost 60% of managers noted that strengthening the positive impact their organizations have on society is one of the five priority areas within the framework of Industry 4.0; only 35% of senior managers, in comparison, believed two years ago that the leading organizations of the future should devote more time to analyzing the impact of new solutions on society. Today, 48% of respondents believe that solving the problems associated with climate change is one of the main tasks that the current generation of leaders is going to face, while 38% of them consider the pursuit of sustainable development as a priority. It is expected that by 2025, the primary resources for the chemical industry will be biomass and processed materials instead of oil and gas. Every year, the environmental agenda and the topic of sustainable development become increasingly relevant for all companies and all consumers. The relationship between sustainable development, environmental conservation, and the opportunities provided by the Fourth Industrial Revolution requires the closest attention of researchers.

The future is closer than it seemed a few years ago. For example, significantly accelerated digitalization has been caused by the COVID-19 pandemic. A very interesting research problem is the effect of this pandemic on the digital strategies of companies and states. Digitalization began about 25 years ago, while the active phase of the modern stage of globalization started about 30 years ago; the pandemic only intensified these processes, primarily digitalization. The coronavirus has transformed consumers' perception of technology, with people increasingly shopping online, spending more time for leisure online, and learning more often using video conference software. The most developed technologies under the influence of COVID-19 will be technologies for remote access (VDI, videoconferencing, online communication, employee performance monitoring); artificial intelligence and machine learning; virtual and augmented reality; cybersecurity; MedTech, telemedicine; RPA, Internet of Things; E-commerce Robotics; E-learning, LMS, HRTech; Unmanned vehicles; and Cloud technologies.

The pandemic has pushed many companies to accelerate digital transformation, and there has been a rapid, enforced transition to the maximum use of digital technologies in all spheres of society and business. This trend will continue after the crisis, long into the Fourth Industrial Revolution.

References

Drucker, P. (1964). *Managing for Results: Economic Tasks and Risk-taking Decisions*. New York: Harper and Row.

Drucker, P. F. (1992). *Managing for the Future: The 1990s and Beyond*. New York: Truman Talley Books.

Kelly, K. (1998). *New Rules for the New Economy: Ten Radical Strategies for a Connected World*. New York: Penguin Books.

Konina, N. (2018). Issues of Modern Geoeconomics. *Mezhdunarodnye Protsessy, 16*(2), 186–196.

McKinsey. (2017). *What the Future of Work Will Mean for Jobs Skills and Wages*. Available at: https://www.mckinsey.com/featured-insights/future-of-work/jobs-lost-jobs-gained-what-the-future-of-work-will-mean-for-jobs-skills-and-wages.

Pissarides, C., & Bughin, J. (2018). Embracing the New Age of Automation. *Project Syndicate*. Available at: https://www.project-syndicate.org/commentary/automation-jobs-policy-imperatives-by-christopher-pissarides-and-jacques-bughin-2018-01.

Renjen, P. (2020). Industry 4.0 Readiness Report: At the Intersection of Readiness and Responsibility. *Deloitte*. Available at: https://www2.deloitte.com/global/en/insights/deloitte-review/issue-22/industry-4-0-technology-manufacturing-revolution.html.

UNCTAD. (2019). *Digital Economy Report*. New York and Geneva: United Nations Publications.

WEF. (2018). Impact of the Fourth Industrial Revolution on Supply Chains. System Initiative on Shaping the Future of Production. *World Economic Forum, Geneva, 2017*. Available at: http://www3.weforum.org/docs/WEF_Impact_of_the_Fourth_Industrial_Revolution_on_Supply_Chains_pdf.

Index

A

B

N. Konina (ed.), *Digital Strategies in a Global Market*,
https://doi.org/10.1007/978-3-030-58267-8

E

The manufacturer's authorised representative in the EU is Springer Nature Customer Service Centre GmbH, Europaplatz 3, 69115 Heidelberg, Germany. If you have any concerns regarding our products, please contact ProductSafety@springernature.com

Printed and bound by CPI Group (UK) Ltd, Croydon, CR0 4YY
22/09/2026
02221066-0008